Claiming Cit
Rights, Participation a
Series editor • J

Around the world, a growing crisis of legitimacy characterizes the relationship between citizens and the institutions that affect their lives. In both North and South, citizens speak of mounting disillusionment with government, based on concerns about corruption, lack of responsiveness to the needs of the poor and the absence of a sense of connection with elected representatives and bureaucrats. Conventional forms of expertise and representation are being questioned. The rights and responsibilities of corporations and other global actors are being challenged, as global inequalities persist and deepen.

In response, this series argues, increased attention must be paid to re-examining contemporary understandings of rights and citizenship in different contexts, and their implications for related issues of participation and accountability. Challenging liberal understandings, in which citizenship is understood as a set of rights and responsibilities bestowed by the state, the series looks at how citizenship is claimed and rights are realized through the agency and actions of people themselves.

Growing out of the work of an international network of researchers and practitioners from both South and North, the volumes in this series explore a variety of themes, including locally rooted struggles for more inclusive forms of citizenship, the links between citizenship, science and globalization, the politics and dynamics of participation in new democratic arenas, and the relationships between claiming rights and ensuring accountability. Drawing on concrete case studies which focus on how people understand their citizenship and claim their rights, the volumes contribute new, empirically grounded perspectives to current debates related to deepening democracy, realizing rights-based development, and making institutions more responsive to the needs and voices of poor people.

Titles in preparation

Claiming Citizenship SERIES
Rights, Participation and
Accountability

Series editor
John Gaventa

Volume 1

Inclusive Citizenship
Meanings and Expressions

Edited by
Naila Kabeer

Foreword by
John Gaventa

Zed Books
LONDON & NEW YORK

Inclusive Citizenship: Meanings and Expressions was first published in 2005 by
Zed Books Ltd, 7 Cynthia Street, London N1 9JF, UK and
Room 400, 175 Fifth Avenue, New York, NY 10010, USA
www.zedbooks.co.uk

Cover designed by Andrew Corbett
Typeset in 10/13 pt Bembo
by Long House, Cumbria, UK
Printed and bound in the EU
by Biddles Ltd, www.biddles.co.uk

Distributed in the USA exclusively by Palgrave Macmillan, a division of
St Martin's Press, LLC,175 Fifth Avenue, New York, NY 10010

A catalogue record for this book
is available from the British Library

US Cataloging-in-Publication Data
is available from the Library of Congress

ISBN Hb 1 84277 548 0
Pb 1 84277 549 9

Contents

Citizenship **and Struggle**

Citizenship and Policy

Acronyms

AAA	American Anthropological Association
ACFOD	Asian Cultural Forum on Development
AFL-CIO	American Federation of Labor and Congress of Industrial Organizations
BOTT	Build Operate Train and Transfer
CAP	community action plan
CBO	community-based organization
CEDAW	Convention on the Elimination of All Forms of Discrimination against Women
CIDA	Canadian International Development Agency
COSATU	Congress of South African Trade Unions
DFID	Department for International Development
DM	district municipality
DWAF	Department for Water Affairs and Forestry
ESRAZ	Escuela Secundaria Rebelde Autónoma Zapatista
FBW	Free Basic Water
ICCPR	International Covenant on Civil and Political Rights
ICESCR	International Covenant on Economic, Social and Cultural Rights
ICPD	International Conference on Population and Development
IFI	international finance institution
LM	local municipality
MDS	Muktidhara Sansthan
MST	landless movement
NAFTA	North American Free Trade Agreement
NGO	non-governmental organization
NK	Nijera Kori
PLA	participatory learning and action
SDM	sub-divisional magistrate
TFD	theatre for development
TNO	trans-national organization
TRIPS	Trade Related Aspects of Intellectual Property
UN	United Nations
UNDHR	Universal Declaration of Human Rights
UNICEF	United Nations Children's Fund
USAID	US Agency for International Development

Notes on Contributors

Oga Steve Abah is Professor of Theatre for Development at Ahmadu Bello University, Zaria, Nigeria. One of Abah's main interests is the exploration of conversations between methodologies, especially Theatre for Development (TFD) and Participatory Learning and Action (PLA) in doing citizenship research. He is the Nigeria Country Coordinator for the Development Research Centre on Citizenship, Participation and Accountability.

Fran Ansley lives in Knoxville and teaches at the University of Tennessee College of Law in the US. She is particularly interested in finding ways for her teaching and scholarship to support bottom-up organizing for social change and horizontal networks among internationalist opponents of neo-liberal globalization.

Carlos Cortez Ruiz (Doctor in Anthropology, UNAM) teaches postgraduate studies on Rural Development at the Universidad Autónoma Metropolitana (UAM) in Mexico. He acts as Coordinator of the Interdisciplinary Research Program on 'Human Development at Chiapas' of the UAM. During recent years he has researched and published on social strategies of sustainable human development and on public policies.

Evelina Dagnino teaches Political Science at the University of Campinas, São Paulo, Brazil. She has written extensively on social movements, relations between culture and politics, civil society and citizenship.

Rosalind Eyben has been a Fellow at the Institute of Development Studies in Sussex since mid-2002. By background a social anthropologist, she has spent her professional life working for development organizations, including at the UK Department for International Development, where she was DFID's first Chief Social Development Adviser.

Shireen Huq is an activist in the women's movement in Bangladesh, a founder member of Naripokkho, and for the last nearly twenty years a trainer on gender, rights and development in Bangladesh and elsewhere. She has also worked, since 1987, as Adviser, Women's Development, for Danida, Bangladesh and is currently working in Danida's Human Rights and Good Governance Programme.

Naila Kabeer is Professorial Fellow at IDS and a member of the Poverty and Social Policy Team. Her research interests include gender, population and poverty issues. Her recent books include *The power to choose: Bangladeshi women and labour market decisions in London and Dhaka* and *Mainstreaming gender equality in poverty eradication and the Millennium Development Goals*.

Ruth Lister is Professor of Social Policy in the Department of Social Sciences, Loughborough University. She is a former Director of the Child Poverty Action Group. Her publications include *Citizenship: feminist perspectives* (2nd edn 2003, Palgrave) and *Poverty* (forthcoming, Polity Press).

Lyla Mehta is a sociologist and has worked as Research Fellow at the Institute of Development Studies, University of Sussex since 1998. She has conducted extensive research on the dynamics of water scarcity, forced displacement and resistance to large infrastructure projects and conceptual issues around the 'public' and 'private' nature of water. She is author of *The naturalisation of scarcity: the politics and poetics of water in western India*.

Celestine Nyamu-Musembi is a Kenyan lawyer with a background in legal anthropology. She is currently a Fellow at the Institute of Development Studies, Sussex. She researches and writes on land relations and gender equity in resource control, the functioning of formal and informal justice institutions at the local level, implementation of international human rights standards, rights-based approaches to development, and integrating participatory approaches into rights advocacy. Her geographical focus is Eastern Africa.

Jenks Zakari Okwori is a lecturer in Drama at Ahmadu Bello University, Zaria. He is one of the lead researchers on the Citizenship DRC in Nigeria. Jenks has focused a great deal on exploring the identity question in Nigeria. He is also very interested in communication strategies.

Dr Mandakini Pant currently works in the Research and Academia Linkage Programme of the Society for Participatory Research in Asia (PRIA), New Delhi, India. She was earlier a Reader in the Research Centre for Women's Studies, SNDT Women's University, Mumbai. She also taught Sociology as Senior Lecturer at undergraduate level in SNDT Women's University, Mumbai. She gained a doctorate in Sociology from Rajasthan University, Jaipur in 1992.

Neil Stammers has been Senior Lecturer in Politics at the University of Sussex since 1980. His research and publications focus on issues around power, human rights, social movements and globalization. These are tied together by a concern to examine the future of radical politics and the possibilities for transformative social change.

Joanna Wheeler is the research manager for the Development Research Centre on Citizenship, Participation, and Accountability at the Institute of Development Studies in Brighton, UK. She was awarded a Fulbright Scholarship to conduct research on citizenship and gender in Brazil in conjunction with her postgraduate studies at the University of Massachusetts Amherst in the United States.

Dr John Williams is a Principal Town Planner in the City of Cape Town and lecturer in the School of Government, University of the Western Cape. He has published various interdisciplinary articles in journals such as *Cities, Development Southern Africa, Critical Arts, South African Labour Bulletin, Ecquid Novi,* and *Visual Anthropology* and internet-based journals, such as http//www.nu.ac.za/ccms/

Foreword

John Gaventa

This book is about how poor people understand and claim citizenship, and the rights they associate with it. Edited by Naila Kabeer, a scholar long committed to exploring issues of empowerment, collective action and social movements, the volume contributes new insights, rooted in local realities, to global debates about concepts of rights and citizenship.

Citizenship, as the essays in this volume remind us, is a highly contested term, with differing meanings ascribed by different cultures, interests and ideologies. Despite the differences, looking across the case studies in this volume Kabeer argues that aspirations for citizenship often entail common core values, including an impulse for social justice and self-determination – both of groups and individuals – and a sense of horizontal solidarity with others. Taking a comparative and historical approach to struggles for greater inclusion, citizenship is understood as an emergent concept, whose realization will vary across contexts and historical moments. Challenging liberal understandings – in which citizenship is understood as a set of rights and responsibilities bestowed by the state – the case studies in this volume, grounded in everyday experience, give a more robust understanding of citizenship as a multi-dimensional concept, which includes the agency, identities and actions of people themselves.

To be meaningful, any concept of citizenship carries with it a conception of rights. In recent years, the 'rights–based approach' has emerged in the development context as a 'new' approach, which has the potential to strengthen the status of citizens from that of beneficiaries of development to its rightful and legitimate claimants. As the essays in this volume articulate, the rights approach goes beyond a 'human rights approach', which often focuses on debates about global legal covenants, to focus on rights in practice. As Nyamu-Musembi points out, such 'actor-oriented perspectives are based on the recognition that rights are shaped through actual struggles informed by peoples' own understandings of what they are justly entitled to'.

While scores of donor and policy documents have been written in recent years about the rights-based approach, few studies have attempted to go beyond the conceptual debates to examine the meanings of expressions of rights and citizenship 'from below', and how these meanings are acted upon through political and social mobilization. Through contributing new, concrete and empirical case studies from countries spanning North and South – including Bangladesh, Brazil, India, Mexico, Nigeria, Peru, South Africa, the UK and the United States – this volume seeks to remedy that gap.

The approaches found in these cases are far-ranging, including, for instance, the use of popular theatre to explore the links between ethnicity and citizenship in Nigeria, in-depth interviews to understand perceptions of the rights of women in Chiapas or the *favelas* of Brazil, action research with nomads in Rajasthan, or focus groups with young people in the UK. The contributors to the volume are highly diverse as well, with disciplines ranging from sociology and anthropology to theatre, political philosophy, planning and law, and including both academics and practitioners who are deeply engaged in the cases about which they are writing. This diversity of methods and voices – which spans North and South, academic and activist, and a range of disciplinary approaches – gives a richly textured and robust view to struggles for inclusive citizenship in different contexts around the globe.

All the researchers in this volume have been associated in some way with the Development Research Centre on Citizenship, Participation and Accountability, an international research partnership based at the Institute of Development Studies in the UK (www.drc-citizenship.org). Founded in 2000, the Citizenship DRC is funded by the UK Department for International Development (DFID), with additional funding from the Rockefeller Foundation, which enabled participation of some of the northern contributors to this project.

Most of the researchers were involved in one of the Centre's first thematic working groups, which focused on meanings and understandings of citizenship. This group worked together over two years to gather, discuss and refine the studies presented in this volume. It met first for a workshop in Bangladesh in early 2002, where members shared preliminary ideas about the formal architectures and structures of citizenship in their countries, about the tensions between these formal constructions and the realities of everyday life, and about how citizenship could be understood as a dynamic and multi-dimensional concept, rooted in different historical contexts, while simultaneously in the process of being constructed through social action and social movements. The group's members – who were largely from the South – felt that the universal, and often Western, concepts of rights and citizenship risked having little meaning in the daily lives of people in their countries, or were used as a basis to exclude, rather than include, poor and powerless groups.

At the meeting in Bangladesh, the group decided to pursue a series of case studies on these themes, following a broad set of common questions. In June 2003 the working group met again, this time in a writing retreat outside Cape Town, South Africa, to share and critique drafts of their work. At this meeting, following concern that the work of the group should recognize that struggles for more inclusive rights and citizenship cut across both North and South, we were joined by other researchers who worked more in northern contexts, and who could share, for instance, the historical struggles in which rights have been shaped in the UK, or the ongoing struggles of immigrant workers for inclusive forms of citizenship and recognition in the USA.

Through its focus on locally grounded meanings and expressions of rights and citizenship, this book appropriately forms Volume 1 of this Zed Books series on Claiming Citizenship: Rights, Participation and Accountability. Other volumes will explore related issues of knowledge and citizen engagement in the context of science and globalization; the politics and dynamics of institutionalized participation in new democratic arenas; and the relationships between claiming rights and ensuring accountability. Also drawing from concrete case studies from around the globe, the volumes will contribute fresh perspectives from both South and North on current debates related to deepening democracy, realizing rights-based development, and making institutions more responsive to the needs and voices of poor people.

As series editor and as director of the DRC, I would like to thank the editor of this volume, Naila Kabeer, as well as each of the authors, for their contribution to the Claiming Citizenship series. The inclusive process of creating this book has been reflective of its thematic content. The collaboration and commitment to mutual learning and partnership across disciplinary, geographic and professional boundaries that have characterized the group's work have created a product that we hope will enrich others as well. In addition to the authors and editors, special thanks should also be given to those who have helped in the production of the manuscript and given support to the working group, including Alexandra Hughes, Lucila Lahitou, Kathryn Perry, Alexander Shankland, Joanna Wheeler, and of course our colleagues and editors at Zed Books, whose support for this series is deeply appreciated.

John Gaventa, series editor
Institute of Development Studies
July 2004

Introduction • The search for inclusive citizenship: Meanings and expressions in an interconnected world

Naila Kabeer

Although the idea of citizenship is nearly universal today, what it means and how it is experienced are not. Nor have they ever been. As a reading of the literature quickly reveals, the history of citizenship in both North and South has been a history of struggle over how it is to be defined and who it is to include. However, what is also clear is that a great deal of the theoretical debate about citizenship today is taking place in an 'empirical void' (Lister and others, in Chapter 7), where the views and perspectives of 'ordinary' citizens are largely absent. We do not know what citizenship means to people – particularly people whose status as citizens is either non-existent or extremely precarious – or what these meanings tell us about the goal of building inclusive societies.

The contributions to this volume go some way towards addressing this void. They explore the meanings and experiences of citizenship in different parts of the world, giving particular attention to the perspectives of the poor and socially excluded. Their contributions thus touch on the different mechanics of exclusion which consign certain groups within a society to the status of lesser citizens or of non-citizens, and on the struggles by such groups to redefine, extend and transform 'given' ideas about rights, duties and citizenship. They therefore help to shed light on what *inclusive* citizenship might mean when it is viewed from the standpoint of the excluded. They also touch on some of the important debates in the field of citizenship studies.

These debates have tended to be conducted as a series of binary oppositions, in which one term in the opposition is associated with classical liberal theory, and, by extension, 'Western' theory, while the other term reflects a critique of that theory from a variety of different political, cultural and philosophical traditions (see Stammers, in Chapter

1

3). Classical liberal theory claims that all human beings have rights by virtue of their humanity: such rights are consequently universal. One set of debates in the field of citizenship studies challenges this claim to universalism with a counter-claim of the particularity or cultural relativism of rights.

Classical liberal theory takes the individual as conceptually and ontologically prior to society and hence as the ultimate bearer of these rights, regardless of their status in society. A second set of debates challenges the idea of individual rights by pointing to contexts in which it is the rights of groups which are relevant and which should take priority over the rights of individuals.

Classical liberal theory recognizes civil and political rights as the only 'true' rights because they promote the freedom of individuals to act. The duty of the state is to defend this freedom. Social and economic rights are seen as entailing excessive state intervention, drawing on public resources and hence constituting an infringement of individual liberty. A third set of debates challenges this view and suggests that economic, social and cultural rights give substance to political and civil rights for the poor and marginalized: these different categories of rights are therefore interdependent and indivisible.

A fourth set of debates touched on in this book concerns the relationship between rights and duties. While liberal theory has always recognized that rights carry correlative duties, classical liberal theory treated rights as unconditional and hence prior to duties. Individuals enjoyed rights by virtue of their citizenship, regardless of whether they owned property, participated in public life, paid taxes or any of the other qualifications associated, for instance, with republican notions of citizenship. This has been challenged in recent times by neo-liberal thinkers for whom citizens must 'earn' their rights and for whom, therefore, duties precede rights. A number of contributions in this book consider the implications of this revised emphasis for patterns of inclusion and exclusion in the practice of citizenship.

In the rest of this introductory chapter, I will elaborate on these points in greater detail in order to draw out some of the unifying themes of the book. The next section explores some of the values and meanings associated with the idea of citizenship in the different narratives which appear in the book. The third section considers how key debates about citizenship, rights and duties have been interpreted by the authors in this book in the light of these values and meanings. The fourth section discusses the emergence of an explicit rights-based approach within the development agenda, and the challenges associated with its implementation. The final section draws together various strands of the discussion to consider what they suggest about the meaning of citizenship from the standpoint of excluded groups.

Values and meanings in the expression of citizenship

The narratives about citizenship in this book offer us certain insights into how excluded groups define themselves in different contexts, how they see themselves in relation to others and what this implies for their understanding of citizenship in the world as they know it. While their experiences clearly vary a great deal both by context and by the nature of their exclusion, their testimonies and actions suggest there are certain values that people associate with the idea of citizenship which cut across the various boundaries that divide them. These values may not be universal but they are widespread enough to suggest that they constitute a significant aspect of the organization of collective life and of the way in which people connect with each other. And because they are being expressed by groups who have experienced exclusion in some form or other, these values also articulate their vision of what a more inclusive society might imply.

Justice

First and foremost, the ideas about citizenship to be found in these chapters express adherence to some notion of *justice*. This is not the retributive notion of justice – or revenge – which Rentlen (1990), for instance, claims has near-universal status, but rather a notion of justice which revolves around when it is fair for people to be treated the same and when it is fair that they should be treated differently. The villagers who made up the audience for the various scenarios about citizenship enacted by the Theatre for Development in Nigeria prioritized ethnicity as the basis of their identity and their primary affiliation (Abah and Okwori, Chapter 4). Nevertheless they protested at examples where individuals were discriminated against by those in authority on grounds of their ethnicity. Whatever their own particular affiliation, they expected the state and its representatives to act fairly and impartially towards its citizens.

In the state of Tennessee in the United States, the campaign to give undocumented immigrants, or 'non-citizens', the right to a driver's licence was couched for pragmatic reasons as a matter of the health and safety of the citizens of Tennessee, but it was also used to open up a public dialogue in which the very visible labour contributions that undocumented immigrants made to the prosperity of the state could be compared to the lack of rights and recognition accorded to them by that state (Ansley, Chapter 12). It was the search for justice which led members of the Wallacedene community in South Africa to seek enforcement of the constitutional right to housing in the highest court of the land (Williams, Chapter 13). For some, their claims were based on the principle of equivalence with others: 'We want suitable houses to be built for us like it is happening elsewhere'. For others, their claims reflected a more historical sense of equivalence: that they should be restored to their rightful land and place in society now that the *apartheid* state was gone.

For the landless women and men organized by Nijera Kori in Bangladesh, the knowledge that the constitution of the country recognized their rights to basic food, land, shelter, education and health was the basis of their struggle for equality, for 'substantive' rather than formal citizenship (Kabeer, Chapter 11). For Naripokkho, a feminist organization in Bangladesh, the constitution itself was found to be flawed because it allowed religion to dictate the lesser status of women (Huq, Chapter 10). However, while the organization wanted equality before the law for women – a uniform civil code – it also wanted the state to recognize what was 'different' about women and what this implied for law, for policy and for their citizenship.

Recognition

This raises a second set of values associated with the idea of citizenship in the narratives in this book. Closely bound up with the demands for justice by many disempowered groups is a demand for recognition: recognition of the intrinsic worth of all human beings, but also recognition of and respect for their differences. There are, as Fraser (1997) points out, forms of injustice which are rooted in hegemonic cultural definitions which deny full personhood to certain groups – definitions which may be formalized in law or built into policy. The search for recognition by such groups often first takes the form of the demand for what Hannah Arendt (1986) called 'the right to have rights', to be recognized as full persons, despite their difference, and hence as full citizens. Thus, for members of Naripokkho, as Huq points out: 'Our experience of discrimination as women led us to demand fair treatment and respect for our dignity as human beings, and only thereafter to claim our rights and entitlements as *citizens*'.

The 'right to have rights' was at the heart of the Zapatista struggle (Cortez, Chapter 8): their demand for the right to difference was encapsulated in the vision of the world they aspired to achieve:

In the world of the powerful there is no space for anyone but themselves

and their servants. In the world we want everyone fits. In the world we want many worlds fit. The nation which we construct is one where all communities and languages fit, where all steps may walk, where all may have laughter, where all may live the dawn.
(Henriquez and Rochas 1995, cited in Yudice 1998, p. 365).

The agreement they signed with the Mexican government included acceptance of multicultural education which would refashion the nation's culture and history from the perspective of its Indian citizens because, as a Zapatista memorandum put it, 'By speaking in its Indian heart, the nation maintains its dignity and its memory' (Henriquez and Rochas 1995, cited in Yudice 1998, p. 366).

The Zapatistas were able to use their command of some of the most advanced means of representation available today – the news media and the Internet – to speak to the global imagination and to mobilize global support for the historical struggle of the Indian community in Mexico for dignity and respect. Other contributions in this book testify that dignity and respect are also essential to the idea of citizenship in less visible, more quotidian moments of life. When residents of the *favelas* in Brazil mobilized in the 1980s to demand the right to use the land on which they lived, their first act was to seek to publicize the results of their own survey to show the other citizens of their city that they too were decent, hard-working citizens – in other words, deserving of rights – rather than 'idle people, marginals or prostitutes' as the popular stereotypes suggest (Dagnino, Chapter 9).

However, the power of stereotypes derives from their persistence, regardless of evidence: the *favela* residents interviewed by Wheeler some years later (see Chapter 6) continued to experience their lack of citizenship, not so much as economic deprivation, but as the lack of respect that characterized their everyday interactions with society and state: 'Dignity is everything for a citizen – and we have no dignity. We are treated like cattle in the clinics, on the buses, and in the shops'.

Self-determination
A third set of values which features in the accounts in this book relates to *self-determination*, people's ability to exercise some degree of control over their lives. Where rights are seen to promote the capacity for self-determination, the struggle for rights is expressed in ways that reflect particular experiences of being denied self-determination. In many cases, it is the individual's right to self-determination that is the object of struggle. As Stammers points out, the right to property was, in the early struggles for citizenship in Europe, as much about the right to

'property in oneself' as it was about ownership and control over resources, and it was claimed as a means of restraining the absolute power of the monarchy over all persons as well as things within its realm. Many of the early political and civil rights, including freedom of movement and religious belief and to dispose of one's labour and property, all helped to express and uphold the rights of individuals over their own lives in this struggle against absolute power.

The desire for individual self-determination is also evident in the demands of indigenous women in Mexico. As Belausteguigoitia (2000) notes, the First Declaration of War of the Zapatistas' National Libera-tion Army, issued within days of the uprising in January 1994, also contained the Revolutionary Women's Laws, which spelt out what indigenous women considered to be essential to their dignity as human beings: these included demands about their public participation – the right to be elected to the community's decision-making positions, to go to meetings and to participate in community councils – as well as demands relating to the private sphere: women's right to choose whom they would marry, and when (also phrased as the right to go on studying if they wanted), the right not to be beaten within the home and the demand that rape within the family be punished. Not all these demands found their way into the subsequent agenda of the Zapatista movement, but the opportunity to express them brought new hope to women who had hitherto been denied any voice: 'Yes, the situation has changed a little. I think that there will be a time when we, as young women, at least will have the right to decide what we want to do with our lives, whether we want to study or have different responsibilities' (Cortez).

In Bangladesh, Naripokkho is concerned with women's right to self-determination in a context where, along with gender inequalities in access to resources such as education, property, jobs, health care and so on (of the kind which can found in most of the world), patriarchal power is also exercised through various forms of control over women's bodies: how their bodies are defined, what physical activities they are permitted, what physical space they can occupy and the punitive actions which are taken against them should they fail to comply with these strictures.

Not surprisingly, body politics has played a central role in Naripokkho's activities in the form of campaigns against violence against women both within the home and in the public domain; solidarity with sex workers, transsexuals and other groups whose marginalization is defined in gendered terms; and advocacy around health and reproductive services. Naripokkho's body politics is personal as well as public: it has led its members to reflect on how they experience their own bodies, their own freedom of movement, their own physical deportment and their own attitudes to sexuality.

Solidarity

A final set of values which emerges out of the narratives about citizenship in this book is to do with *solidarity*, the capacity to identify with others and to act in unity with them in their claims for justice and recognition. The form that solidarity takes varies, not only according to the 'included' or 'excluded' status of particular individuals and groups, but also the extent to which they hope to transcend their excluded status. For those who do not have such hope, solidarity can take a very narrow form, limited only to those who experience the same daily struggles or, even more narrowly, to one's own family and kin.

These differing circles of solidarity are evident in the narratives of the young people interviewed in the British city of Leicester (Lister with others). While for the majority, who did not necessarily regard themselves as 'outsiders', the idea of 'British-ness' as the basis of citizenship appeared too remote from their everyday lives to have much resonance, they did identify citizenship with ability to make a contribution to society as they understood it. For some, this contribution was defined in very general terms: participation in paid work or payment of tax. For others, it was defined more specifically as some form of involvement with their communities: they defined the 'good citizen' in terms of 'respect', for themselves, for others and for their environment, and 'caring' – looking out for others, helping people in the neighbourhood, giving something back to society. Significantly, however, those groups who constituted 'outsiders' tended to define their obligations far more narrowly in terms of looking after themselves or their immediate families.

Similarly, in the *favelas* of Rio de Janeiro, strong feelings of alienation from formal politics and from the idea of 'Brazilian-ness' as the basis of their identity had led residents, who saw themselves as 'lacking citizenship' in the wider society, to define themselves either in relation to their extended family networks or else in terms of their immediate neighbourhood, those who shared the same habitat and experienced the same frustrations (Wheeler).

The elderly black man in Cape Town who explained to Williams that his neighbourhood wanted support but not welfare from the state also expressed a solidarity with his immediate community and a desire for localized forms of self-determination. He wanted the state to respect the constitutional entitlement of his community to shelter; he wanted them to be told how things worked and then he wanted that they be left to get on with their own lives.

However, when solidarity takes more overtly political forms, it is expressed as a demand for collective self-determination which extends beyond those who share the frustrations of daily life. Such solidarity may be on the basis of the shared experience of oppression, or it may be in response to perceived injustice to others. The mobilization of dispossessed groups historically (Stammers) and today (Kabeer) to exercise collective power over the terms and conditions on which they sell their labour; the struggles of indigenous people to claim their place in their nation's history (Cortez); the attempts by women's organizations to challenge the manifestations of patriarchal power in public and private domains and thereby redefine the boundaries between the two (Huq) are all examples of solidarity based on a shared sense of oppression.

Examples of solidarity based on perceived injustice to others can be found in the role of external catalysts like Nijera Kori in Bangladesh, which organizes landless men and women to claim their rights (Kabeer), and MDS in Rajasthan, working with nomadic groups towards the same end (Pant, Chapter 5). Such external catalysts are often critical, as Pant points out, in situations where disempowerment is manifested as a lack of agency and organizational capacity. The citizens of Tennessee who participated in the campaign to provide undocumented migrants with driving licences were also expressing solidarity in response to perceived injustice with a group of people who were outside their immediate circle of family and friends.

And it is worth noting that while the Zapatistas were fighting for the right to collective self-determination for indigenous communities in Mexico, they also saw themselves as fighting for the rights of *all* marginalized groups, not just in Mexico but in the rest of the world. As a leading figure put it: 'Marcos is gay in San Francisco, Black in South Africa, Asian in Europe, Chicano in San Isidro, anarchist in Spain, Palestinian in Israel, Indian in the streets of San Cristobal…' (EZLN, *Documentes y Communicados*, 1994, cited in Belausteguigoitia 2000).

Rights and duties in debates around citizenship

The values and meanings of citizenship discussed above are drawn from the narratives of groups who have been assigned a marginal status within their societies. They therefore offer a particular standpoint from which to consider some of the central debates in the field of citizenship studies. However, just as excluded groups are not homogenous either in the mechanisms by which they are excluded or in their concrete experience of exclusion, so too the standpoints that their narratives offer will not necessarily lead to converging positions on these debates. They may share similar values at the abstract level – the values described above are, after all, particular ways of talking about *liberty, equality, fraternity*, the 'meta-values' which inspired the French Revolution over two centuries ago – but these values will be ranked differently and interpreted differently by different people at different times. In this section, we consider what the contributions to this book have to say about some of the key debates in the field of citizenship studies.

Universalism versus particularism

The contributions which touch explicitly on the debate over the universality versus the particularity of human rights acknowledge the tension between the two positions but suggest that the two sets of claims can be treated as the abstract and concrete sides of the same coin, rather than as opposing principles of a dichotomy. In a globally differentiated world, universalism cannot be taken for granted. It has to be worked for in different contexts, and these different contexts will shape the concrete forms that are given to abstract rights. Actor-oriented approaches to the question of rights make this clear. Such an approach is captured, for instance, in Mamdani's argument that rights are defined by struggle, and that rights-struggles are born of experiences of deprivation and oppression:

> Without the experience of sickness, there can be no idea of health. And without the fact of oppression, there can be no practice of resistance and no notion of rights ... Wherever there was (and is) oppression – and Europe had no monopoly over oppression in history – there must come into being a conception of rights.
>
> *Mamdani, 1989, pp. 1–2, cited in Nyamu-Musembi*

As Nyamu-Musembi comments: 'Viewed from this perspective, human rights are both universal and particular: universal because the experience of resistance to oppression is shared among subjugated groups the world over, but also particular because resistance is shaped in response to the peculiarities of the relevant social context'.

A similar point is made by Stammers. He notes that the universalist construction given to rights in the Western context can be traced to the particularities of the historical struggle of the oppressed against their oppression within that context. The claim for the universality of 'natural' rights, premised on the universality of the human condition, served a strategic purpose in challenging prevailing claims to power by an absolute monarch: 'Given that claims to absolutist power were legitimized transcendentally – by monarchs claiming Divine Right – it is not hard to see why oppositional social actors would seek to develop equally strong transcendent claims in efforts to de-legitimize them'. However, despite the universalism claimed for human rights, he suggests that whenever rights are instantiated as the rights of citizens within specific legal, political and state formations, they necessarily take on a 'particularistic' form.

Of course, it is widely recognized that the status of human being was often selectively rather than universally applied, so that even within Western society itself, citizenship was not a fully inclusive concept: quite aside from the 'exclusions from without' practised on the basis of slavery and empire, there were exclusions from within on grounds of gender, class and ethnicity. Nevertheless, the promise of universality contained in the idea of rights has proved to be a useful resource for groups seeking to pursue their claims for justice and recognition.

It was the promise of universalism contained in the idea of human rights which led to the extension of the political franchise to the previously excluded working class and in turn allowed them to demand the economic and social rights which would guarantee their access to the basic necessities of life, independent of their status in the market. This process of 'de-commodification' allowed labour to rescue itself from the status of just a commodity to be bought and sold in the marketplace (which unregulated market forces were threatening to reduce it to) and to gain the status and dignity of human beings and citizens (Marshall 1950). As Mehta points out, the language of universal rights may once again provide an important counter-discourse to the neo-liberal discourse of commodification which dominates current policy agendas across the world and is being used to legitimate the extension of market forces to every area of social life, including the provision of basic needs.

Women's groups throughout the world, including Naripokkho (although this is not mentioned in Huq's contribution), have also responded to the promise of universalism, seeking to re-frame women's rights as human rights as a way to underscore their claims for equality (sameness) and equity (difference). As Bunch with others (2001) notes: 'Human rights language creates a space in which different accounts of women's lives and new ways of demanding change can be developed. It provides a set of overarching principles to frame alternative visions of gender justice, without dictating the precise content of those visions' (p. 223).

By using the large body of international conventions, agreements and commitments as political leverage, women have been able to gain recognition and ratification for new kinds of rights, rights which reflect an 'embodied' rather than a disembodied understanding of what it is to be human, and hence an embodied, rather than an abstract, view of citizenship. Reproductive rights and recognition of human rights violations within the family are examples of these new kinds of rights, whose history is tied up with the emergence of women as collective actors in the public arena and their willingness to challenge pre-defined notions of the boundaries between public and private.

Individual versus collective rights

However, the implications which can be drawn from some of the contributions in this book, as well as the wider literature on debates about group versus individual rights, serve to illustrate the continuing tensions between the universal and the particular (see, for instance, Kabeer 2001). As Parekh (1993) has pointed out, for all its claims to universalism, liberal individualism as philosophical tradition and legal practice is the product of a particular history, the history of industrialization, in a particular context, 'the West'. Hence its adherence to the idea of the individual as the bearer of rights which are independent of their social relations and place in society does not have universal resonance. Even within the Western tradition, established liberal philosophers such as Isaiah Berlin (1969/1958) have noted the importance of group identity and affiliation as an aspect of citizenship for those who have been marginalized by society.

> What oppressed classes or nationalities, as a rule, demand is neither simply unhampered liberty of action for their members, nor, above everything, equality of social and economic opportunity, still less assignment of a place in a frictionless, organic state devised by the national lawgiver. What they want, as often as not, is simply recognition (of their class or nation or colour or race) as an independent source of human activity, as an entity with a will of its own, intending to act in accordance with it ... and not to be ruled, educated, guided ... as being not quite fully human, and therefore not quite fully free.
> *pp. 156–7, cited in Isin and Wood 1999*

Historically, struggles for national independence in the 'Western' context, including the American war for independence, were struggles for the right to collective self-determination, in this case, by 'the people' of the United States. Many of the struggles of workers and socialist activists were also struggles for collective rights: the right to organize and to bargain collectively (Stammers). More recently, the influx of immigrants from very different cultural backgrounds has given rise to multicultural engagement with the idea of collective rights. In any case, Western societies vary considerably between the more solidaristic cultures which prevail in the Nordic countries and the greater individualism of the Anglo-Saxon countries, particularly the United States (Fraser and Gordon 1994).

Nevertheless, these are all societies in which individual rights are solidly enshrined in their constitutions, institutions and cultural sensibilities and form the backdrop against which much of daily life is conducted. By contrast, as Parekh notes, individualism as a way of being has little or no place in societies which have a strong sense of kin and community ties, where individuals meet their needs on the basis of a shared morality of claims and obligations and define their identities in relation to other members of their community: he suggests a number of Arab and African countries as example. It also runs into problems in societies which are made up of multiple communities, each of which represents affiliations which have greater meaning in the lives of their members than membership of the larger society.

Most of these societies strive after some balance between individual and group rights, but with far greater emphasis on collective rights than in most Western societies. In some cases, the balance is between different *spheres* of life, so that certain spheres are governed by liberal principles of individual equality before the law while others are governed by religious or tribal principles which may differentiate between individuals on the basis of age, gender or social status or curtail certain individual freedoms in the interests of the collective. Pakistan, for instance, combines primarily individual rights in the economic sphere with religious law in the sphere of the family. Other countries may differentiate between different *groups*, defining certain rights for all individuals belonging to a particular nation-state but according other rights on the basis of group membership. Group rights may be on the basis of ethnicity or lineage, as in a number of African states, or on the basis of religion or caste, as in South Asia.

The recognition of collective rights reflects the reality that, in many situations, individuals have multiple affiliations, and nationhood may not be the most important; but it can also result in a fragmented and divided polity rather than the 'imagined unity' which is the basis of viable nationhood. In Nigeria, for instance, where certain rights of citizenship are associated with ethnic descent, it is possible to have been born and spent one's entire life in a particular state of Nigeria without qualifying for such rights in that state. Instead, these rights can only be sought in the ancestral home state, irrespective of the weakness of ties retained with that home. Under these circumstances, individuals who are not indigenes experience various kinds of discrimination: in their children's access to school, voting rights and so on.

Not surprisingly, it is to their kin and ethnic community that people turn for social, political and economic support. In a context where there is no public social security, such behaviour has allowed politicians from different ethnic communities to make huge capital from poverty and 'the politics of the belly', excluding minorities from representation in government and hence from an avenue for material accumulation and the location of economic and social facilities (Alubo 2000). As Abah and Okwori suggest, it is not clear whether the problem that Nigerians face today is that of a state without citizens – because there is no real basis for a common Nigerian identity – or that of citizens without a state, in that the possibility of a common identity is thwarted by powerful sections of the elite who benefit from reinforcing ethnic divisions.

The double-edged nature of group rights is also evident in the matter of reservations of a quota of government jobs for members of 'untouchable' castes in the Indian context in recognition of their historically disadvantaged status. Betteille (1983) pointed out that oppressed groups are not necessarily internally homogeneous, and job reservations could simply reinforce these internal inequalities. There are not enough government jobs to benefit more than a minority of lower-caste groups, those who were least disadvantaged, so that a policy which set out to decrease inequalities between different castes may have ended up by increasing inequalities between individuals within these castes. Parry, however, offers a modified 'two cheers' for this practice, because 'for all their barbed jibes about "quota-wallahs" the higher castes have found it far more difficult to dominate and discriminate against a low-caste population, many of whom have secured decent jobs and incomes, than it had been to dominate and discriminate against an impoverished population which was still tied to its traditional, stigmatized occupations' (Parry 2001, p. 162).

Feminists have also focused on the tensions between group and individual rights which emerge once the 'groups' in question are de-constructed to reveal their internal inequalities, of which gender is the most pervasive. As Nyamu-Musembi notes, the demand for individual self-determination by women as subordinate members of their communities is particularly problematic when their communities are themselves positioned as socially subordinate groups. She cites ethnographic work by Khare (1998) among 'untouchable' women in India who spoke of the most important right as the 'right to survive', which they defined in terms of access to food, clothing, housing, education, and secure life, 'but *not* at the expense of [their] personal and community honour'. As she observes, 'when status as a member of a particular group is so central to how one is defined in a particular social context, it leaves little room to speak of such an individual's rights without addressing the broader issue of the group's status as a rights–holding community' (p. 14).

However, this interdependency between individual and group rights can often serve to undermine the capacity of subordinated members of subordinated groups to press for their individual rights when to do so appears to divide the collective struggle for recognition or to play into hegemonic discourses which denigrate such groups. In the context of Mexico, Belausteguigoitia (2000) draws attention to some of the difficulties that indigenous women have had in asserting their rights as individuals within the Zapatista movement. As we noted earlier, the First Declaration of War of the Zapatistas' National Liberation Army, issued within days of the uprising in January 1994, also contained the Revolutionary Women's Laws which expressed a range of demands for indigenous women, many relating to their individual rights within the family and the community. Not all of the demands expressed in informal forums by these women – such as 'the right to rest' – found their way into these laws, and a further dilution took place in subsequent months. After the first round of negotiations between the Zapatistas and the government, a special communiqué delivered by the official representatives of the Zapatistas contained a very different set of 'women's issues': child care centres, food for their children, kitchens and dining halls, corn mills and *tortilla* pressing machines for the community, livestock, technical assistance, bakery projects, artisan workshops, fair prices for their crafts and transportation.

This dilution may have been a product of tactical agreement on the part of indigenous women to give priority to the 'larger' struggle, or it may have been imposed on them by the leadership in the interests of the larger struggle, but it repeats a familiar pattern. It suggests to Belausteguigoitia that, despite the leadership's sophisticated command of the interconnections between global, national and local inequalities, it was unable or unwilling to consider patriarchy as being as able as capitalism, racialism and other hierarchies to marginalize and oppress: the specificities of women's demands were reduced to their roles as food providers, educators and mothers.

It is this experience of women's interests being constantly subsumed within, or subordinated to, other agendas which helps to explain the rise of 'autonomous' women's organizations in different parts of the world. Deere notes, for instance, in the context of Brazil, that until the

1980s, women agricultural workers did not have the option of joining the trade unions if their husbands were already members, while women who attempted to raise the issue of women's land rights within the Movement for the Landless were told they were being divisive and advised to join the autonomous women's movement (Deere 2003, cited in Meer with Sever 2004). During the transition to democracy, women workers did precisely this, joining an autonomous rural women's movement to organize around their interests as women, including a successful campaign to include women's rights to land within the new Brazilian constitution.

In the Bangladesh context, Naripokkho allows women activists to explore their own priorities and determine their own trade-offs in an organizational space that is not dominated either by the zero-sum politics of the mainstream parties or by the instrumentalist agendas of the development community. Indeed, the organization's early experiences of attempting to work with women from political parties (in which their feminist politics was constantly subordinated to partisan politics) has led them to steer clear of coalition politics and opt for a strategy of alliances based on shared stands on particular issues.

Hierarchy versus indivisibility of rights

A third set of debates touched on in some of the contributions to this book concerns the privileged status granted by mainstream liberal theorists to civil and political rights over economic, social and cultural rights. By contrast, the perspectives offered by these contributions support the view that these rights are indivisible: each is essential for the realization of others. The rationale for this is quite simply the multi-dimensionality of power itself. Power may be fused in the person of the absolute monarch, as in the early European context, or it may operate through institutionally differentiated relations of state, market, community and family – in both situations, political disenfranchisement, social marginalization, cultural devaluation and economic dispossession come together in various combinations to define the condition of exclusion and marginalization.

Consequently, as Nyamu-Musembi points out, 'people do not experience rights – or their deprivation – in a bifurcated manner, distinguishing between rights of a civil-political nature and rights of an economic-social nature'. When they protest, their protests are not confined to one or other of these spheres, but tend to straddle them both. Thus indigenous women in the Chiapas in Mexico framed their demands in terms which subverted conventional demarcations of spheres. The social-economic right to education was intimately linked with the political-civil right to decide who and when to marry. The 'public' right of voice within their community was merged with the 'private' right for voice within the family. Fair returns to their labour in the market-place, a demand that male workers across the world are likely to have recognized, was premised on the right to rest from their labour, a demand that few male workers have felt the need to articulate.

However, the indivisibility of rights does not necessarily imply their simultaneous realization. In some cases, there may be a sequential pattern which reflects the balance of political power in particular contexts. In Britain, the success of the struggles of the working class for political enfranchisement paved the way for a welfare state which ensured the basic economic and social rights necessary to transform workers from 'commodities' into citizens. In Germany, on the other hand, modern welfarism was introduced by Bismarck in order to undercut the growing power of the German trades unions and the Social Democratic Party: social and economic rights thus preceded full political enfranchisement.

In other cases, the sequence may reflect a strategic assessment of priorities. Thus while Nijera Kori's analysis of injustice in Bangladesh defines it in economic, political and social terms, the organization's strategy has been to begin by mobilizing poor people to claim their economic rights as a way of building their capacity to act in more overtly political ways, including putting up their members for local elections. In Latin America, on the other hand, it has been observed that earlier social movements conducted largely by peasant unions, political parties and church groups seeking to forge class, partisan, religious and other identities failed to politicize indigenous groups, consequently feeding into stereotypes of Indians as submissive and backward (Yashar 1998). However, indigenous groups have mobilized actively in the most recent round of democratization, and it has been demands around cultural rights – territorial autonomy, respect for customary law, multicultural education and new forms of political representation – which have galvanized them. Finally, in some contexts, the sequence of struggle may simply reflect an institutional logic: the need to possess a ration card, a land deed or a driving licence in order to enjoy other, larger rights.

Rights and duties

While most approaches to citizenship recognize that rights imply correlative duties, they diverge on the relationship between rights *vis-à-vis* duties and on the role of the state in this relationship. Classical liberal notions of citizenship have generally focused on rights, mainly civil and political rights (Foweraker and Landman 1997). Such rights are not conditional on the fulfilment of duties: individuals enjoy them by virtue of their status as citizens, regardless of any action or inaction on their part. Within this view, it is the duty of the state to ensure that these rights are *protected*.

The role of the state was expanded with the emergence of social-democratic welfare regimes and the extension of the definition of citizenship to encompass social and economic rights. It was required to assume a more proactive role which included the *promotion* of the basic social security of citizens. However, the rise of neo-conservative thinking in the political domain in both the US and the UK in recent years has been associated with a strong attack on the purported dependency bred in individuals when they can rely on the state to meet their basic needs rather than their own efforts in the market-place. It has led to a renewed emphasis on the duties of citizenship. It is argued that since rights are not sustainable without duties, duties have to be regarded as prior to rights and the condition for rights.

The priority given to the duty of individuals to take care of themselves has also led to a re-definition of the role of the state to a protective role, that of maintaining the freedoms necessary for such self-reliance, intervening only to support those who are incapable of meeting their citizenship obligations through the market. Even this latter group must however 'earn' their right to state support through participation in various forms of 'workfare' programmes. As a result, debates about the relationship between universality and particularism in the sphere of public policy, which earlier took the form of a debate over universalism versus diversity in service provision, are increasingly conducted as a debate between 'universalism' of provision and 'residualism' (means-testing).

It is in this context that the expressions of citizenship articulated by young adults in Britain have to be understood (Lister and others). Their views appear to echo the growing emphasis on economic self-reliance as the hallmark of citizenship which is being articulated in the country's policy circles. Indeed, ethnicity and race seem to play less of a role in defining a sense of citizenship than do economic prospects: in other words, regardless of race and ethnicity, those who appear to be on their way to an economically assured future are more likely to identify themselves as full citizens than those who appear destined to experience long periods of unemployment or employment in poorly paid, unskilled work. Citizenship has thus come to be associated with economic respectability, with owning a house and paying taxes.

This new emphasis on self-reliance through individual effort in the market-place is also evident in the contributions of those writing about the South. It informs the neo-liberal structural adjustment policies which have led to the promotion of market forces in many parts of the Third World and the accompanying transfer of responsibility for social service provision from the state to various versions of the private sector, including various non-profit civil society organizations. In Brazil, Dagnino points out, this has led to the co-optation of many organizations which had been at the forefront of the struggle for citizenship rights during its transition from dictatorship to democracy. It has displaced questions of poverty and inequality from their proper place in the arena of public politics alongside questions of justice and citizenship, and assigned them to the domain of technical management or philanthropic responsibility and (as Wheeler comments) left poor and excluded groups without the capacity to articulate their demands. In Bangladesh, Nijera Kori has consistently refused the role of service delivery which now characterizes most non-governmental organizations in the country, on the grounds that such a role creates relations of dependency between civil society organizations and their marginalized constituencies, diverting the energies of both from the larger goals of transforming society and democratizing the state (Kabeer).

Rights-based approaches within the policy agenda

The rise of neo-liberal versions of citizenship in the international policy agenda has been partly countered by the parallel rise of 'rights-based' approaches to development, both within a number of international development agencies as well as within national agendas. This new discourse of rights in the context of development integrates concerns with sustenance (economic and social rights) and freedom (political and civil rights): while these have long been developmental concerns, a rights-based approach adds 'an element of accountability and culpability; an ethical/moral dimension' (Nyamu-Musembi).

The new 1994 constitution in South Africa is widely held up as a model for its strong commitment to the universal basic rights of its citizens. It is therefore appropriate that the two chapters on South Africa in this book both grapple with the struggles to implement such an approach in a country whose past history is one of the brutal denial of rights to the majority of its citizens. The challenges of implementation discussed by both Williams and Mehta make it clear that while winning the constitutional recognition of universal rights is an important step in the construction of inclusive citizenship, it is only a first step.

The chapter by Mehta discusses the tensions between the 'universal' and the 'particular' as they play in the context of a commitment to universalism as the foundation of basic social needs. How, she asks, does one operationalize the commitment to universal provision – in this case of water – as a right, when the needs of different groups are so different. The need for water, for instance, varies considerably in drought-prone areas from areas which are rain-fed or irrigated. And while defining water as a basic need appears to imply use for human consumption rather than commercial purposes, for poor farmers, water for productive purposes may be critical to the means by which they meet their basic needs, so the dichotomy between commercial purposes and human consumption becomes artificial.

One answer, of course, is that universality does not necessarily imply uniformity. It is possible to meet a generic set of basic needs in a variety of different ways – not simply by varying amounts allocated, but also through very different resources. It is also worth noting that liberal theory does not necessarily rule out 'selectivism' in policy provision. Titmuss, for instance, one of the key theorists of the British welfare state, rejected negative 'selectivism', or the targeting of services on the basis of individual means, because it stigmatized recipients, turned them into clients and treated them as failures (cited in Thompson and Hoggett 1996). However, he favoured 'positive' selectivism, or active discrimination in favour of certain groups, because of the specificity or urgency of their needs, because he saw it as a redistributive mechanism.

It is this second approach which was reflected in the constitutional judgement on the right to housing in the Wallacedene case documented by Williams. Aware of the constraints imposed by the country's socio-economic conditions, the court did not require the state to go beyond its available resources or to realize the right to housing immediately. But it did insist that the state had failed in its duties because it had not addressed the plight of the poorest and most desperate sections of the community: 'Those whose needs are the most urgent and whose ability to enjoy all rights are therefore most in peril must not be ignored by the measures aimed at achieving realization of the right'. It recommended, in other words, a 'bottom-up' incrementalist approach to universal coverage rather than an instantaneous one that could be more easily captured by elite groups. And it pointed to some of the practical conditions that would have to be in place to assure even this basic incrementalism, including provisions to plan, to budget and to monitor the meeting of basic needs and the management of crisis.

In Chapter 15 Eyben deals with the somewhat different challenge of operationalizing the rights-based agenda faced by DFID, a bilateral donor agency, in Peru, a country where its presence was small and whose government's commitment to such an agenda was uncertain. One key challenge such agencies face, of course, is the issue of national sovereignty. International convention considers interventions by external actors (such as donor agencies) in domestic matters acceptable if such interventions are couched in 'technical' terms and requested by recipient governments. As Eyben points out, such requests are most likely to come from governments that are concerned with strengthening democratic processes and the respect for rights in their own countries and are prepared to work with donors within mutually agreed frameworks.

Quite apart from the challenges posed by changes of government and the government officials it was dealing with, the DFID office also had to work out what exactly was implied by a rights-based approach in the context of Peru. The particular interpretation it adopted appears to accord closely with the actor-oriented approaches to rights from the perspective of excluded actors which have featured in this book: strengthening the organizational capacity of poor people to realize their rights and mobilize support from influential allies within government and civil society to promote their voice and presence within policy processes. How this interpretation was then acted on was derived, as Eyben puts it, from learning through practice. Some of this learning was from attempts to build participatory processes within the policy domain which were being carried out elsewhere in the region. As Dagnino's contribution also notes, some of the most innovative work in this regard has been attempted in Brazil and includes participatory budgeting and monitoring in local government along the lines initiated in Porto Alegre, as well as the establishment of management councils for social policy provision, with membership equally divided between civil society and government at city, state and federal levels.

DFID's experience in Peru raises an important issue. Like other collectives, nations are not internally homogeneous and many are characterized by extreme inequalities and repressive practices. This is another example of the tension we noted before, where the rights of self-determination of the collective – in this case, of the nation – may come into direct conflict with the rights of groups and individuals within that collective. There is, of course, a great deal of cynicism on the part of many within the Third World – governments as well as civil society – about the rise of rights-based approaches within bilateral and multilateral agencies; they are seen as yet another 'donor' fad, or simply old conditionalities repackaged with a new, more human face.

On the other hand, it is also the case that attempts by external actors with a genuine (as opposed to symbolic) commitment to promoting the struggles of poor and excluded groups to fight for their rights are likely to be resisted most vehemently by regimes which have least commitment to the poor in their country and are least accountable to their people. Insistence on the principle of national sovereignty offers a useful alibi for such regimes, while appeals to the international community over the heads of repressive governments are increasingly resorted to by the victims of their repression. One approach that DFID has taken in Peru to reconcile its own agenda with that of the government has been to invoke internationally agreed conventions which embody the principles that it is seeking to act on and to which both Britain and Peru are signatories. To that extent it can argue that it is merely acting within a shared framework of ethics. In the end, however, as Eyben points out, it is the extent to which donors open themselves up to the same principles of transparency, coherence and accountability that they are currently demanding of recipient countries – and the extent to which that accountability extends to the governments and citizens of recipient countries rather than to their own taxpayers alone – that will determine the extent to which their commitment to a right-based approach will be perceived as legitimate and genuine.

Inclusive citizenship in an interconnected world

The narratives in this book, taken together, challenge the conventional political science understanding of citizenship in terms of the relationship between individuals and the state from both a sub-national (local) as well as a supra-national (global) perspective. First of all, from a sub-national perspective, it is apparent that membership of the nation-state often means little to its members, compared to other forms of sub-national communities with which they identify and through which they exercise their claims and obligations. This is as true for citizens of countries like Britain, where independent nationhood has a long history, as it is for the various countries of the South who won their independence within the past half century.

In some cases, the communities that people acknowledge, the claims and obligations they recognize, may be very narrowly defined, restricted to their immediate circle of family, kin, lineage and neighbours. In others, the sense of connectedness transcends immediate or primordial identities and coheres around shared experiences of oppression or in solidarity with those who experience such oppression. This is a 'societal' understanding of the citizen as someone who belongs to different kinds of collective associations and defines their identity from participation in activities associated with these different kinds of membership. Their sense of citizenship lies in the terms on which they participate in this collective life and the forms of agency they are able to exercise. And where they are only able to participate on highly unequal terms, or are denied access altogether, citizenship relates to their attempts to challenge these exclusionary processes and bring about change. As a number of contributions to the book make clear, while the capacity to exercise agency at the individual level may be an important pre-condition, it is the collective struggles of excluded groups which have historically driven processes of social transformation.

Ansley's contribution spells out this societal notion of citizenship very well. Although, as she says, the example of mobilization that she discusses was initiated by, and designed to benefit, a population of *non-citizens*, and hence could not be described as an expression of their citizenship, we can interpret her own involvement, and that of her fellow citizens in the state of Tennessee, in the campaign to ensure the rights of undocumented immigrants as an expression of *their* under-standing of citizenship. As she points out, a great deal of the social justice work carried out by organizations and citizens' movements in the US has been concerned with the rights of marginalized or sub-ordinate groups in relation to the state as well as to other members of society:

> In good times, they have fought for more expansive understandings about things that all citizens should be able to expect from the state and from each other, and in bad times they have defended what rights they had against incursions by public and private power.

Dagnino is also explicit about the importance of such constructions of 'citizenship from below'. She points out that in Latin America (and, it could be said, elsewhere), struggles for recognition by those groups who were subject to cultural rules that denied them the right to have rights led to a broadening of the terms in which the struggle for citizenship is conducted: 'beyond the incorporation into the political system in the restricted sense of the formal-legal acquisition of rights' and into 'a project for a new sociability, a more egalitarian framework for social relations at all levels, new rules for living together in society … recognition of "the other" as a subject bearer of valid rights and legitimate interests'. This active engagement in the wider political struggle was seen by many as a central dimension of citizenship: for some, she points out, it constituted the essence of citizenship, even in the absence of formal rights.

What emerges from these narratives is what might be called a 'horizontal' view of citizenship, one which stresses that the relationship *between* citizens is at least as important as the more traditional 'vertical' view of citizenship as the relationship between the state and the individual. Indeed, in situations where the state has proved consistently unresponsive to the needs of its citizens, it is through the collective action of citizens, particularly those who have been disenfranchised by the prevailing regime, that a more democratized vertical relationship can be established or restored. The conundrum, of course, is how such collective action for inclusion or transformation con be organized by those whose exclusion is premised precisely on their lack of organizational power. In some cases, support may come from allies within the nation-state who may act on behalf of, or with, excluded groups. In others, it may take on more global forms of solidarity.

This takes me to the second challenge to conventional state-centred views of citizenship presented by some of the contributions in this book, one which is posed by growing interconnections at the global level. These interconnections take a number of different forms. Interconnections which reflect the shared global environment reflect the fact that decisions taken within the boundaries of a nation-state regarding the management of non-renewable resources can have impacts that go well beyond national boundaries (Eyben). The forces of economic globalization are evident in Ansley's discussion of the flow of undocumented migrants into the United States, and touched on briefly in Kabeer's discussion of the emergence of export-oriented shrimp production in Bangladesh. A number of chapters deal with the globalization of the neo-liberal economic worldview through the ascendance of these ideas within national governments or their imposition through donor conditionalities.

However, counteracting these processes are various global interconnections of a different kind, interconnections which represent an active solidarity across national boundaries. The phenomenal ability of the Zapatistas to mobilize international support, partly through their mastery of the new forces of technology, not only brought their cause to the attention of the world but served to provide them with some protection in the face of a repressive state. Other examples of such global interconnections discussed in the book include the attempts by the DFID office in Peru to support nascent struggles for citizenship by excluded groups within the country; Nijera Kori's participation in international networks to oppose the unregulated industrialization of shrimp production and the consequent human rights violations; and the way in which women's organizations across the world have sought to negotiate their way between the customs and laws within their countries and those spelt out in international conventions (Nyamu–Musembi). Nor is it only women's organizations in the South that can make strategic use of international conventions. As Calman (1987) points out, US feminists could benefit from pushing the US to ratify many of the key international human rights conventions, including the Convention on the Elimination of All Forms of Discrimination Against Women (which it has not yet ratified, although it was signed by Carter in 1980), because many of these are far more favourable to women than US law.

To some extent, it is the construction of global policy/political regimes 'from above' to ensure the free flow of international capital which has made an alternative set of global interconnections 'from below' necessary. A great deal of the politics of globalization from above as well as below is focused on contestations around the kinds of rights and duties that are appropriate in an increasingly globalized world. One obvious focus concerns the rights of labour to the same kind of unfettered mobility that is currently enjoyed by capital (Ansley). While an apparently logical solution to, on the one hand, the need of richer countries for labour to do the jobs its own citizens are unable or unwilling to do and, on the other, the need of poorer countries to find employment for their citizens, such a right still remains an apparent political impossibility. Contestations also focus on the rights of indigenous groups to their collective knowledge, the rights of labour to some degree of protection from global market forces, the rights of citizens to unpolluted environments and so on.

The other important question concerns the duties associated with globalization. Globalization increasingly means that many policy decisions taken within one country about the environment, about taxation, about social protection, about labour standards – are likely to have repercussions in others. There is clearly a need for greater co-ordination of responsibility at the global level. However, for nations to buy in to the idea of global responsibility comes up against the problem of resources and incentives. Why should individual nations act in globally responsible ways, to take (or refrain from taking) actions in the interests of the global community, if such actions go against their national interests or strain their national capacity?

Clearly there has to be a framework of global citizenship which induces countries to act in globally responsible ways and which ensures that they have the resources necessary to carry out these responsibilities. A framework of global clientelism based on foreign assistance, which is essentially how relations between rich and poor countries are presently constructed, is unlikely to command the allegiance of client governments or of their citizens. Foreign assistance is exactly that; it is premised on the same dependency relationships at the global level that charity entails at the national, similarly subject to whims and arbitrary decisions,[1] incapable of sustaining a long-term vision of global responsibility.

Despite various controversies, including controversies over its 'fortress' mentality, the European Union has received a great deal of attention in this regard because it is one – perhaps the only – attempt in the contemporary era to forge a supranational association which is based on more than trading relationships (Mishra 1998; UNRISD 1997; Linklater 1998). It embodies a vision of political, social and economic integration between member states bound by common rules, including a charter of fundamental human rights, backed by necessary redistributive mechanisms. There is no doubt that the reality falls short of the vision – the Common Agricultural Policy, for instance, penalizes EU taxpayers and consumers as well as Third World farmers – but it nevertheless serves to make an important point. Members of the Union may not exercise the same clout as each other but they are members, nevertheless, not clients. They are required, as the basis of membership, to subscribe to certain common principles and practices, including the principles and practices of citizenship, and there are redistributive mechanisms to ensure that all members are able to fulfil their obligations.

Global citizenship also requires rules which spell out the claims and obligations of membership and ensure redistribution as a matter of right rather then discretion. It requires measures of the kind proposed by the Brandt Commission at the end of the 1970s, and more recently by a number of countries at the Monterey conference on financing for development, namely that countries be taxed on a sliding scale related to national income in order to generate revenue for a global social fund. Ultimately it is only within this framework of a global community based on mutual rights and responsibilities that the idea of a 'rights-based' approach to development will make sense. Short of this, attempts to promote the idea of rights in development will continue to appear to many poor countries as simply conditionality with a human face'.

Note
1. It is worth noting as a footnote to Eyben's chapter on DFID's activities in Peru that the office has now been closed down as DFID transfers its resources and capacity to waging peace in Iraq.

References

Alubo, O. (2000) 'Gaps and, potholes in Nigeria's political practice: issues of who is in and who is out', Department of Sociology, University of Jos: Mimeo Jos

Arendt, H. (1986) *The origins of totalitarianism*, New York: Andre Deutsch

Belausteguigoitia, M. (2000) 'The right to rest: women's struggles to be heard in the Zapatistas' movement', *Development* 43 (3), pp. 81–7

Berlin, Isaiah (1969/1958) 'Two concepts of liberty' in *Four Essays on Liberty*, Oxford: Oxford University Press

Betteille, A. (1983) *The idea of natural inequality and other essays*, New Delhi: Oxford University Press

Bunch, C. with P. Antrobus, S. Frost and N. Reilly, 'International networking for women's human rights' in M. Edwards and J. Gaventa (eds) *Global Citizen Action*, Boulder, Colorado: Lynn Reinner Publishers

Calman, L. J. (1987) 'Are women's rights "human rights"?' Working Paper No. 146, Michigan State University

Deere, C. D. (2003) 'Women's land rights and rural social movements in the Brazilian agrarian reform', *Journal of Agrarian Change* 3 (1 & 2), pp. 257–88

Foweraker, J. and T. Landman (1997) *Citizenship rights and social movements: a comparative and statistical analysis*, Oxford: Oxford University Press

Fraser, N. (1997) *Justice Interruptus: critical reflections on the 'post-socialist condition'*, London and New York: Routledge

Fraser, N. and L. Gordon (1994) 'Civil citizenship against social citizenship? The condition of citizenship' in B. V. Steenbergen (ed.) *The condition of citizenship*, London: Sage Publishers

Henriquez, E. and R. Rojas (1995) 'Queremos ser parte de la nacion mexicana, como iguales', *La Jornada*, Nov. 18

Isin, E. F. and P. K. Wood (1999) *Citizenship and identity*, London: Sage Publications

Khare, R. S. (1998) 'Elusive social justice, distant human rights: untouchable women's struggles and dilemmas in changing India' in M. Anderson and S. Guha (eds) *Changing concepts of rights and justice in South Asia*, Calcutta, Oxford: Oxford University Press

Linklater, A. (1998) *The transformation of political community: ethical foundation of the post-Westphalian era*, Cambridge: Polity Press

Mamdani, M. (1996) *Citizen and Subject: contemporary Africa and the legacy of late colonialism*, Princeton: Princeton University Press

Marshall, T. H. (1950) *Citizenship, social class and other essays*, Cambridge: Cambridge University Press

Meer, S. with C. Sever (2004) *Gender and citizenship: overview report*, BRIDGE, Brighton: IDS

Mishra, R. (1998) 'Beyond the nation state: social policy in an age of globalisation', *Social Policy and Administration* 32 (5), pp. 481–500

Parekh, B. (1993) 'The cultural particularity of liberal democracy' in D. Held (ed.) *Prospects for democracy: north, south, east, west*, Oxford: Polity Press with Blackwell Publishers

Parry, J. (2001) 'Two cheers for Reservation. The Satnamis and the steel plant' in R. Guha and J. Parry (eds) *Institutions and Inequalities, Essays in honour of André Betteille*, New Delhi: Oxford University Press

Rentlen, A. D. (1990) *International human rights: universalism versus relativism*, London: Sage Publications

Thompson, S. and P. Hoggett (1996) 'Universalism, selectivism and particularism:

towards a postmodern social policy', *Critical Social Policy* Vol. 46, pp. 21–43

UNRISD (1997) *Report of the UNRISD International Conference on Globalisation and Citizenship*, Geneva 9–11 December 1996

Yashar, D. J. (1998) 'Contesting citizenship: indigenous movements and democracy in Latin America', *Comparative Politics* 31 (1), pp. 23–42

Yudice, G. (1998) 'The globalisation of culture and the new civil society' in S. E. Alvarez, E. Dagnino and A. Escobar (eds) *Cultures of politics, politics of cultures*, Boulder, Colorado: Westview Press

Citizenship and Rights

Two

Towards an actor-oriented perspective on human rights

Celestine Nyamu-Musembi

Summary

This chapter[1] argues that rights are shaped through actual struggles informed by people's own understandings of what they are justly entitled to. Examining rights from the perspective of actual struggles makes it possible for analysis to transcend accepted normative parameters of human rights debates, question established conceptual categories and expand the range of claims that are validated as rights. The chapter draws out these 'actor–oriented perspectives' in the course of reviewing key debates in the field of international human rights to show how they question underlying assumptions in these debates, and offer the possibility of breaking through the impasse that some of them have reached.

Introduction: What does an actor-oriented perspective mean?

Actor-oriented perspectives are based on the recognition that rights are shaped through actual struggles informed by people's own understandings of what they are justly entitled to. They imply an approach to needs, rights and priorities that is informed by the concrete experiences of the particular actors who are involved in, and who stand to gain directly from, the struggles in question. The understanding of actor-oriented perspectives in this chapter is drawn in part from a legal literature that does not necessarily position itself within the human rights tradition, but which calls for an evaluation of legal principles in terms of their particular effects in a social setting, rather than only in terms of the conceptual coherence of abstract principles.[2] It goes beyond a call for attention to context to an emphasis on consequences for less powerful groups and/or individuals in society. To quote one of the contributors to this literature: 'When we ask ourselves whether a social or legal practice works, we must ask ourselves, "works *for whom?*" Who benefits and who loses from existing political, economic, and legal structures?' (Singer 1990, p. 1841).

Such an approach thus explicitly acknowledges the reality of power differences and hierarchical relationships in society, and points to the need to look beyond abstract formal equality principles to the effect of those principles in entrenching or challenging hierarchy from the perspective of the subordinated (Matsuda 1990, p. 1768; Minow and Spelman 1990, p. 1650). When people ask the question 'works for whom?' and translate this question into action, they change the terms of institutionalized understandings of rights and make rights real in their own context. They use an otherwise legalistic discourse of rights in a transformative manner that translates it into an effective challenge to power inequalities. They shift the parameters of the discourse and expand the possibilities for action.

The discussion in this chapter is organized around three key debates that have gone on among legal practitioners and scholars in the field of human rights: debates about universalist versus relativist views about rights; about individual versus group rights; and about the hierarchy versus the indivisibility of rights. The chapter elaborates on each of these debates and then draws on critical responses to the debates and on accounts of concrete struggles over rights in order to highlight the ways in which actor-oriented perspectives challenge the premises underlying these debates and expand the range of claims that can be validated as rights.

Universalism versus cultural relativism

Do human rights principles provide a universal standard to be applied uniformly, or are they contingent on social context? This debate has characterized the post-Second World War human rights movement since the enactment of its founding document, the Universal Declaration of Human Rights (UDHR) 1948, and continues to be intense. I will map out some of the positions represented on a spectrum that has 'universalist' arguments at one end and 'cultural relativist' arguments at the other.

Universalist arguments

The *first* type of universalist argument is the normative claim that human rights *should* provide a universal standard because rights inhere in every human person simply by virtue of being human. Rights flow from the inherent dignity of every human person. They are not given by the sovereign and therefore cannot be taken away by a sovereign. Nor are rights pegged to status based on age, gender, race or caste. This argument is influenced by the idea of 'natural rights' attributed to natural law theorists such as Kant (Wilson 1997, p. 8). Contemporary variants of this position can be found in Donnelly (1989), Howard (1992) and Schachter (1983).

It also finds expression in international human rights documents such as the 1993 Vienna Declaration on Human Rights, adopted at the first United Nations (UN) Conference on Human Rights. The preamble to the declaration states that 'all human rights derive from the dignity and worth inherent in the human person' and that the UDHR 'constitutes a common standard of achievement for all peoples and all nations'. Article One reinforces this by asserting that 'human rights and fundamental freedoms are the birthright of all human beings' and that the universal nature of rights and fundamental freedoms 'is beyond question'. Since rights flow from the inherent dignity of the human person, they are not contingent on particularities such as political, social, economic or cultural context.

The *second* category of universalist arguments is the formalist one: since most states have ratified and agreed to be legally bound by international human rights law, human rights standards are universal. In addition, some argue, the UDHR, though simply a declaration that is not legally binding, is such a widely accepted landmark instrument in human rights that it has (or parts of it have) become customary international law (Steiner and Alston 2000, p. 367). Customary international law refers to norms that have evolved from state practice over time, norms that bind even those states that have not entered into specific treaties on those aspects of international law: in this case, human rights.

This argument resonates with Howard's (1992) contention that human rights must be seen as universal because even if their Western origins are acknowledged, most states around the world have adopted the liberal state framework. This framework makes rights inevitable and indispensable in regulating state–citizen relations. This category of argument is not concerned with the legitimacy of human rights standards; formalist criteria such as the fact of ratification alone, or the existence of a liberal state framework, will suffice to make the case for universality.

Multicultural universalism or weak cultural relativism

I refer to this category of arguments as 'multicultural universalism' or 'weak cultural relativism' because it does not reject universality out-right, neither does it insist that rights are contingent on cultural context. Rather, it refers to the incompleteness of international human rights discourse as currently constituted. Its proponents argue that human rights could be truly universal if as many world cultures as possible contributed to shaping the universal discourse of rights. Every society has a valuable contribution to make because every human society has some fundamental idea about human dignity and social justice, of which the particular concept of human rights is just one aspect (Schachter 1983). An-Na'im expresses this argument as follows:

> Current and foreseeable new human rights cannot be seen as truly universal unless they are conceived and articulated within the widest possible range of cultural traditions ... As normative propositions, human rights are much more credible and thereby stand a better chance of implementation if they are perceived to be legitimate within the various cultural traditions of the world.
>
> *An-Na'im, 1992: p. 2*

Human rights principles as expressed in existing human rights laws and institutions are not universal because they are shaped by a distinctly Western experience. Their origin can be traced to an Enlightenment mindset, and their modern institutions have roots in the specific historical circumstances of post-Second World War Europe (Wilson 1997, p. 4). Some emphasize the absence of non-Western representatives at the drafting of the landmark human rights instrument, the UDHR (Mutua 1999).[3] Others cite the inadequate representation of indigenous peoples in the process of formulation of rights at the international level. Since they are not adequately represented in this state-oriented system, their values and needs are not taken into account, and therefore the norms so formulated cannot claim to be universal (Falk 1992, p. 48).

According to these authors, the project for the modern human rights movement is to make human rights truly universal by accommodating these fundamental ideas in as many cultures as possible, particularly non-Western cultures. The modern human rights movement should build on them, rather than work from a Western conception of rights as the starting point (Mutua 1995). 'Retroactive legitimation' is not only possible but desirable, and the existing human rights standards should be open to revision and reformulation (An-Na'im 1992, p. 6; Mutua 1995, p. 346).

Radical cultural relativism

Radical cultural relativist arguments are at the other end of the spectrum from normative and formalist universalism. They hold that there can be no transcendent idea of rights and they view culture as 'the sole source of the validity of a moral right or rule' (Wilson 1997, p. 2). International human rights norms therefore reflect a particular cultural viewpoint – a Western one. A good example of radical cultural relativism is the statement from the American Anthropological Association (AAA) in reaction to the draft UDHR in 1947. The AAA cast doubt on the UDHR's claim to represent a universal perspective. It stated:

> How can the proposed Declaration be applicable to all human beings and not be a statement of rights conceived only in terms of the values prevalent in the countries of Western Europe and America? ... Standards and values are relative to the culture from which they derive so that any attempt to formulate postulates that grow out of the beliefs or moral codes of one culture must to that extent detract from the applicability of any Declaration of Human Rights to mankind as a whole.
> *AAA 1947*

Aspects of the declaration that the AAA regarded as typifying the Western worldview included the centrality of the individual as opposed to the community (discussed under a separate heading below), and the emphasis on rights as opposed to duties.

In the arena of state practice of international law, cultural relativism is expressed in the reservations that various states have made to some human rights instruments. The UN Convention on the Elimination of All Forms of Discrimination Against Women (CEDAW) registers the highest number of reservations, most of which relate to the provisions that stipulate equality in family relations and state obligation to reform customs and practices that discriminate against women.[4] The phrasing of the reservations shows clearly that the states concerned see these provisions as inherently contradictory to their cultural and/or religious values. For example, Bangladesh, Tunisia, Libya and other Muslim countries cite conflicts with Islamic law as the reason for their reservations, and give no indication that this situation could change to permit withdrawal of the reservations any time in the future.

The radical cultural relativist argument has provided ammunition for governments bent on deflecting criticism of their governance practices. A frequently cited example is what has come to be referred to as the 'Asian values' argument, contained in the Bangkok Declaration that was issued by a summit of Southeast Asian leaders meeting just before the UN Conference on Human Rights held in Vienna in 1993. The

Bangkok Declaration states that rights must be understood within the context of national and regional particularities, and must be informed by specific cultural, religious and historical backgrounds. It condemns the 'imposition of incompatible standards' through political pressure or conditionality in development assistance.

In a move that was clearly intended to counter the Bangkok Declaration, over 200 non-governmental organizations (NGOs) took part in the drafting of an Asian Human Rights Charter in commemoration of the 50th anniversary of the UDHR in 1998. The charter reaffirms the relevance of fundamental human rights in the Asian context, and the universality of such rights (Ghai 1998).

Challenges to the universalist versus cultural relativist polarity

One example of the challenge to the assumptions underlying the universalist versus cultural relativist debates – specifically the question of whether rights are of Western origin – posed by an actor-oriented perspective comes from Mamdani. He argues that rights are defined by struggle, and rights struggles are born of experiences of deprivation and oppression.

> Without the experience of sickness, there can be no idea of health. And without the fact of oppression, there can be no practice of resistance and no notion of rights … Wherever there was (and is) oppression – and Europe had no monopoly over oppression in history – there must come into being a conception of rights.
> *Mamdani 1989, pp. 1–2*

Viewed from this perspective, human rights are both universal and particular: universal because the experience of resistance to oppression is shared among subjugated groups the world over, but also particular because resistance is shaped in response to the peculiarities of the relevant social context.

The polarities of the universalist versus cultural relativist debate have also been criticized for obscuring manifestations of local understandings of rights – 'vernacularization' of rights, in the words of Sally Engle Merry (1997). She uses ethnographic data drawn from Hawaiian struggles for independence to show that even though the discourse of human rights is based on 'Western liberal-legalist ideas', when specific struggles in non-Western societies utilize the discourse in framing their demands, the concept is reinterpreted and transformed. This transformation is a two-way process of incorporation of local understandings and the addition of global discourses, and it is this two-way process that she refers to as 'legal vernacularization'.

A similar challenge has come from accounts that undertake a situated analysis of how people actually live in a context of legal and cultural pluralism, and strategically draw from both their cultural or religious norms and formal rights regimes in dealing with real-life situations. Both cultural norms and formal rights regimes provide opportunities and challenges in dealing with specific situations. The lines are not so clear-cut in reality and therefore rule out the possibility of a clear-cut demarcation that places the blame for human rights violations on culture and posits universal human rights principles embodied in formal laws as the solution (Nhlapo 1995; Nyamu 2000; WLSA 1995).

Individual versus group rights

A second set of debates revolves around the relationship between individual and group rights. Is there space for group-based claims in the liberal individualist conception of rights? Or alternatively, how are individual freedoms to be protected in the context of group rights? One of the arguments made in the AAA statement of 1947 and other radical cultural relativist critiques is that human rights discourse downplays the importance of community. It therefore seeks to impose an individualist model of rights that is at odds with non-Western ways of life. This individualist emphasis is present in the constitutions of countries that have adopted the liberal state framework. The relationship between individual and group rights has been the subject of debate in the broader conversation between liberals and communitarians. The former conceptualize people/citizens as self-interested autonomous individuals, while the latter view individual identity as being defined through relations with others and embedded in community (for further elaboration of these arguments, see Jones and Gaventa 2002; Mulhall and Swift 1992).

The debate is really between an abstracted view of the rights-bearing individual as a universal construct and a contextual view of the individual as defined by his/her ethnic, cultural or religious community (Steiner and Alston 2000, p. 365). The abstracted view of the individual tends to view group rights as being in opposition to the very concept of human rights. Rhoda Howard, for instance, views collective rights as 'a claim for something very different from human rights; it is a claim that reasserts the value of the traditional community over the individual' (1992, p. 83). The individual holder of rights holds them against his or her community 'or even family'. The contextual view holds that a collective conception of rights is consistent with the liberal conception of rights, because membership in a community plays an important role in enabling meaningful individual choice and supporting self-identity (An-Na'im 1999, p. 59; Kymlicka 1995, p. 105).

This philosophical debate aside, there are some international human rights documents that embody human rights whose holders are groups as well as individuals. An early example is the 1948 Convention on the Prevention and Punishment of the Crime of Genocide. The 1981 African Charter on Human and Peoples' Rights designates some rights as individual (dignity, recognition of legal status as a person, right to receive information, freedom of association and movement, right to work, etc.), and others as peoples' rights. Peoples' rights include the right to existence and self-determination, to economic, social and cultural development, and to a general satisfactory environment favourable to their development.

Challenges to the antagonistic conception of the relationship between individual and community rights

One struggle that has changed the terms of the debate on individual and collective rights is the struggle for the rights of indigenous peoples. In the early stages of its engagement with the international human rights arena, the struggle had to overcome immense ideological opposition (mainly from the USA and Australia) to the use of the term 'peoples' in the draft UN Declaration on the Rights of Indigenous Peoples (1994). The plural form – 'peoples' – suggests group rights as opposed to the rights of aggregated individuals. The declaration is still being discussed by a working group of the UN Sub-Commission on the Promotion and Protection of Human Rights.

Like the African Charter, it incorporates both rights regarded as belonging individually to members of indigenous communities (for example, nationality, life, physical and mental integrity, liberty, security) and rights regarded as collective (for example, right to live freely as distinct peoples). Some rights are phrased as both individual and collective. These include freedom from genocide and other forms of violence (such as the removal of children from their homes), deprivation of cultural values and identities, imposed assimilation and dispossession of their lands.

New developments have made it quite clear that there are some rights claims that can only be conceived of in collective terms. For instance, in arguing for compensation to indigenous communities for use of their knowledge in medicine, developing new plant varieties, or films and other forms of art based on oral traditions, it would be impossible to ascribe ownership to particular individuals. These claims have been framed in terms of packages or programmes that benefit the community as a collective (Posey 1990). Thus, collective action by indigenous communities around these emerging issues calls into question the rigid distinction between individual and community in thinking about human rights.

In addition to the movement for indigenous peoples' rights, there have been other calls for a conception of rights that does not treat collective rights, such as the claims of family and kinship groups, as inherently antagonistic to individual rights. Contrary to the dominant tendency in liberal human rights discourse, which is to present state–citizen relations in abstracted individualist terms, people are constantly negotiating between an internal moral system (shaped by factors such as culture and religion, and represented by institutions such as kinship) and the formal legal regime of the liberal state (Khare 1998, p. 199). Far from subsuming individual concerns under community interests, 'situated analyses of rights' point to people's own experience of these concerns and interests as overlapping and intertwined, sometimes in harmony and sometimes in tension.

One example is drawn from Khare's ethnographic work among 'untouchable' women in a Lucknow neighbourhood in India (1998). These women's perception of primary or fundamental rights integrated a vision for the individual and the community. They spoke of the most important right as the 'right to survive', which consists of access to 'food, clothing, housing, education, and secure life, but *not* at the expense of [their] personal and community honour' (Khare 1998, p. 200). Concern about personal insult went hand in hand with concern about humiliation of their parents and husbands, as did concern for physical violence, including violence committed by those same parents and husbands. This latter concern points to the reality of simultaneous harmony and tension between individual and group rights. This is the lived reality.

Khare's account of the experiences of untouchable women reveals a more general point on the relationship between individual and group rights. When status as a member of a particular group (for example, low caste) is so central to how one is defined and treated in a particular social context, it leaves little room to speak of such an individual's rights without addressing the broader issue of the group's status as a rights-holding community.

Adopting the perspective of people situated within the reality of this complex web of relationships regulated primarily by social norms changes not only the way we think about human rights but also the way we 'do' human rights. This has certainly been the case for activists engaged in community-based human rights work with Muslim women, and for advocates of Islamic family law reform. A group of women's human rights activists from various Islamic backgrounds have developed a *Manual for Women's Human Rights Education in Muslim Societies* (Afkhami and Vaziri 1996). The manual covers a broad range of 'rights situations' such as rights within the family, autonomy in family planning decisions, rights to education and employment, and rights to political participation. What makes the manual different from conventional human rights education manuals is that its interactive and interpretive exercises interweave excerpts from international human rights agreements with verses from the *Qur'an, shari'a* rules, stories, idioms and personal experiences.

Take as an example the session on women's rights and responsibilities within the family: the session begins with an exercise where participants give their views on where rights come from, which opens a discussion on the family as a source of rights, and/or what role the family plays in protecting or denying rights. Then follows an exercise on 'talking to the men in your family', which teases out differences and similarities in the way various women in the group relate with their male family members. An exercise on 'negotiating your rights and responsibilities within your family' focuses on a woman's freedom to choose whom and when to marry. The exercise is facilitated through the story of a woman named Leila, her father and the man to whom she has been betrothed. A series of questions based on the scenario culminate in a reflection on two verses from the *Qur'an* and Article 16(2) of the Universal Declaration of Human Rights (UDHR),[5] which invites the participants' comments on what aspects of their cultural and religious experience support women's rights within the family (Afkhami and Vaziri 1996, pp. 5–9).

Recognition of the reality of community, and of plural moral orders, also forces us to think more broadly about sites for human rights engagement and come up with more innovative strategies. For instance, access to formal types of remedies under statutes and constitutional bills of rights may be placed beyond the reach of weaker social groups due to factors such as cost, bias or perception of the formal system as far removed from people's day-to-day lives. In addition, the social cost of pursuing formal remedies may be prohibitive, as in the case of a widow deprived of access to inheritance by her in-laws. She knows that she has legal standing to apply for the necessary letters to administer the estate, and that she has legal rights to the property as a widow, which she could enforce in court. But it is also in her interest and that of her children to maintain good relations with her in-laws, and this restrains her from taking legal action.

Scenarios such as these have led to activist strategies and scholarship that engage with the norms that sustain and regulate these relationships (such as kinship) 'on their own terms'. This engagement with community norms (also referred to as customary law) has prompted attention to micro-level forums, such as intra-family and community-based dispute resolution processes, and made them sites for human rights struggles. These forums play a key role in enabling or constraining people's ability to claim whatever rights are available to them under custom, national laws or international human rights principles (Griffiths 1997, 2001; Hellum 1999; Hirsch 1998; Nyamu 2000; Nyamu-Musembi 2002; Stewart 1998).

The challenge lies in crafting a legal framework of rights and citizenship that adjudicates fairly in the complex reality of harmony and tension between individual and group claims. This would be one that does not disregard the community context in which people are embedded, but at the same time does not legitimize a narrow definition of personhood based on status in hierarchical social relationships.[6] The latter would thereby deny the very agency that rights and citizenship should enable (Kabeer 2002, p. 20).

The hierarchy or indivisibility of rights

A final set of questions in international debates about human rights revolves around the relationship between different sets of rights. Is the relationship a hierarchical one, with political and civil rights – which have been accorded stronger recognition in most legal frameworks – taking precedence over economic, social and cultural rights? Or are all rights interdependent, inter-related, indivisible and therefore non-hierarchical?

The founding document of international human rights, the UDHR, makes no distinction between rights of a civil–political nature and rights of an economic–social nature. It provides for rights in both categories. The debate on hierarchy between the two categories of rights originated in the post-UDHR attempt to draw up a single, binding charter of rights, and became a defining feature of international human rights discourse throughout the Cold War era. The Western bloc argued for the primacy of civil and political rights, while the Eastern bloc argued for the primacy of economic and social rights. The conflict resulted in the enactment of two separate human rights covenants: the International Covenant on Civil and Political Rights (ICCPR) and the International Covenant on Economic, Social and Cultural Rights (ICESCR) in 1966.

Some recent academic accounts still continue to contest the 'rights status' of economic and social concerns and their relevance to discussions on citizenship rights. A recent study on the link between social movement activities and the enjoyment of citizenship justified the omission of 'so-called social rights' from the discussion as follows:

> Whatever the virtues of these rights (and there are many), they do not qualify as integral to the discourse of rights, and therefore cannot serve the purposes of a comparative study of citizenship'
> *Foweraker and Landman 1997, p. 14*

The authors go on to argue that while civil and political rights are universal and amenable to formal expression in the rule of law, 'social rights' are fiscally constricted and require distributional decisions and therefore they are best described not as equal and universal rights but as 'conditional opportunities', more realizable in the developed welfare capitalist states (1997, p. 15).

The reality, of course, is that people do not experience rights – or their deprivation – in a bifurcated manner, distinguishing between rights of a civil–political nature and rights of an economic–social nature. In an organized protest in 1987, street vendors in Ahmedabad, Gujarat, expressed their struggle as being about 'dignity and daily bread'. Police harassment, irregular allocation of trading spaces, city laws enacted without public participation, uneven distribution of resources among neighbourhoods were all integrated in their demands (IHRIP and Asian Forum for Human Rights and Development 2000, p. v).

All rights, including civil and political rights, require the allocation of resources that are presumed in the Foweraker and Landman (1997) quote to be free of distributional consequences. For instance, guaranteeing the right to a free trial and the right to vote require state resources, as do rights to health and education. There have been some significant attempts to institutionalize the idea that all human rights are interlinked; that rights guaranteeing political freedom and civil liberties are dependent on rights guaranteeing sustenance or economic and social development, and vice versa. One example is the 1986 UN Declaration on the Right to Development. The declaration recognizes that development is a comprehensive economic, social, cultural and political process, whose purpose is the improvement of the well-being of all individuals on the basis of meaningful participation and fair distribution of the benefits of development.

The declaration was largely the initiative of developing countries. Most industrialized states were opposed to the framing of some of the rights as belonging to states. Article 2(3) for instance, gives states 'the right and the duty to formulate appropriate national development policies'. But the real opposition at the adoption of the declaration was to the overall radical politics of the New International Economic Order that spawned the declaration. This is expressed in the strong language on peoples' sovereignty over their natural resources, which was viewed suspiciously as reminiscent of past nationalization policies.

By the time of the UN Conference on Human Rights in Vienna in 1993, the idea of interdependence of rights was being popularized increasingly in post-Cold War human rights circles. Paragraph 5 of the 1993 Vienna Declaration states that '[A]ll human rights are universal, indivisible, interdependent and interrelated' and calls on the international community to treat all rights fairly and equally, on the same footing and with the same emphasis. Recent focus on a 'rights–based approach to development' suggests further significant attempts to bridge the gap between freedom and sustenance.

Rights-based approach to development

The 1995 Copenhagen Declaration on Social Development seeks to use the framework of rights to achieve goals such as poverty eradication. Among the aspirations in employing this 'rights–based approach' is that groups hitherto disadvantaged socially and economically will be empowered (Ghai 2001). An underlying proposition is that a society that is committed to achieving social justice must implement social and economic rights. This seems commonplace on the face of it, but is proved controversial by the lack of political will in making this simple idea a reality (2001, p. 49).

The rights-based approach suggests an integrated view of sustenance (economic and social rights) and freedom (civil and political rights): each one is necessary for the full realization of the other – again, a fact that should be self-evident but one that has been obscured by Cold War politics and decades of controversy within the human rights movement. Kabeer (2002) writes of this linkage from the perspective of the *purpose* of rights. The purpose of rights is to ensure 'freedom of action'. Viewed from this perspective, both freedom from coercion (civil and political rights) and the freedom to access material resources serve the complementary purposes of *protection* and *promotion* of the ability to act. None is adequate without the other.

The *Human Development Report 2000* had as its theme this linkage between human rights and human development, emphasizing that although these two fields have followed separate disciplinary paths, they share the same goals: securing freedom for a life of dignity and expanding people's choices and opportunities (UNDP 2000). A rights-based approach adds an element of accountability and culpability: an ethical/moral dimension to development. It therefore demands a shift from viewing poverty eradication as a development goal to viewing it as a matter of social justice; as the realization of a right and the fulfilment of a duty.

Within the framework of a rights-based approach to development, NGOs and bilateral programmes committed to its implementation have come up with lists of rights they regard as basic, which cut across the spectrum of economic, social, cultural, civil and political rights.[7] However, systematic inquiry needs to be conducted among these organizations to generate answers to the question 'how does the adoption of a rights-based approach make us "do development" differently?'[8]

Expanding the rubric of rights: environment, knowledge and participation

Groups working on the implementation of economic and social rights have become involved in community struggles against economic injustices such as environmental degradation, threats to health posed by industrial and mining activities, and the exploitation of indigenous knowledge about natural resources by pharmaceutical companies and seed developers.[9] This has contributed to the articulation of these issues as rights concerns, thus expanding the range of 'moral claims' that can be termed rights, as well as expanding the content of existing rights. One example of such expansion of meaning has been the broad interpretation of the right to life and the right to an adequate standard of living (which are provided for under existing human rights treaties) in order to embrace the right to a clean environment, which is not expressly provided for in a binding instrument.[10]

The horizons of rights discourse have also been expanded by contestation over 'knowledge rights'. These have taken place largely within the context of natural resources, where two types of questions have arisen. First, how should local (indigenous) knowledge be valued and adequately compensated when used for commercial purposes?[11] This question has been made all the more urgent by the strong protection of the intellectual property rights of commercial entrepreneurs under the Trade Related Aspects of Intellectual Property (TRIPS) agreement under the World Trade Organization framework. Community awareness and activism have been awakened. In 1999, a coalition of indigenous communities living in the Amazon successfully prevailed upon the US Patent and Trademark Office to revoke a patent that had been awarded to a US citizen over an Amazonian plant that held religious significance for the communities (IHRIP and Asian

Forum for Human Rights and Development 2000, p. 131).

The stakes in such conflicts are both political and economic: indigenous peoples' rights to information and full participation in the relevant policy processes, and their right to the tangible economic benefits that derive from any commercial use of their knowledge, since entrepreneurs clearly 'piggy-back' on indigenous knowledge. Second, how should policy-making balance between local knowledge and 'scientific knowledge' in making key decisions? It is now becoming commonplace to state that these matters are democratic and not technocratic, as Geoff Wood remarks with respect to water management in Bangladesh (Wood 1999). People have demanded broadened participation, not something narrowed down to those who claim to have scientific and technocratic expertise. Conceiving of participation as a right has politicized economic and social rights. It is no longer a 'welfarist' concern with provision of services to passive beneficiaries. Rather, it is the participation of empowered citizens in the key processes of decision-making that enact policies on how to distribute social and economic resources – a process that is inherently political (Cornwall 2000).

Conclusion

> Citizenship must be an active condition of struggling to make rights real.
> *Phillips 1991*

The discussion so far bears witness to the relevance of this statement. Specific social movement struggles at particular times have been crucial in moving the discourse and practice of human rights beyond the impasse of conventional debates, and shaping actor-oriented perspectives. These struggles have transformed the pre-defined normative parameters of human rights, questioned established categories, expanded the range of claims that could be characterized as rights, and in some cases altered institutional structures.[12] The insights arising from these social movements cut across all of the debates discussed above.

Indigenous peoples' struggles have transformed approaches to group rights as well as broadened the arena of rights to cover issues of ownership of knowledge and a more robust interpretation of the right to a healthy environment. Communities' challenges to multinational corporations continue to expand spaces for holding powerful non-state actors accountable, both through formal legal processes and informal non-binding measures such as codes of conduct, 'citizen juries' and street protests. Demands for 'dignity and daily bread' reject the compartmentalization of rights into the political and economic spheres. Rights claims in a rapidly changing world continue to expand the rubric of rights to cover new concerns such as knowledge rights.

By way of conclusion, I would like to draw out some of the key lessons that emerge from actor-oriented perspectives on the meaning of rights and citizenship. First, they suggest that we would obtain a better understanding of these issues if we sought to investigate them through pluralistic approaches which capture the everyday experiences of citizenship as mediated by factors such as gender, ethnicity, caste and kinship structure. Such a holistic analysis of citizenship and rights ought to explore how these expressions of diverse and overlapping identities function simultaneously as forces of inclusion and exclusion (Kabeer 2002).

Second, while we need to pay attention to the particular, as defined by gender, ethnicity, religion and so on, we should not lose sight of the relevance of 'across-the-board' notions of citizenship and how the mutual interaction between these notions of citizenship enables or constrains agency. It is crucial to ask, for instance, how formal state law (public) has validated and reinforced structures of inequality that have come to be viewed largely as resulting from or being dictated by (private) custom or religion.

Third, lessons from experience suggest that the rejection of a hierarchy of rights should not rule out the need to be attentive to the reality that at times the realization of one right is contingent on the existence of another. From the outset, it is instructive to approach the inquiry with an open question about how people articulate rights claims in specific situations, rather than ask which types of rights are important and how they reinforce or weaken each other. The open question is more likely to bring out the complex overlap between demands for rights as 'things' and demands for the power to make decisions concerning the 'things' (participation).

Notes

1. This chapter was first published as an IDS working paper: Nyamu-Musembi, Celestine (2002), *Towards an actor-oriented perspective on human rights*, IDS Working Paper No. 169, October.
2. See for example scholarly work in the 'critical pragmatic' framework: Joseph Singer, 'Property and Coercion in Federal Indian Law: the Conflict Between Critical and Complacent Pragmatism'; Margaret Radin, 'The Pragmatist and the Feminist'; Mari Matsuda, 'Pragmatism Modified and the False Consciousness Problem'; Martha Minow & Elizabeth Spelman, 'In Context' – all in *Southern*

California Law Review (1990).

3. Remarks at a plenary session of Harvard Human Rights Program's 15th anniversary celebration, September 1999.
4. CEDAW: Articles 2(f), 5(a) and 16.
5. Article 16(2) of the UDHR guarantees the right to marry and equal rights between men and women in marriage.
6. Constitutions that exempt religious or customary family law from the anti-discrimination clause are one example of legitimization of status hierarchy. People assigned a less favourable status in any specific situation, for instance a widow in an inheritance dispute, have no recourse to the fundamental rights of equality and non-discrimination guaranteed to all citizens. For examples from specific African constitutions, see Nyamu (2000).
7. Oxfam, for instance, now organizes its work around five types of rights: the right to a sustainable livelihood; to services (primarily health and education); to life and security; to be heard (to organize and speak out); and to an identity (free from discrimination on grounds such as gender or ethnicity) – see www.oxfam.org/eng/ campaigns_aims.htm.
8. This inquiry is the subject of an IDS Participation Group project on 'Exploring Linkages Between Rights and Participation' in seven countries; see www.ids.ac.uk/ids/particip/research/randp.html. See also Cornwall and Nyamu-Musembi, 'Putting the "Rights-Based Approach to Development" into Perspective' (forthcoming, *Third World Quarterly*, 28 (4), 2004).
9. For specific examples, see *Basic Rights*, the newsletter of the Center for Economic and Social Rights (available at www.escr-net.org/EngGeneral/ news letterarchive.asp).
10. The right to a clean environment is recognized in non-binding declarations such as the 1972 Stockholm Declaration and the 1992 Rio Declaration on Environment and Development. Some national constitutions recognize the right to a healthy environment. These include those of South Africa, the Philippines, Peru, Ecuador, Hungary and Portugal (see IHRIP and Forum-Asia 2000, p. 291).
11. See for example William Lesser (1994), 'An Approach for Securing Rights to Indigenous Knowledge', International Academy of the Environment, *Working Paper No. 15*; Darrel Posey (1990), 'Intellectual Property Rights and Just Compensation for Indigenous Knowledge', *Anthropology Today*, 13.
12. For instance, resistance to the Sardar Sarovar project to dam the Narmada river in India led to the establishment of the World Bank Inspections Panel, which oversees projects' compliance with the Bank's own operating procedures (see Fisher 1995; Rajagopal 2000; http://wbln0018.worldbank.org/ipn/ipnweb.nsf).

References

Afkhami, M. and H. Vaziri (1996) *Claiming Our Rights: A Manual for Women's Human Rights Education in Muslim Societies*, Bethesda, MD: Sisterhood is Global Institute

American Anthropological Association (AAA) (1947) 'Statement on human rights', *American Anthropologist* 49: 539

An-Na'im, A. (1992) 'Introduction', in *Human Rights in Cross-Cultural Perspectives: Quest for Consensus*, Philadelphia PA: University of Pennsylvania Press

An-Na'im, A. (1999) 'Promises we should all keep in common cause', in J. Cohen, S. Okin and M. Nussbaum (eds) *Is Multiculturalism Bad for Women?* New Jersey: Princeton University Press

Bangkok Declaration on Human Rights, www.rwgmechanism.com/asia.html

Cornwall, A. (2000) 'Beneficiary, consumer, citizen: Perspectives on participation for poverty reduction', *Sida Studies* 2

Donnelly, J. (1989) *Universal Human Rights in Theory and Practice,* Ithaca: Cornell University Press

Falk, R. (1992) 'Cultural foundations for the international protection of human rights', in A. An-Na'im (ed.) *Human Rights in Cross-Cultural Perspectives: A Quest for Consensus,* Philadelphia: University of Pennsylvania Press

Fisher, W. (ed.) (1995) *Toward Sustainable Development: Struggling Over India's Narmada River,* Armonk, NY: M.E. Sharpe

Foweraker, J. and T. Landman (1997) *Citizenship Rights and Social Movements: A Comparative and Statistical Analysis,* Oxford: Oxford University Press

Ghai, Y. (1998) *Asian Human Rights Charter: A People's Charter,* Hong Kong: Asian Human Rights Commission

Ghai, Y. (2001) 'Human rights and social development: Toward democratization and social justice', *UNRISD Democracy, Governance and Human Rights Programme Paper* 5

Griffiths, A. (1997) *In the Shadow of Marriage: Gender and Justice in an African Community,* Chicago: University of Chicago Press

Griffiths, A. (2001) 'Gendering culture: Towards a plural perspective on Kwena Women's Rights', in J. Cowan, M. Dembour and R. Wilson (eds) *Culture and Rights: Anthropological Perspectives,* Cambridge: Cambridge University Press

Hellum, A. (1999) *Women's Human Rights and Legal Pluralism in Africa: Mixed Norms and Identities in Infertility Management in Zimbabwe,* Tano Aschehoug: Mond Books

Hirsch, S. (1998) *Pronouncing and Persevering: Gender and the Discourses of Disputing in an African Islamic Court,* Chicago: Chicago University Press

Howard, R. (1992) 'Dignity, community, and human rights', in A. An-Na'im (ed.) *Human Rights in Cross-Cultural Perspective,* Philadelphia: University of Pennsylvania Press

International Human Rights Internship Program (IHRIP) and Asian Forum for Human Rights and Development (2000) *Circle of Rights: Economic, Social and Cultural Rights Activism. A Training Resource,* Washington DC: International Human Rights Internship Program

Jones, E. and J. Gaventa (2002) 'Concepts of citizenship: A review', *IDS Development Bibliography 19*

Kabeer, N. (2002) 'Citizenship, affiliation and exclusion: Perspectives from the South', *IDS Bulletin* 33(2): 12

Khare, R. S. (1998) 'Elusive social justice, distant human rights: Untouchable women's struggles and dilemmas in changing India', in M. Anderson and S. Guha (eds) *Changing Concepts of Rights and Justice in South Asia,* Delhi: Oxford University Press

Kymlicka, W. (1995) *Multicultural Citizenship,* Oxford: Oxford University Press

Lesser, W. (1994) 'An approach for securing rights to indigenous knowledge', *International Academy of the Environment* Working Paper 15

Mamdani, M. (1989) 'Social movements and constitutionalism in the African context', *Centre for Basic Research Working Paper* 2, Kampala: Centre for Basic Research

Matsuda, M. (1990) 'Pragmatism modified and the false consciousness problem', *Southern California Law Review* 63: 1763

Merry, S. E. (1997) 'Legal pluralism and transnational culture: The *Ka Ho'okolokolonui Kanaka Maoli* Tribunal, Hawai'i, 1993', in R. Wilson (ed.) *Human Rights, Culture and Context: Anthropological Perspectives,* London: Pluto Press

Minow, M. and E. Spelman (1990) 'In context', *Southern California Law Review* 63: 1597

Mulhall, S. and A. Swift (1992) *Liberals and Communitarians,* Oxford: Blackwell

Mutua, M. (1995) 'The Banjul Charter and the African cultural fingerprint: An evaluation of the language of duties', *Virginia Journal of International Law* 35: 339

Mutua, M. (1999) Remarks at plenary session of Harvard Human Rights Program's 15th anniversary celebration, September 1999

Nhlapo, T. (1995) 'Cultural diversity, human rights and the family in contemporary Africa: Lessons from the South African constitutional debate', *International Journal of Law and the Family* 9: 208

Nyamu, C. (2000) 'How should human rights and development respond to cultural legitimization of gender hierarchy in developing countries?', *Harvard International Law Journal* 41: 381

Nyamu-Musembi, C. (2002) 'Are Local Norms and Practices Fences or Pathways? The Example of Women's Property Rights' in A. An-Na'im (ed.), *Cultural Transformation and Human Rights in Africa,* London: Zed Books

Phillips, A. (1991) 'Citizenship and feminist theory', in G. Andrews (ed.) *Citizenship,* London: Lawrence and Wishart, pp. 76–7

Posey, D. (1990) 'Intellectual property rights and just compensation for indigenous knowledge', *Anthropology Today* 6: 13

Radin, M. (1990) 'The pragmatist and the feminist', *Southern California Law Review,* 63

Rajagopal, B. (2000) 'From resistance to renewal: The Third World, social movements and the expansion of international institutions', *Harvard International Law Journal* 41: 531

Schachter, O. (1983) 'Human dignity as a normative concept', *American Journal of International Law* 77: 848

Singer, J. (1990) 'Property and coercion in federal Indian law: The conflict between critical and complacent pragmatism', *Southern California Law Review* 63: 1821

Steiner, H. and P. Alston (2000) *International Human Rights in Context: Law, Politics, Morals,* Oxford: Oxford University Press

Stewart, J. (1998) 'Why I can't teach customary law', in J. Eekelaar and T. Nhlapo (eds) *The Changing Family: Family Forms and Family Law,* Oxford: Hart Publishing, pp. 217–30

UNDP (2000) *Human Development Report 2000,* New York: Oxford University Press

Wilson R. (1997) 'Human rights, culture and context: An introduction', in R. Wilson (ed.) *Human Rights, Culture and Context: Anthropological Perspectives,* London: Pluto Press

Women and Law in Southern Africa (WLSA) Research and Educational Trust (1995) 'Beyond research: WLSA in action', *WLSA Working Paper* 10, Harare: WLSA

Wood, G. (1999) 'Contesting water in Bangladesh: Knowledge, rights and governance', *Journal of International Development* 11: 731

Three

The emergence of human rights in the North: Towards historical re-evaluation

Neil Stammers

> '... without the fact of oppression, there can be no practice of resistance and no notion of rights.'
> *Mamdani, cited in Nyamu-Musembi 2002*

Introduction

Most contributions to this volume work from a perspective that is able to incorporate the insight from Mamdani above. In contrast, the dominant discourses on human rights effectively block such considerations by failing to give proper analytical weight to the link between social movement struggles and the historical emergence of human rights. In my view, the very dominance of such accounts has led to important conceptual difficulties and incapacity to assess properly the potentials and limits of human rights.

What I want to do in this chapter, therefore, is to demonstrate the necessity for a proper re-evaluation of the historical praxis through which human rights emerged in the North. The argument that follows is illustrative and provisional since it will range over a 350-year time span and select issues and examples from both European and American history. My task here is not to provide a new substantive historical account of the Northern history of human rights, rather simply to show that such an alternative historical account is possible. That said, illustrative and provisional though it is, the evidence presented here (drawn largely from authoritative historical scholarship) is already sufficient to raise serious questions regarding the accuracy of the standard accounts from both proponents and critics of human rights.

Social movement struggles against power: a history obscured

The mainstream literature on human rights does not explicitly deny a connection between human rights and social movement struggles. Indeed, on occasion, the existence of such a link has been acknowledged (for example, Weston 1992). Yet the dominant discourses from both proponents and critics are not analytically equipped to grasp the way in which human rights have been socially constructed in the context of social movement challenges to extant relations and structures of power. This analytical closure arises from a range of embedded assumptions in the academic disciplines and theoretical perspectives from which the vast bulk of the literature on human rights arises.

In a previous paper (Stammers 1999) I identified four such perspectives, labelled 'metaphysical abstraction', 'legal positivism', 'strong particularism' and 'structuralism'. The first two of these are deeply embedded in the discourses from proponents of human rights, while the latter two are crucial elements of discourses from critics of human rights.

The problem with metaphysical abstraction lies quite simply in attempts to construct supposedly timeless and universal understandings of human rights that are entirely independent of social context and thus social movement struggles. Associated in disciplinary terms with philosophy and political theory, variations of metaphysical abstraction lie at the heart of virtually all liberal and social democratic attempts to justify and ground the concept of human rights theoretically.

The term 'legal positivism' is not to be understood here in its technical sense. Rather, it signals the intent and ambition of what might be termed the global 'human rights industry'. There is an enormous literature arising from this industry: a literature overwhelmingly concerned with the establishment, implementation and enforcement of human rights as state and international public law. In this perspective, it is not that social movement struggles are unrecognized – they would probably be acknowledged as having provoked important recent debates on human rights. Yet they are not considered to have any analytic value because these approaches focus on the institutionalization and legal codification of human rights. Thus, this perspective precludes any serious consideration of the non-legal or pre-legal dimensions of human rights. While obviously associated with the discipline of law, such approaches also represent the 'realist'[1] orientation of these state and non-state actors: those international agencies and organizations who are in the business of 'doing' human rights in an institutionalized context.

Approaches grouped under the heading of 'strong particularism' emphasize the particularities of the social construction of human rights. But they do so in an overly homogenized way. This perspective fails to grasp the full extent to which relations and structures of power are multifaceted and necessarily operate both within and between what are assumed to be (or assumed should be) sealed and homogenized cultural formations and political communities. Associated most obviously with the discipline of anthropology, strong particularist perspectives are also derived from elements of post-structuralist and post-modernist thought, and have been utilized by a range of politicians and activists in the South to resist the encroachment or imposition of 'Western' values.[2]

Structuralist approaches see human rights as a 'product' or an 'effect' of what are believed to be more fundamental structural dynamics within social relations. While rightly grasping the importance of structure in shaping social relations, such approaches then typically rely on overly simplistic monocausal models to explain social change, while at the same time denying the capacity for human action to constitute meaningful agency. Unsurprisingly, advocates of this perspective see little or no positive potential in social movement struggles for human rights. Structuralist explanations can be found in a range of academic disciplines, but here they are probably more usefully understood as specific strands within broader schools of social and political thought such as Marxism and post-structuralism.

Despite their very significant differences, all these perspectives share an important characteristic. Each for their own reason fails to take proper account of historical praxis and processes. In each case, *a priori* assumptions take the place of concrete historical analysis. Such assumptions result in arguments from proponents and critics tending to mirror and contest each other, rather than making any effective connection to history and social reality. We can see this at work in three areas of debate crucial to contemporary debates on human rights. These are the relationships between:

- civil and political rights on one hand, and economic and social rights on the other;
- individual rights and collective rights;
- universal and particular dimensions of human rights.

While there are signs of an increasing stress on complexity and interdependence (for example, Mahoney and Mahoney 1993; Pollis and Schwab 2000), much of the specialist literature on human rights over the last 50 years or so has focused on claimed fundamental differences between the categories identified in each of these three areas of debate. Furthermore, these differences have typically been set up as incompatible binary oppositions.

In terms of the relationship between civil and political rights and economic and social rights, key liberal theorists and powerful Western states have argued that only civil and political rights are real human rights on the grounds, for example, that correlative duties to such rights simply require the state not to interfere with individual freedoms (the notion of negative rights). Concomitantly, economic and social rights are unreal rights because correlative duties require state intervention (the notion of positive rights) that may be impractical and likely to interfere with other people's freedoms (for more detail see Beetham 1995; Cranston 1973; Steiner and Alston 2000, pp. 181–85, 249–61). Critics have argued that such claims illustrate the deep ideological nature and limits of human rights as Western/bourgeois notions, and that, if human rights are useful at all, economic and social rights are more real because, for example, our basic physical and material existence relies upon them. Thus it can be argued that economic and social rights should be privileged over civil and political rights (for example, Halasz 1966; Pollis and Schwab 1980; Steiner and Alston 2000, p. 237)

In a parallel set of arguments, liberal theorists and politicians argue that only individual human rights are 'real' human rights. This is rooted in their abstracted understanding of individual freedom and their suspicions about the authoritarian potential embedded in concepts of collectives. Here, critics respond that such arguments demonstrate the possessive, egoistic nature of individual rights, and that again, if anything, collective rights should be privileged over individual rights on the basis, for example, that outside of some understanding of some collective entity/community, the very notion of the individual is meaningless (Freeman 1995, pp. 25–40; Robinson 2002).

Finally, some proponents have made strong, sweeping and uncritical claims regarding the universality of particular declarations of human rights (such as those set out in the UN Declaration). Their task, as they see it, then becomes to ensure that such rights are implemented and enforced globally. Critics respond that such claims simply confirm human rights as a dangerous form of Western imperialism. They would point out, for example, that the UN Declaration of 1948 was primarily the product of the victorious Western allies at the end of the Second World War and not based on any genuinely negotiated worldwide agreement (for example, Evans 1998).

While of a somewhat different order, we should also make note of the 'generations' perspective within the mainstream literature on human rights. This perspective usually identifies three generations of human rights: the first, civil and political rights; the second, economic and social rights; and the third, collective or solidarity rights (Donnelly 1989, p. 143). Such arguments are not necessarily derived from the perspectives discussed above, and could potentially historicize human rights in a way that could recognize the relevance of social movement struggles. Yet, at the same time, such arguments still assume that different generations are separable as categories of rights (for a recent example of this, see Frost 2002), and certainly the metaphor of 'generations' strongly implies a historical chronology and, to a lesser degree, progressive linear development. What follows suggests significant limits to the utility of this perspective too.

Many of these debates are closely connected to what has happened to human rights globally over the last 50 years, and, of course, this cannot be separated from the geopolitical realities and structures of power in the contemporary world order. Yet these arguments are also, typically, projected backwards in time and claimed to apply to the entire history of human rights. What I want to do in the sections that follow is to begin to show that the veracity and usefulness of such historical claims are far from self-evident. An alternative historical account could cast a very different light on the potentials and limits of human rights.

Economic dimensions in struggles for natural rights

The 150 years spanning the period from the English Civil War (1640–51) to the French Revolution (1789) witnessed the emergence of strong claims to 'natural rights' in both Europe and North America. These ideas and claims significantly cross-fertilized, and there is little disagreement today that natural rights were an important precursor of what we now call human rights. But what these natural rights comprised, where they came from and what they signified have been highly contested. Despite this, the standard accounts from proponents and critics share important assumptions. First, natural rights are seen as quintessentially civil and political rights. Second, there is an underlying conceptual separation of the economic from the political, with the cultural being ignored altogether. For proponents, natural rights mark the beginning of developments that led to the establishment of liberal states – state power being constrained by the constitutional set-up and the institutionalization of a range of rights belonging to individual citizens. In this sort of perspective, the political is privileged over the economic. In contrast, especially for many structuralist Marxist critics, these civil and political rights were the political and legal frameworks that arose to consolidate and legitimize new patterns of capitalist economic relations. While the economic and political appear to be connected here, in fact such a connection still ultimately relies on a conceptual separation within which the economic is privileged over the political.

To examine history is to study structured but contingent complexity, and even a cursory examination of the emergence of natural rights suggests that the basic assumptions of the above accounts are nowhere near as watertight as their advocates claim. Indeed, the economic, political and cultural dimensions of these social struggles can be seen to be deeply intertwined throughout this whole period. So this section considers a key economic dimension of struggles for natural rights, that of property relations

As a starting point, it is important to recognize the extent to which, within the ideology and reality of absolutism in this historical period, different facets of power were fused or claimed to be so. In other words, in contrast to the differentiation of political, economic and cultural forms of power typical of the trajectory of Western modernity, traditional forms of power were assumed to be undifferentiated and were legitimized in terms of an absolute monarch acting as a direct servant of God *via* the doctrine of the Divine Right of Kings. Put simply, the monarch claimed absolute power (Burns 1990; Mann 1986, pp. 475–83). The importance of this point lies in the fact that, while on one level a challenge to monarchical power could reasonably be described as political, on another it was also a challenge to prevailing forms of economic and cultural power.

From here it is possible to re-examine the place of property rights in articulations of natural rights. When natural rights are only understood as civil and political rights, the place of property rights is manifestly anomalous, and this anomaly does seem to point to the pivotal role of private property rights in understandings of natural rights, as both liberal and Marxist theorists have argued. However, once it is recognized that claims to natural rights sought to challenge economic as well as political power, the anomalous position of property rights disappears. Clearly, whether taken as meaning 'property in oneself',[3] or ownership and/or control of economic resources, claiming the right to private property was a very radical demand in the context of monarchical claims to absolute power over every object and person within the realm. But it does not follow that such claims must necessarily be understood as 'bourgeois rights'.

Interestingly, there is a further and connected key issue of contestation here. Were such claims to private property a challenge to power, or were they, rather, designed to consolidate and legitimate new relations and structures of power that had already emerged? If true, the latter argument would buttress explanations of property rights as inherently bourgeois. If false, in what sense could such rights claims then be said to consolidate and legitimate new relations and structures of power (see also Stammers 1999, p. 996)? These two points will be briefly examined below, using the modern understanding of property rights.

Hampsher-Monk (1992) takes up these questions in respect of Locke's *Two Treatises of Government*, often argued to be the key founding text of liberal/bourgeois political thought in respect of property rights. He notes that many writers interpret Locke as providing a theoretical justification for the capital accumulation of a triumphant bourgeois class, but he points out that 'we must not credit Locke with prescience. His purpose at the time of writing was to defend the claims of private property against royal appropriation' (1992, p. 93). In fact, the *Two Treatises* was written to rebut the advocacy of absolute monarchy in Filmer's *Patriarcha*, and, in the context of Locke's involvement with radical politics, led him to fear for his life and flee the country. Hampsher-Monk points out that 'the work was thus not originally written to justify the successful revolution of 1688 but almost wholly to incite a future one' (1992, p. 72).

More generally, Arblaster (1984) and Richardson (1997) have identified important forms of social movement praxis that they say cannot be reduced to a defence of bourgeois property relations. This is in the context of wide-ranging surveys discussing the nature of liberalism and movements associated with it. Discussing England in the middle decades of the seventeenth century, Arblaster unsurprisingly identifies the gradual formation of an essentially bourgeois social philosophy that was to become the middle-class orthodoxy of the eighteenth century. But, he argues, 'these ideas were challenged by a more democratic and popular standpoint by the short-lived popular movements of the period' (1984, p. 147). Richardson's point is a wider one. He identifies what he calls 'contending liberalisms', saying that these can be traced back to the seventeenth century. Pointing out that the term 'liberalism' only emerges in the nineteenth century to cover a wide range of movements and ideas, he argues that one strand of liberalism is a liberalism of privilege, private property and power. He sees the other strand as much more radical, seeking to universalize ideas of liberty, equality and fraternity (1997, pp. 7 and 10). Within this formulation, far from defending bourgeois property relations, the radical rights-based strand of liberal thought and activism has always challenged power, property and privilege, in much the same way that the earliest articulations of natural rights sought to challenge absolutist power.

If we now turn our attention to the specific social transformations that took place in England, America and France, we find interesting patterns of historical evidence that support the above arguments. In each case, there is evidence that the advocates of natural rights did not represent bourgeois property interests, and that claims to natural rights were consistently attacked and denounced by both the old and the emerging propertied classes.

In England, the radicalism of the Levellers' and Diggers' movements during the English Civil War has been well documented (Arblaster 1984; Wootton 1991, 1992). Indeed, Manning argues that 'popular movements played a part, perhaps the decisive part, in the revolution' (1996, p. 5). More provocatively perhaps, in reviewing the work of Marxist historian Christopher Hill, who specialized in this period of English history, Eley and Hunt describe the revolutionary radicals of the time as 'the rank-and-file who originated the democratic and socialist history of our civilisation' (1988, p. 25).

Much less well known is the extent to which key natural rights theorists were influenced by the ideas of these relatively short-lived movements of the English Civil War. Yet both Laslett (1988, p. 22) and Hampsher-Monk (1992, Chapter 2) note the strong resemblances between Locke's writings and the activism of the Levellers. Rather more surprising is the suggestion, in a classic study of the more radical Diggers movement, that Diggers' leader Gerrard Winstanley laid the groundwork for the thinking of John Locke and Thomas Paine, Locke being described as Winstanley's 'immediate successor' (Berens 1906/1961, p. 71).

At first sight, the American transformation looks the most evidently conservative and bourgeois in character. Indeed, some accounts do argue that nothing very much changed internally: a propertied elite led the revolution, won the revolution and maintained power thereafter. But there are analyses that suggest that the revolutionary period at least was a far more radical affair. Reviewing historical research of this period, Greene identifies a 'progressive conception' of American history that identifies a fundamental conflict between 'an upper class elite who advocated property rights and the political predominance of special interests' and 'the little men … who stood for human rights and democracy' (1979, p. 8). Historical accounts of the revolution from this perspective see the revolutionary period itself as a struggle for democracy on the part of disenfranchised and underprivileged groups, and some accounts argue that, by the time of the Declaration of Independence and the revolutionary war, it was the radicals, not the elites, who had won. On the other hand, this victory was apparently short-lived, progressive accounts then arguing that the constitution-building of the late 1780s delivered a decisive victory for the propertied elites. Referring to Beard's study of the economic interests of members of the Constitutional Convention of 1787, Greene notes:

> Implicit in Beard's conclusions was the idea that the constitution, instead of being the logical culmination of the revolution ... was actually a repudiation of it, the counterrevolutionary instrument conceived by Conservatives to curb the democratic excesses of the war and confederation periods.'
>
> *Greene 1979, p. 12*

It should be said that Greene is clearly unconvinced by such accounts. He argues that more recent research undermines such explanations (1979, pp. 27–31) and that a central concern of the 'men of the American Revolution' was the search for the means (citing Morgan) 'to check the inevitable operation of depravity in men who wielded power' (p. 73).

But even if Greene is right, the relevance of these accounts for this chapter is that they again show that there is serious historical scholarship that disrupts suppositions that the nature of the American transformation was simply the consolidation of the power of an American propertied elite. Also, in stressing the notion of struggle between social forces, such accounts point towards contingency rather than inevitability in terms of outcomes.

In England it was some fifty years before notions of natural rights were institutionalized in the constitutional settlement of 1688–89. In the American case, it took just over a decade. In the French case, as a number of scholars have noted, the French Declaration of the Rights of Man and Citizen was, at least in part, about legitimizing and institutionalizing a new form of political power from the very outset (Baker 1990, pp. 261–7; Van Kley 1994, p. 6).

The French Revolution has of course been depicted in many ways. It has been seen as the first 'popular revolution', the starting point of 'modern politics', and as marking the 'unexpected invention of revolutionary politics' (Doyle 1999; Hobsbawm 1962, pp. 1–4; Hunt 1986, p. 3). Curiously, and apparently paradoxically, the classic explanation of the French Revolution (shared by Marxists and liberals) was one that saw it as a bourgeois revolution, establishing a regime that more closely reflected the new distribution of economic power (Doyle 1999). But just as in the American case, the assumption that the revolution was inherently bourgeois ignores the contingency of historical processes and downplays the struggles of key social actors (see, for example, Hunt 1986, pp. 4–5). Indeed, Williams, writing at the end of the 1980s, stated that in France the classic account of the Revolution had collapsed under the weight of evidence-gathering built upon the previous major advances achieved by Marxist historical scholarship (1989, p. ix).

To summarize, there are important historical accounts (including those of radical and Marxist historians) that provide substantive evidence that the transformations in each of these countries should not simply be understood as 'bourgeois' in terms of historical processes, even if the ultimate outcomes were so. Rather, in terms of social struggles, these transformations – particularly in their revolutionary moments – may be better understood as struggles against absolutist state power. In each case, these alternative accounts identify social move-ments as important agents of transformation. Such accounts indicate that it was movement activists that generated discourses of natural rights, and that they did so as a way of challenging absolutist power. This is particularly clear in the English and American cases, perhaps less so in the French case. Seen in these terms, claims to natural rights are not simply reducible to an ideological defence of bourgeois property rights. Indeed, these alternative historical accounts suggest (again, particularly in the English and American cases) that it was the most radical currents of activism that developed and deployed the idea of natural rights. Far from relying on them, the newly emerging propertied classes saw such rights talk as dangerous and revolutionary – anarchical fallacies, as Bentham neatly summed it up at the time (Waldron 1987).

Political dimensions of workers' struggles of the nineteenth century

Claims to basic economic rights were very much part of the package of rights claims that moved to centre stage in the nineteenth century as social relations were radically transformed in Europe and the United States with the development of industrial capitalism. The point of this section, though, is not to examine 'the social question', as it was then often termed. Rather, it is to look at the way in which economic and political claims were inter-linked in the workers' struggles of this period. Interestingly, the details of such struggles hardly ever figure in the accounts of the emergence of human rights found in the dominant discourses, despite the fact that these struggles were clearly foundational for the subsequent construction of economic and social rights in the

North.

The first point to stress is the extent of the continuity between earlier understandings of natural rights and the rights claims that emerged in the nineteenth century. From an understanding of how power was fused within absolutism, it is not difficult to see how the critique of privilege and power underpinning claims to natural rights could be translated and applied to the changing circumstances. This is what seems to have happened as rights claims were reformulated in the nineteenth century (Thompson 1963, Chapters 4 and 5).

Of course, part of this reformulation involved a more explicit emphasis on economic power. For example, in his study of radical artisans in England and France from 1830 to 1870, Prothero notes that the privilege the radicals assailed was often seen in terms of particular economic interests, and that rights claims were used to challenge the 'logic of political economy' (1997, Chapter 2 and pp. 134–7). But equally, the political and cultural identities that emerged in earlier movement struggles for natural rights could also be reconfigured in respect of the new realities. E. P. Thompson brilliantly shows how the changing productive relations and working conditions of the Industrial Revolution were imposed not upon raw material but upon a culturally embedded understanding of being a freeborn Englishman (1963, Chapters 4 and 5). Thus in England at the beginning of the nineteenth century, working people could identify with their apparent historical predecessors. Thompson argues that even the Luddites understood themselves to be defending 'ancient right' (1963, pp. 587–602).

Despite the greater and explicit emphasis on the problems of economic power, the centrality of demands for civil and political rights to the workers and socialist movements can hardly be underestimated. These struggles were about extending the civil and political equality of natural rights to the working class and, for some activists at least, such political reform was seen as a necessary first step that would then pave the way for economic reform and the achievement of economic rights. However, that said, it is also important to note that many of the specific demands for civil and political rights arose as a form of resistance to the implementation of repressive legislation designed to construct a free market for the new industrial capitalist economy. Thompson notes that no less than 63 new capital offences against property were created in England between 1760 and 1810 (1963, p. 60) and Prothero summarizes a range of repressive legislative changes in England and France that affected employment contracts and the legality of trades unions, movements and trade societies (1997, pp. 134–5). Even these few examples make it clear that such rights claims need to be under-

stood as having political, economic and cultural dimensions, and constituted challenges to the combined weight of economic and political
power in early-nineteenth-century Europe.

The historical link between collective and individual rights

A reader of contemporary literature on human rights could be forgiven
for thinking that the notion of collective or group rights was a recent
invention. Yet even a cursory examination of historical materials
suggests that such assumptions are untenable, that a notion of collective
rights derived from conceptions of collective identity was embedded
even in the earliest articulations of natural rights. As far as I am aware,
this has never even been acknowledged within the dominant discourses,
let alone given the analytical scrutiny it deserves.

In his study of 'Leveller democracy and the puritan revolution',
Wootton notes that the Levellers' document of 1647, the *Agreement of
the People*, was the 'first proposal in history for a written constitution
based on inalienable natural rights' (1991, p. 412). But it is also in this
programme that we can see the first suggestion of a notion of a
collective right, because the people who are said to have these rights are
'the people of England' (*Agreement of the People*). The American
Declaration of Independence goes a step further, clearly articulating a
notion of collective right. It states that whenever any form of government becomes destructive of inalienable rights, 'it is the *right of the people
to alter or abolish it*' (in Ishay 1997, p. 127; my emphasis).

By the time of the French Revolution, the notion of collective right
appears in a considerably stronger form. Clause 3 of the French Declaration of the Rights of Man and Citizen states, 'the source of all
sovereignty resides essentially in the nation; no group, no individual
may exercise authority not emanating expressly therefrom'. Clause 6
begins, 'Law is the expression of the general will' (Ishay 1997, p. 138).
This emphasis on nation, law and the general will indicates the rather
more state-centric concerns and institutional focus of the French
Revolution at its ruptural moment compared to the English and
American cases. More interestingly here, though, is an apparent
articulation of collective right that is seen as superior to individual
right.

Indeed, it has been argued that it was precisely the French
Revolution that fired nineteenth-century Western Europe with
nationalist fervour, and resulted in struggles for national self-
determination. Ronen argues that the 1848 revolutions were primarily
revolutions that sought either to unify a supposedly national community

or else liberate such a community from an imperial power like the Hapsburg Empire (1979, pp. 3–4). This suggests a direct link between the twentieth-century notion of a people's right to national self-determination and its apparent origins in the French Revolution.

What is more, both Hobsbawm and Ronen have noted that 'the social question' and 'the national question' were two sides of the same coin throughout Europe in the nineteenth century. In particular, Hobsbawm points to what he calls the 'popular-revolutionary' notion of a nation, within which the link between the national and the social questions is understood 'from below' as a struggle for the common interests of the people against particular interests. Using a language strongly resonant of Paine and earlier articulations of natural rights, Hobsbawm argues that these struggles need to be understood as struggles against arbitrary power and privilege (1992, pp. 19–20). Furthermore, by 1880, debates around the national question had become crucial for socialists. Subsequent struggles by anti-imperialist movements in the twentieth century were then influenced strongly by these socialist and Marxist understandings of a right to national self-determination (1992, pp. 123–4, 149–51).

Of course, this is not the only important way in which individual and collective notions of rights are connected in the nineteenth century. As noted in the previous section, many of the struggles by workers and socialist activists were struggles for rights to organize collectively in trade unions or friendly and co-operative societies. These often long, protracted and bitter struggles laid the groundwork for the recognition of trades union and related rights as fundamental human rights in the twentieth century. Yet, again, they barely figure in accounts of the development of human rights in the dominant discourses.

The universality and particularity of rights claims

> Our experience of discrimination as *women* led us to demand fair treatment and respect for our dignity as *human beings*, and only thereafter to claim our rights and entitlements as *citizens*
>
> Huq 2003: p. 10, emphasis in original

The above statement relates to contemporary women's struggles in Bangladesh, and indicates a process of a particular collective identity being universalized as part of the human condition, and then re-particularized in terms of claims to citizenship rights within a particular political community. Fascinatingly, this observation appears to resonate with elements of the historical development of human rights discussed in this chapter.

The outline sketch offered here casts serious doubt on arguments based on a binary separation of the universal and the particular. From the very earliest of claims and struggles for natural rights, some conception of a particular collective identity – a 'we the people' – already appears to have been present. In the construction of their claims and demands, activists and movements in England, America and France then developed and adopted understandings of universal natural rights. Of course, claims for universal natural rights were also claims for, and could only be instantiated as, particular citizenship rights – institutionalized within specific political, legal and state formations. The nineteenth-century workers' struggles seem somewhat different, insofar as emergent class identities appear to have been connected to (by then stronger) notions of national identity. As we saw, rights claims still appealed to notions of universal rights understood as challenges to power and privilege, but struggles during this period seem to have become more explicitly focused on struggles for citizenship rights within the legal jurisdictions of particular nation-states.

While further substantive and detailed research would be necessary to consider whether the sequencing indicated by Huq is a common and persistent feature of the development of human rights in the North, the fact that it can be identified in this initial survey suggests that it may be highly significant. If so, what are the implications of this for thinking about human rights?

First, in contrast to the claims of liberal political theorists and their Marxist critics, it appears that claims to the universality of natural rights were constructed on the basis of recognition of the vulnerability of human beings situated within a matrix of relations and structures of power. So, despite the language of natural rights sometimes being couched in strongly egoistic terms, a key aspect of the claimed universality of rights nevertheless needs to be understood in terms of situated social actors struggling against power. Given that claims to absolutist power were legitimized transcendentally (by monarchs claiming Divine Right), it is not hard to see why oppositional social actors would seek to develop equally strong transcendent claims in efforts to de-legitimize them. Additionally, of course, one way of challenging power within a specific regime would be to articulate universalized claims that could potentially 'trump' any such particular legitimations of power.

All of this points to a quite different way of thinking about the universality of human rights. If claims to universality seek to challenge and overcome particularities of power, perhaps it is also the ubiquity, the universality, of power in the world (political, economic and cultural power) that lies behind the continuing claims and demands for human rights from grassroots movements worldwide.

Yet we have also seen that the historical struggles considered here had important particular dimensions, both in terms of the construction of particular collective identities and in terms of particular instantiations of citizenship rights. Throughout this historical period, these two types of particularities appear to be connected *via* the notion of an emergent 'sovereignty of the people'. And this, of course, needs to be understood in the context of the historical development of the modern nation state. Thus, it is undoubtedly the case that a crucial trajectory of such rights claims was towards their institutionalization within the positive law of particular nation states. In an earlier paper (Stammers 1999) I argued that the institutionalization of rights produces a paradox. On the one hand, the instantiation of human rights as positive law can protect rights and punish violations. Yet at the same time, because the very process of institutionalization necessarily enmeshes them within existing relations and structures of power, institutionalized rights can be 'turned' or 'switched', being used to sustain power both within the particular community and also, importantly, beyond it.

As many authors in this volume note, citizenship and citizenship rights can be exclusionary. This may be explained by the specific particularities of collective identity construction. Essentialist and exclusionary dimensions of collective identity were clearly embedded within historical struggles for human rights in the North. It was through these that indigenous peoples, slaves and women could be excluded from so-called universal natural rights. Whilst physically within a legal jurisdiction, they were not considered part of the institutionalized 'we the people'. They were 'othered' and placed outside the boundaries of citizenship.

There is another vital dimension here, too, because the particularity of citizenship rights within a specific state also excludes those people outside the territorial jurisdiction where citizenship rights have been instantiatied. A strong case could no doubt be made to show that the very building of citizenship rights in the North was, in crucial ways, dependent upon massive violations of human rights in the South. One tragedy of human rights at the beginning of the twenty-first century is the continuation of that story.

While the above discussion certainly suggests that there are crucial problems with the traditional constructions of human rights in the North, they are hardly the ones pointed to by most critics of 'Northern' or 'Western' human rights. What has been suggested here is that it is in the exclusionary potential of collective identity construction and the institutionalization of human rights as citizenship rights that the key difficulties are located. In contrast, what may be most positive about the history of struggles for human rights in the North is to be found in claims to their universality, providing that universality is understood not in terms of the rights themselves, but in terms of the universality of power in the world that such rights claims seek to challenge.

Conclusion

This chapter has tried to show that a plausible and substantive alternative historical account of the emergence of human rights in the North could be developed through a proper engagement with existing historical scholarship. Even the provisional and illustrative outline provided here casts doubt on the veracity and utility of many of the standard accounts. In my view, these dominant discourses are both historically inaccurate and analytically flawed. By failing to examine the emergence of human rights in terms of the historical praxis of social movement struggles, both proponents and critics have engaged in debates that are largely spurious and only serve to limit a more thorough understanding of the potentials and limits of human rights.

The evidence presented here has been highly selective and focused on action rather than any systematic attempt at analysing historical processes of structuration. Yet part of the reason for this lies precisely in the limits of the existing literature. Historical research on human rights has to be a sort of archaeology. This is not meant in a Foucauldian sense, but the metaphor is a good one to the extent that it points to the necessity of delving into a range of historical materials beyond the human rights literature in order to unearth relevant fragments. I hope the way in which some of these fragments have been assembled here is sufficient to demonstrate that a more thorough historical re-evaluation of the emergence of human rights in the North is desperately needed.

The stakes are high. My contention is that the greatest problem with human rights is not those usually identified by critics. It is not that they are 'Northern' or 'Western'. Rather, it connects to deeper problems of the organization of human relations historically and globally. It connects back to the problem of power in the world – economic, political and cultural – and to the continuation of historical struggles to prevent its abuse.

Notes

I would like to thank Gurminder Bhambra, Marie Dembour, Ariadna Estevez-

Lopez, Naila Kabeer and Zdenek Kavan for their helpful comments on an early draft of this chapter.

1. I am using the term 'realist' here as it is used within the discipline of International Relations.
2. The very term 'Western' here demonstrates the problem, as does the use of 'Northern' and 'Southern' in this chapter and volume. While undoubtedly both a convenient shorthand and offering some analytical purchase on the asymmetries of power in the world, closer consideration makes it quickly clear that the 'North' and 'South' cannot even begin to capture the degree of heterogeneity in social relations in their supposed areas or regions.
3. As Hampsher-Monk puts it, '"property" in the 17th century was often used more widely to denote any rights of a fundamental kind, and fundamental rights were often claimed to be inalienable' (1992, p. 88). So rather than seeing the right to property as one right amongst others, property in this sense relates to all those rights that people might have as potential constraints on power, and this connects to the extensive debates on the development of possessive individualism during this historical period (for example, Tully 1993, Chapter 2).

References

Agreement of the People (1647) website copy accessed July 2003 at www.fairfax.org.uk/main/ARTICLES/RESEARCH/levellers/agreement%20164 7.HTM

Arblaster, A. (1984) *The Rise and Decline of Western Liberalism*, Oxford: Blackwell

Baker, K. M. (1990) *Inventing the French Revolution: Essays on French Political Culture in the 18th Century*, Cambridge: Cambridge University Press

Beetham, D. (1995) 'What future for economic and social rights?', *Political Studies* (special issue) 43, pp. 41–60

Berens, L. (1906/1961) *The Digger Movement in the Days of the Commonwealth*, London: Holland Press and Merlin Press

Burns, J. H. (1990) 'The idea of absolutism', in J. Miller (ed.) *Absolutism in Seventeenth Century Europe*, Basingstoke: Macmillan

Cranston, M. (1973) *What Are Human Rights?* New York: Taplinger

Donnelly, J. (1989) *Universal Human Rights in Theory and Practice*, New York: Cornell University Press

Doyle, W. (1999) *Origins of the French Revolution*, Oxford: Oxford University Press

Eley, G. and W. Hunt. (1988) *Reviving the English Revolution*, London: Verso

Evans, T. (ed.) (1998) *Human Rights Fifty Years On*, Manchester: Manchester University Press

Freeman, M. (1995) 'Are there collective human rights?', *Political Studies* (special issue) 43, pp. 25–40

Frost, M. (2002) *Constituting Human Rights: Global Civil Society and the society of democratic states*, London: Routledge

Greene, J. P. (1979) *The Re-interpretation of the American Revolution 1763–1789*, Westport, Connecticut: Greenwood Press

Halasz, J. (1966) (ed.) *The Socialist Concept of Human Rights*, Budapest: Akademiai Kiado

Hampsher-Monk, I. (1992) *A History of Modern Political Thought*, Oxford: Blackwell

Hobsbawm, E. J. (1962) *The Age of Revolution*, London: Weidenfeld and Nicholson

Hobsbawm, E. J. (1992) *Nations and Nationalism since 1780*, 2nd edition, Cambridge: Cambridge University Press

Hunt, L. (1986) *Politics, Culture and Class in the French Revolution*, London: Methuen

Huq, S. P. (2003) Untitled working paper presented at an authors' workshop in Stellenbosch, South Africa, 6–8 June 2003, by the Development Research Centre on Citizenship, Participation and Accountability, Institute for Development Studies, University of Sussex

Ishay, M. R. (1997) *The Human Rights Reader*, London: Routledge

Keane, J. (1996) *Tom Paine: A Political Life*, London: Bloomsbury

Laslett, P. (1988) 'Introduction', in J. Locke, *Two Treatises of Government*, edited by P. Laslett, Cambridge: Cambridge University Press

Mahoney, K. E. and P. Mahoney (eds) (1993) *Human Rights in the Twenty-First Century: A Global Challenge*, London: M. Nijhoff

Mann, M. (1986) *The Sources of Social Power*, Vol. I, Cambridge: Cambridge University Press

Manning, B. (1996) *Aristocrats, Plebeians and Revolution in England*, London: Pluto Press

Nyamu-Musembi, C. (2002) 'Towards an actor-oriented perspective on human rights', IDS Working Paper 169, Brighton: Institute of Development Studies

Pollis, A. and P. Schwab (1980) (eds) *Human Rights: Cultural and Ideological Perspectives*, New York: Praeger

Pollis, A. and P. Schwab (2000) (eds) *Human Rights: New Perspectives, New Realities*, Boulder, CO: Lynne Reinner

Prothero, I. (1997) *Radical Artisans in England and France, 1830–1870*, Cambridge: Cambridge University Press

Richardson, J. (1997) 'Contending liberalisms: Past and present', in *European Journal of International Relations* 3(1), pp. 5–33

Robinson, F. (2002) 'Human rights discourse and global civil society: Contesting globalization?', paper presented at the annual conference of the International Studies Association, New Orleans

Ronen, D. (1979) *The Quest for Self-Determination*, New Haven, London: Yale University Press

Stammers, N. (1999) 'Social movements and the social construction of human rights', *Human Rights Quarterly* 21, pp. 980–1008

Steiner, H. and P. Alston (2000) *International Human Rights in Context*, 2nd edition, Oxford: Oxford University Press

Thompson, E. P. (1963) *The Making of the English Working Class*, London: Victor Gollancz

Tully, J. (1993) *An Approach to Political Philosophy: Locke In Contexts*, Cambridge: Cambridge University Press

Van Kley, D. (1994) (ed.) *The French Idea of Freedom: The Old Regime and the Declaration Rights of 1789*, Stanford CA: Stanford University Press

Waldron, J. (1987) *Nonsense Upon Stilts: Bentham, Burke and Marx on the Rights of Man*, London: Methuen

Weston, B. H. (1992) 'Human rights', in R. P. Claude and B. H. Weston, *Human Rights in the World Community*, Philadelphia, PA: University of Pennsylvania Press

Williams, J. (1989) *Artisans and Sans-Culottes: Popular Movements in France and Britain during the French Revolution*, 2nd edition, London: Libris

Wootton, D. (1991) 'Leveller democracy and the puritan revolution', in J. H. Burns (ed.) *The Cambridge History of Political Thought*, Cambridge: Cambridge University Press

Wootton, D. (1992) 'The Levellers', in J. Dunn (ed.) *Democracy: The Unfinished Journey, 508BC to AD 1993*, Oxford: Oxford University Press

Citizenship and Identity

Four

A nation in search of citizens: Problems of citizenship in the Nigerian context

Oga Steve Abah and Jenks Zakari Okwori

Introduction: framing citizenship in colonial Nigeria

In exploring issues of citizenship in Nigeria, we need to begin with the history of how we came to be Nigerians (or how we are not!). What is now known as Nigeria is the product of the British colonial imagination; a patchwork country whose component parts have refused to fuse as one (Okwori 2003). Although the interest in Nigeria began with trade, it moved to conquest and ownership. The British first showed a serious interest in Nigeria after Sir George Goldie (Goldie 1898) promoted the Niger Delta area: 'This heart of Africa was not a barren desert. They found that it was filled with populous and organised States, that it possessed a fertile soil and intelligent and industrious inhabitants'. This interest was pursued first as trade, when Sir George Goldie and his Royal Niger Company were drawn to the region by the attractions of trade in rubber, timber, palm oil and, later, slaves. In return for these goods, they provided local chiefs with gunpowder, mirrors and other trivia. The gunpowder later proved useful for slave raiding and disciplining the population. The transition from a source of valued, traded goods to an owned territory was an interesting business transaction. Sir George Goldie, the director of the Royal Niger Company, sold the territory around the Niger to the British Crown for £850,000 in 1900. One may argue, therefore, that modern Nigeria began its life both as a commodity and as a corporate slave!

Once this region passed into the hands of the Crown, Nigeria was first organized into protectorates, then extended to the north as the empire expanded. In 1906, the colony of Lagos was merged with the protectorate of the Niger Coast to form the colony and protectorate of Southern Nigeria. The protectorates of Northern and Southern Nigeria merged into the colony of Nigeria in 1914 (Ihonvbere and Shaw 1998). Each of the protectorates 'was a sprawling territory of separate ethno-linguistic groups, each with its own distinctive history, language, social custom, and beliefs. Nigeria is therefore a veritable mosaic of nationalities; it has within its borders several hundred ethnic groups with distinct languages and cultures' (Okehie–Offa and Sadiku 1996, p. 1).

Framing citizenship in post-colonial Nigeria

The project of forming Nigeria and understanding who its citizens are, has been (and still is) riddled with contradictions and tensions arising from the disconnections between a primordial 'indigenous' sense of being (ontology) and the membership of an entity that is defined beyond the confines of autochthony. The former carries a sense of rootedness; the latter merely describes a geographical space. This disconnection is at the heart of what constitutes the major impasse in the 'national question' in Nigeria.

This disconnection is compounded by the second level of impasse, which dates back to 1939, when the southern provinces of the country were split in two, while the North was left intact as a single protectorate. The North occupies about 74 per cent of the entire land mass of the country and, according to (contested) population counts, is home to more than half the population. This lopsided division was retained when Nigeria gained independence in 1960; it has had, and continues to have, consequences for the conduct of elections and for the composition of the central administration. As Okeke (1992, p. 18) argues, 'Since the electoral system adopted in the country was based on the principles of proportional representation and majority rule, Northern Nigeria had a competitive advantage over the Southern regions in Federal politics'. This gave the North domination in political and territorial terms over the divided southern regions. Nigeria thus inherited two architectures of citizenship from its colonial past, both at loggerheads with each other: the architecture of nationhood (an inclusive identity) and that of differing ethnicities (which are exclusive).

A third impasse, exacerbating the tensions between nationhood and ethnicity, was introduced by the definition of citizenship enshrined in the Nigerian Constitution of 1999. This allowed for three, often conflicting, criteria for acquiring Nigerian citizenship. The first is birth, and includes conditions relating to dates, parentage and indigenity. The second is naturalization, with its own set of conditions. The third is through marriage. However, it is only a woman married to a Nigerian man who can acquire Nigerian citizenship. A Nigerian woman married a non-Nigerian man cannot bestow citizenship on her husband. There is an obvious discrimination enshrined in the constitution here. However, in all three criteria for citizenship outlined in the constitution, ethnic belonging is given greatest emphasis in the actual practice of realizing citizenship in Nigeria.

Thus, outside of registration and naturalization, it is ancestral linkage, place of birth or origin – and therefore ethnic belonging – that plays a fundamental role in citizenship. This has practical ramifications, because many of the entitlements bestowed on citizens by the state in Nigeria are tied to such definitions. As a nation, Nigeria would like to promote the sense of oneness for all Nigerians. Yet through its political practices it has not only retained the original differentiated identities that have characterized the area since the colonial period, but has added to the sense of divided identities in its citizens.

The 1999 constitution was adopted when a military government was in power. A constituent assembly was set up with representatives from different parts of Nigeria. While intended to address the divisions of ethnicity, the reliance on a group selected mainly from elites in the different areas, and the lack of grassroots participation in the process, meant that ethnic divisions became further entrenched. Two things were missing from the process. The first was that the consultation was not as wide as it could have been. The second was that some of the most pertinent questions were not asked. They were not asked precisely because the people who might have raised them did not have the chance to do so. Nonetheless, such questions are now being asked outside the process, and the consequences of not putting them on the agenda of the Constituent Assembly are being felt. Among the questions that many Nigerians ask both privately and publicly are whether the different nationalities that form Nigeria need to belong to one nation. They also ask why there is no meaningful and equal participation by all the ethnicities in the governance of Nigeria. And at the local level, many wonder whether there is any meaning at all in being so-called Nigerians. For example, a paramount chief in Otuokpoti, a small riverine community in Bayelsa State, said to us: 'My friend, I cannot tell you that I will beat my chest and say that I am a Nigerian. Look around. Does this village look like a place in Nigeria? What do we get from Nigeria?'

One important reason for not addressing these crucial issues at the time was that they could lead to a break-up of Nigeria. Another was the political and economic interests of the elite, who did not want to lose control of power. Moreover, the northern part of the country was perceived by many as a zone without adequate natural resources to sustain an independent existence. It was also argued that although the southern part of the country had huge natural resources, especially oil, it was a conflict zone, where different ethnicities were not at one with each other. The balancing politics, then, was that the North had political capital and the control of power, while the South, with more natural resources, was characterized by discordant voices and incoherence as a political force. In the end, the avoidance strategy did not work because the problems that the politicians feared might surface have surfaced anyway. The inter-ethnic clashes, the religious riots and the political waywardness that define present-day Nigeria are attestations to a failed vision. Ordinary men and women in villages across the country are still battling to understand the concept of Nigeria and what it means to be its citizen.

Methodology of the research

This chapter is based on research carried out with the objective of exploring the notions of identity and citizenship that ordinary Nigerians subscribe to. To do this, we wanted to adopt a methodology that was open-ended and allowed space for people's voices as they sought to articulate their sense of belonging in their immediate 'acknowledged' communities and the imagined community that is the larger Nigerian entity (Kabeer 2002). We therefore adopted a participatory research approach built around the notion of 'conversations', which brought together three methodologies drawn from theatre, participatory learning and action (PLA), and interviews. The conversations took three forms: between methodologies; between our project ideals and peoples' aspirations; and between different members and groupings within the project communities.

In bringing together these methodologies, we sought to benefit from their interaction. We also wanted to give people the space to reflect on their everyday lives and their communities as a way of assessing where they stood in relation to members of other communities, local government and the state. And finally, we wanted to link these assessments to our overarching goal of promoting critical thinking as a process towards claiming rights. Overall, therefore, the methodological conversations were a means of extending boundaries of understanding – and in some cases, they meant transgressing boundaries, first in the imagination and then in reality. These conversations gave us stories of people's personal lives, and their community issues and problems, which became the subject of further analysis. This chapter draws on these stories and the processes of reflection that produced them, and which they in turn gave rise to.

In each village, we started by seeking out local community-based organizations (CBOs). With their support and participation, we would begin the 'conversation' in each community with a transect walk. This is a cross-sectional walk that takes the participants across the village and allows them to note down key features of the community, its people and their relationships. The route of the walk was always chosen by the members of the community to allow us to build a picture of their geographical and social space. But in addition, it enabled us to note problem areas and significant absences. We used our conversations with community members to add detail to the picture as we went along. It was also a means of triangulating what the members of the CBOs had told us.

The next stage was to translate what we saw into a community map. The map was drawn on the ground, usually by CBO members, and helped visually to 'fix' structures and people in relation to each other. The CBOs decided the important structures that needed to be reflected in the map, such as churches, mosques, wells, clinics and so on. When the map was done, it provided a picture of the social structure, settlement patterns and geography of amenities within the community. In each place, as the map was drawn, we would interpret and analyse it, noting the resources available to the community, where the access roads passed and to what destinations. We were interested to see who lived in which part of the community because of what this revealed about its power relationships. The map also allowed us to see what was absent.

However, the transect walk and the mapping exercise only involved a few members of the community speaking on behalf of the rest, because it is not possible or constructive to attempt to involve the entire community in such exercises. So, to reach out to a wider community, we used an approach called theatre for development (TFD) to 'dynamize' the map, allowing the issues to jump into life and provide space for further discussion. TFD is a genre of theatre that constructs its plot from the stories and experiences of ordinary people. As Abah (1997) has argued in his concept of 'perforaltics', TFD also draws its performance style from the performative instincts and practices of the communities. It is, in other words, a theatre of songs, stories, dance and dialogue that draws from everyday life. It is usually performed by the members of the community, addressing their own concerns in their own voices and languages. The use of theatre allowed us to expand the conversation on issues of citizenship, entitlements and exclusion, and to explore different factors that influence rights claims.

The construction of each dramatic performance began with interviews carried out within people's homes or at their places of work that were based on a checklist of issues developed by the research team and CBO members. In each community, a minimum of fifty people were interviewed. Later, members of the CBOs and the research team sat down together to analyse the various stories we had heard from different people and the issues they raised. The key issues and concerns prioritized by the CBOs became materials out of which the drama was made. This drama was then subjected to critique and analysis when the wider community watched it. The critique would usually happen in two ways. One was when members of the community who were not part of creating the drama entered into the performance space to make changes to the argument in the drama. In making such interventions, people not only changed the narrative of the drama, they also intervened in the community's perceptions of citizenship issues. Their intervention was part of the process of analysing the issues and adding important details. The second form of critique and analysis occurred when we asked our audience to break into small groups to further interrogate the issues raised by the drama and to explore how it resonated with their own realities.

In general, therefore, the approach adopted in the research was to maximize participation from a wide spectrum of the population, to allow as much debate and reorganization of ideas as possible, and then to let the communities in which we worked develop their own future action plans on the various issues identified. Overall, the combination of TFD, PLA and semi-structured interviews that made up our method-ological conversations continues to be used to explain and make visible the complexity of issues around citizenship, to promote understanding of citizenship, to challenge perceptions and to explore what people want for their future.

Citizenship stories

We argue that the project of forming a unified Nigeria with a common identity requires the translation of the principles guiding citizenship within the constitution into the reality of people's lives. However, there are many conflicting factors that continually serve to thwart this transla-tion, including ethnicity, religion, gender and governance. Usually these factors work together, and they have multiple layers of meaning that contribute to defining people's understanding of their own identities. Our research teased out these meanings through walking, mapping, acting and talking. The stories of citizens' frustrations that we heard in the areas in which we worked were many.[1] We tell one here and provide a summary of the drama that sought to enact the problems it raised.

Sunday Ogbaka's story

Sunday Ogbaka was born in Otukpo, Benue State, about 30 years ago to an Igala father and an Idoma mother. He has lived all his life in this Benue town and married an Idoma woman from the place. All their children were born here, like Sunday himself. He is an active member of the Eupi community where he lives, in Otukpo. He is, in fact, one of the advisers to the chief. Based on the length of time he has lived here, his involvement in community activities and the fact that he is married to an Idoma woman from Eupi, Sunday ought to be regarded as a truly bona fide *member of this community. But, as he declares, 'I am Igala because my father is from Igala land. I must return to my place, which is Igala land. That is my real place.' When asked why, he said, 'Here I cannot be chief but in Igala land I can be chief. Politically, I do not have a problem, but when it comes to cultural options, I am not accepted and cannot take part... All my children are Igalas too ... My wives are like my tail; they must go where I belong'. Sunday Ogbaka is no more than an Igala man living in Idoma land.*

The story of Sunday Ogbaka raises many issues. His identity in Idoma land remains that of an Igala man because he cannot be regarded as an indigene of Idoma since his father was Igala. This means that Sunday's ethnicity is Igala, and that he cannot claim the entitlements of someone born to an Idoma father. The story thus illustrates the significance of ethnicity as a factor in the citizenship question in Nigeria. However, there are other dimensions as well. There is gender. Although Sunday was born to an Idoma woman, that does not make him an Idoma person because ethnic identity is traced and bestowed through the father's lineage. And it is this that determines the entitlements that one has access to and the spaces for action within which one can participate. The impossibility of Sunday being considered an indigene of Otukpo, the limited nature of his entitlements in the place where he was born and bred, despite the fact that his mother is a full-blooded Idoma, reflects the second-class status of women in that society.

This is not only true in Benue but all over the country. An example of the implications of this exclusionary notion of citizenship was demonstrated during the April 2003 elections. Then, a man from Benin Republic, Deinde, married to a Nigerian woman and living in Adedoro village in Ogun State, was prevented from voting. His wife and the members of the community in which he lived argued that he had lived among them for ten years, had three children by a 'daughter of the community' and that the community accepted him. However, as an account by John Ikubaje of the episode in *This Day Newspapers* relates, community members who were ready to argue forcefully on his behalf had to back down when it was explained to them that the Electoral Act, which is based on the Nigerian Constitution, stipulates that 'a person shall be qualified to register as a voter if such a person is a citizen of Nigeria' (Federal Republic of Nigeria 1999). And since marriage to a Nigerian woman does not confer citizenship on her husband, Deinde could not be considered a Nigerian.

It was stories like the ones above that informed a drama that we enacted, in which Agaba, who had settled in another part of the country from where he was born, experiences discrimination and abuse:

Agaba charges into the office of the local government chairman, where a budget meeting is in session. He is wielding a machete and prancing about as if possessed. All the councillors and the chairman run for cover. Agaba demands to know who the chairman is as he has urgent matters to discuss with him. As he charges forwards and backwards, he swears, 'I am going to kill someone today, in fact more than one! As many as will tell me that I do not come from this place! What does it take to come from this place after I have lived here for 30 years and had twelve children here? If it is a football team they want I have produced it! So, what is it? What have I not done for this community? I will truly kill someone!'

When one of the councillors finally manages to calm him down he narrates the story behind his 'madness'. He has lived in this community for 30 years, paid all his tax here and had all his twelve children in this town. He has used his wealth to build roads, help pay teachers' salaries and other such community development needs. Now, three of his children have gained admission to the university and the state would not give them scholarships. 'Do you know why? They are telling them that they do not come from this state! Where do they come from, every one? That is why I am going mad, and I am right to do so, do you hear!'

The chairman crawls out of hiding to listen to Agaba's story. He is, however, not sympathetic. He acknowledges Agaba's contribution to the development of the community. But he concludes his narrative by emphasizing 'difference' rather than 'integration' in Agaba's behaviour, when he points out that the money he had ploughed into community development had been made in his place of sojourn, not in his place of birth. In other words, the community has a claim on his wealth. He drives the point of difference home when he finally declares that, 'No matter how long a wild cat stays in the homestead it is still not a home cat!' The message is clear: Agaba would never be completely accepted in this community. After a deep breath, and in a very subdued voice, he asks, 'If they say I am not from here, what about the children? Where do these children come from?'

Agaba's story points to several factors of importance in the realization of citizenship rights in Nigeria. It is a story about the denial of rights and about the forces at play in that denial: ethnicity, location and gender.

Although religion does not come out prominently in Agaba's story, it is part of its sub-text and was a strong issue outside the fiction of the drama. In the follow-up discussion that took place after the performance, one of the ways suggested for Agaba to be fully accepted in Kubau, Giwa and some parts of Sabon-Gari was to *saki jiki* (relax the body), which is a euphemism for taking on the dominant cultural identity in the place where one lives. In the parts of Kaduna State where this suggestion was made, *saki jiki* meant adopting the Islamic way of life and believing in the *Qur'an* and *shari'a*.

Reflections from the field

Whenever we sat down with groups of people after the performance to discuss the issues raised in the drama, one clear point that always emerged was that while ethnicity, gender, religion and location were key factors in the citizen story in Nigeria, the discussions of solutions by ordinary Nigerians invariably located the crisis within a larger frame of politics and governance. Many believed that the political class was manipulating ethnicity and religion for political ends. Therefore, they saw good governance – by which they meant principles and practices that neither played on nor emphasized ethnicity and religion – as the route to citizenship rights.

So each time in the performance that Agaba asked his last question, about where his children come from and whether they should be entitled to a scholarship, we found that members of the audience who intervened always began by re-making government and changing the governance process. They always removed the corrupt chairman, they allowed room for more debate and they sought to balance the distribution of development projects in the wards. And each time this 'rewrite' took place by the community members who entered into the fiction of the drama, three things happened:

- Whenever the drama was revised, the new performance that the audience now watched offered a different perspective. The first version offered a lived reality; the second an altered and desired one.
- The community members symbolically broke through a number of barriers by entering into the drama space. In Anchau, one woman looked at the community map, and after locating the place in which the drama was being enacted observed that it was in the space of *masu arziki* (the rich and influential). When ordinary members of the community entered the drama, they effectively transgressed into a

space to which they were normally denied access. In addition, they had made their voices heard from within that space of influence. This was an empowering act for them, even if only momentarily.

• It provided an opportunity for immediate feedback from the community. The altered narratives they gave to the drama told us where their interests lay. They were articulating messages that policy-makers needed to hear and needed to address in the lives of the community.

Another critical point in the process of reflection initiated by our 'conversations' was in the making and analysis of the community map. The act of condensing what had been seen on the transect walk into a small space on the floor challenged the taken-for-granted ways in which members of the community saw their community. That was why, after looking at the map of Anchau–Takalafiya that the women had drawn, Hajiya Aishatu Goma observed that the Sarkis'[2] palace, the mosque and courthouse were in close proximity to each other and that this consti-tuted a space that ordinary people enter only when they are summoned. They do not go there voluntarily. Another woman said it was a space of power and another observed: 'You go there to face judgement'. These interpretations contrasted with those of the men, who saw the trinity of Sarkis' palace, mosque and courthouse as a 'place for justice'. This dif-ference of perception and interpretation is, of course, reflective of the difference in the power positions of the two groups. The men make the law and the women are at the receiving end.

It was also by looking at the map in Kargi that many of the people saw a critical difference between those who lived inside the walled part of the town and those who lived outside of it. The *yan ganuwa* (those who lived inside the wall) had more entitlements than the *yan karkara* (those who were outside the wall). The *yan karkara* are usually non-indigenes or settler communities (Abah and Okwori 2003).

At the end of our encounters with members of different communi-ties, which would normally take about seven to ten days, one critical question always raised by them was 'What will happen next?' Members of the community organizations and members of the community at large always wanted to know what would be done about the issues raised, what would be the concrete results of the research for them. They had participated actively in the different stages of the research process: mapping and analysing their community, understanding its power struc-tures and identifying the key political and developmental actors in their lives. Their question could be seen as a manifestation of the critical capacity that their participation had helped to build. However, our response to their question was to throw the challenge back to them. We argued that the critical steps were most effective when they were decided on by the community for themselves and not by outsiders on their behalf.

We therefore encouraged the communities to develop community action plans (CAPs). These served as our response to the community's desire to act on issues raised by the research beyond the immediate life of the research. They helped the community to chart its needs and priorities, to determine necessary interventions and to identify who within the community or outside should be responsible for carrying them out. The construction of CAPs was integrated into our interactions with the community. It followed a process of critical examination of the issues and problems generated through the different conversations of our research process: the transect walk; the mapping exercise; the focused group discussion sessions; the interviews; and during the post-performance interactions.

After the various issues and problems had been catalogued, members of the community brainstormed on those they considered to be their priority, what needed to be done, who should do it and where to find support. They also set time-frames within which certain tasks would be done, developed the budget for each action, and worked on where and from whom the community would find the necessary resources. Many of the problems that they identified as priority issues required more resources than most of the communities we worked in could afford on their own. They would need the local government to support them or take over the issue. But their experiences to date with local government did little to encourage them to believe that such support would be forth-coming.

To address this, the Theatre for Development Centre took on the role of relating the stories of these citizens to policy-makers. During this project, we organized a dissemination workshop for 75 serving and aspiring councillors and chairmen in Kaduna State in February 2003. During the workshop, we told the people's stories to illustrate the crises of citizenship and of the 'poverty of governance' through the use of drama. The politicians were asked to break into small groups to discuss the issues we raised, and then to state what they would do to solve the problems if they were voted into office in the next general election.[3]

The workshop gave us a good opportunity to make the politicians publicly spell out their vision of good governance and commit themselves to a certain course of action. So we presented each one of them with a certificate of commitment. This required that each write their promises on the certificate; this would then become an accountability checklist to measure their performance against. What we played on here was the love of certificates by Nigerians, which they always use to enhance their political or other profiles!

On the community side, the CBOs started to use their action plans as a basis for negotiating political power and participation in governance. In the campaigns leading to the April 2003 elections, communities such as Sab-Zuro and Anchau in Kaduna State began to ask political aspirants to enter into a contract with the community that they would address the issues in their community action plan as a condition for voting them into office.

Conclusion

We hoped to use our conversational approach to draw out stories from the ordinary citizens of Nigeria about what they understood by citizenship, how they related their membership of 'acknowledged' communities, defined by ethnicity, religion and so on, to their membership of the 'imagined' community of the nation-state, and what being a Nigerian meant to them. We found that the reality of the Nigerian situation is that, although citizenship is constitutionally determined by both ancestry and by place of birth or sojourn, in practice Nigerians always revert to and insist on ancestry as the true and recognizable determinant of citizenship.

However, the research process evolved along the way into more than the telling and hearing of stories. The combination of TFD and PLA not only served as a powerful medium through which people could tell their stories, and through which others outside their own communities could hear their stories. It also encouraged multi-layered conversations between people and hierarchies of authority at village, district and local government levels – conversations that became forms of empowerment when community members began to map their needs and to use these inventories as a contract for governance and as an accountability checklist.

Our experiences in the field also helped to highlight aspects of the contradictory understandings of citizenship that had not been apparent to us beforehand. On the one hand, when asked about their primary affiliations, most of those we encountered prioritized their ethnic identity over that of their nation. On the other hand, when faced with dramas enacting issues of citizenship and entitlement, those same people identified issues of governance as the main obstacles both to the *just* realization of entitlements as well as to their identification with Nigeria as a nation. Some of these issues of governance revolved implicitly around official practices tying entitlement to ethnic affiliation.

This threw up a conundrum for us. Was Nigeria a state without citizens? Or were Nigerians citizens without a state? If the former was the case, it implied that those who make up Nigeria are still entrenched in their different ethnic nationalities and will resist all attempts to force a common sense of nationhood. On the other hand, if the latter is the case, it suggests that the failure of ordinary Nigerians to see themselves as a single nation reflects a failure on the part of the state. If the state had promoted principles of access and entitlement that were independent of ethnic and other particular identities, rather than subject to divided definitions of citizenship, might it not have brought into existence a sense of common nationhood? This was an important insight for the research team, and it helped us to understand the gap between the theory and practice of citizenship in Nigeria.

We want to conclude by observing that the research has, if anything, raised more questions than answers for us. As we continue to deal with the contradictions and conflicts in the citizenship agenda and the search for good governance, these are the questions that we will continue to seek answers to:

- When a nation is constructed on ethnic foundations and in such a way that the different ethnicities prioritize their own nationalities above the federation, are the people in the geographical space that is now called Nigeria citizens with no state, or is the country a state without citizens?
- Are there forms of governance, or architectures of citizenship, that would overcome this conundrum and allow those who live in the geographical space called Nigeria to attain a common and inclusive identity that transcends their ethnic and other exclusive affiliations?
- Given the disparity between the quest for nationhood, which the concept of Nigeria implies, and the reality of ethnic bases of citizenship and belonging, are we dealing here with several nations in one? And may it therefore not be necessary to renegotiate what Nigeria should or should not claim to be?

While we search for the answers to these and many other questions, Nigeria still remains an experiment after 43 years of independence.

Notes

1. The nine local government areas were: Kubau, Kujama, Sabon Gari, Giwa, Jaba and Zangon Kataf in Kaduna State; Ohimini, Otukpo and Gwer East in Benue State.
2. Sarkis are traditional rulers that exercise power and jurisdiction over a set of villages or communities in a ward.
3. The local government election, in which chairpersons and councillors are voted into office.

References

Abah, Oga S. (1997) *Performing Life: Case Studies in the Practice of Theatre for Development*, Zaria: Shekut Books

Abah, O. S. and J. Okwori (2003) 'Caterwauling citizens: The border limits of citizenship in the north of Nigeria', in Oga S. Abah (ed.) *The Geographies of Citizenship in Nigeria*, Zaria: Tamaza Books

Federal Republic of Nigeria (1999) *The Constitution of the Federal Republic of Nigeria*, Lagos: Federal Government Press

Goldie, G. (1898) *Campaigning on the Upper Nile and Niger*, London: Methuen

Ihonvbere, J. and T. Shaw (ed.) (1998) *Illusions of Power: Nigeria in Transition*, New Jersey: Africa World Press

Kabeer, N. (2002) 'Citizenship, affiliation and exclusion: perspectives from the South', *IDS Bulletin* 33(2): 12–23

Okehie-Offa, M. U. and M. N. O. Sadiku (1996) (eds) *Ethnic and Cultural Diversity in Nigeria*, Trenton, New Jersey: Africa World Press

Okeke, O. (1992) *Hausa-Fulani Hegemony: The Dominance of the Muslim North in Contemporary Nigerian Politics*, Enugu: Arena Publishers

Okwori, J. (2003) 'The patchwork that is Nigeria: Implications and impact on citizenship, participation and accountability', in Oga S. Abah (ed.) *The Geographies of Citizenship in Nigeria*, Zaria: Tamaza Books

This Day Newspapers, 14 May 2003

The quest for inclusion: Nomadic communities and citizenship questions in Rajasthan

Mandakini Pant

Introduction

Citizenship has traditionally been cast as the universal legal and constitutional rights and responsibilities that are defined by the state on behalf of its citizens. However, concepts of citizenship based on universal rights and responsibilities do not in themselves guarantee equality of voice, access or influence within the state or in society. Instead, their interactions with particular identities may act as forces for the inclusion of some groups at the expense of others, and thereby limit the capacities of the latter to articulate and act upon their claims. There are a range of different sections of the population in the Indian context – the poor, low castes, tribals, women – who have not benefited a great deal from the rights provided by the constitution, or from the special provisions set up to rectify certain forms of historical disadvantage. The gap between the formal recognition of rights and their actualization remains substantial.

Renewed concerns about citizenship in recent times have begun to question the standardized formulation of rights within the legal, constitutional and political framework of the country from the perspective of those poor and marginalized groups who are extremely heterogeneous, whose relationships with each other are fluid and shifting, and who have a diverse range of needs and priorities. These concerns have helped to frame one of the research projects pursued by the Society for Participatory Research in Asia in New Delhi as part of its activities under the Development Research Centre. We had a number of questions that we wanted to explore through this research. Was the 'citizen' an abstract and passive subject upon whom the 'state' bestows rights of access to resources and opportunities? Did the formal principle of equality upheld by the constitution promote substantive equality among its citizens, or did it simply gloss over the inequalities generated by the socio-economic positioning of different groups? How did the specific social positioning of citizens determine their experiences as citizens? How did citizens see themselves as citizens? How did they relate their identities as members of social groups to their identities as citizens? What processes strengthened the capacity of these groups to articulate their rights as citizens?

The research process

This chapter is based on one of two research projects that the Society for Participatory Research (PRIA) carried out to explore some of these questions – in this case with nomadic communities in Rajasthan.[1] Nomadic communities are made up of groups whose lives and livelihoods are based on pastoralism, foraging, artisanship, service, trade and limited agriculture, but who carry out these activities through periodic, usually seasonal, movements along long-established routes across the countryside. This research was carried out with the Gadiya Lohar, Banjara, Bhopa, and Bawariya communities in Alwar district in Rajasthan.

The research was organized around two key themes: the problems and priorities of nomad groups, including those that reflect their marginalized status as citizens and their attempts to organize collectively to address these problems. It was carried out in collaboration with Muktidhara Sansthan (MDS), a non-governmental organization (NGO) that works primarily with nomads in Alwar district. The organization, founded in 1993 by social activist Ratan Katyayani, is premised on the belief that the denial of land and shelter to nomads is tantamount to a violation of their constitutional rights, preventing them as it does from claiming their other basic entitlements as citizens. Our collaboration with the organization allowed us access to different nomadic groups on a basis of trust, as well as allowing us to observe MDS's attempts to organize them.

We began our research by discussing our objectives with members of MDS and with the nomadic communities they work with. We then met with members of these communities to discuss their problems and aspirations. We used a combination of focus group discussion, participant observation and in-depth, open-ended interviews to do this because we wanted to understand their experiences as citizens, or as non-citizens, from their own personal perspectives. We also interviewed social activists, researchers, influential community leaders and key informants in the area to deepen our understanding of the issues. Meetings were then conducted with government officials at various levels within the district to elicit their views of their responsibilities towards nomads as a marginalized group.

This chapter reports on the findings of the study. The section following this provides some background to the study, explaining what it means to be a nomad in India: how nomads perceive themselves and are perceived by the wider community. I then go on to report on some of the problems and perceptions articulated by nomads related to how they see themselves and how they interact with the state, as well as with the wider community. I then examine some of the approaches adopted by MDS to support nomads in their quest for more inclusive forms of citizenship. The concluding section locates the issue of marginalized citizenship in the broader concept of citizenship.

Nomadism: a changing way of life

South Asia has the largest nomadic population in the world. They represent nearly 7 per cent of the total population in India, and consist of about 500 different communities of pastoralists, mobile herders, foragers and traditional peripatetics (Rao and Casimir 2003). In Rajasthan alone, there are about two dozen nomadic communities, each characterized by their own distinct livelihood practices and customs. The Bawariya are an example of a foraging community, whose principal economic strategy consists of gathering and collecting or hunting in the forests. Gadiya Lohar, Banjara, Nat and Bhopa are the 'service and technology' nomads of Rajasthan. The Banjaras are trading nomads dealing in salt, *multani mitti* (fuller's earth) and cattle. The Gadiya Lohars are blacksmiths. They fabricate and repair iron tools and utensils, moving shop from village to village. They get their names from their *gadiya* (bullock-driven carriages) and *lohars* (blacksmiths). The Nat are entertainers, performing at village fairs as acrobats. Bhopa are sacred specialists, singing ballads and reciting extempore poetry in worship of *pabuji* (a war hero) and *bhairav* (a demi-god). There are also pastoral nomads, who are economically dependent on livestock. They herd sheep and goats across their trail, and have developed institutions of property in herds, pasture and routes between pastures (Kovoori 1985).

Nomadic communities have generally followed a pre-determined cyclical course, regulated by the seasons, in their physical movements. Banjaras, for instance, moved to other Indian areas (Punjab, Haryana, Delhi, Madhya Pradesh, Uttar Pradesh and Gujarat) along routes which provided for faster and more economical movement of goods and services. As I learnt during the study, some of those routes have now become national highways.

The nomadic way of life has various folklores associated with it, especially with regard to the nomads' origins and their links to the caste system. Castes are a part of Hindu social structure. They are endogamous groups ranked within local hierarchical social systems. Membership of caste is determined by birth. Caste status is ascriptive and unchanging for the lifetime of the individual. Underlying the caste hierarchy are core values of pollution and purity that determine the rank assigned to a particular caste.

The Banjara trace their origin to a *rajput jagirdar* (feudal lord belonging to the warrior caste) of Rail Mangra district of Udaipur, who, along with his followers, was excommunicated for having deviated from certain traditional Rajput customs. They took up trading as their occupation, and moved from place to place in a group of 20 to 30 families. They came to be known as Banjara, for having taken to *banj* (business) as their source of livelihood. Initially, they sold salt to village people. Later, they began transporting goods from one place to another by bullock caravans. Gadiya Lohars claim Chittorgarh as their ancestral home. They maintain that they are the progeny of Rajputs who had to leave Chittorgarh after the Mughal army seized it in 1568. Bhopa believe that they are descended from Pabuji, a legendary hero belonging to Rathore Rajputs.

The fact that all these nomadic groups observe the Hindu rituals, and claim lineage (*gotra*) synonymous with *gotras* of Rajputs, suggests that they are very much part of the caste system. It is their economic peripherality, overall lifestyle and the nature of their occupations that explain their low status in the caste hierarchy (Rao and Casimir 2003). During the pre-colonial period, nomadic communities shared a symbiotic relationship with the sedentary mainstream of society. Food exchange, trade, transport services, hunting and entertainment were the economic activities through which regular interaction between the nomads and sedentary groups took place. In return for their services, they were allowed to live on the village commons and to use natural resources such as water and pasture lands until they moved to their next settlement.

However, nomads have been coming under progressively greater strain in recent years. Changes in the economy, industry, and technology, and attendant effects on social relations, are threatening the livelihood of these communities in unprecedented ways. The changes in question, like many major social changes in India, began with the upheavals of the colonial period and took a number of different forms. For instance, forest regulations put in place during the colonial period prevented the nomads from collecting forest produce, an important item of barter in their trade. These regulations deprived pastoralists and foragers of grazing land and free access to the forest. Their situation has been exacerbated by the pressure of a growing population on shrinking common lands and the commoditization of both land and forest. Shorn of their access to forest produce, Bawariya seek work as agricultural labourers, construction workers, wage sharecroppers, cattle breeders, night watchmen for crops and daytime shepherds for others' cattle.

The construction of roads and the laying of railway lines during the late nineteenth century was particularly disruptive of the migration patterns of Banjaras, who travelled on bullocks or donkeys to physically isolated areas, where they were often the only source of commodities such as salt for the inhabitants of these areas. Today, apart from a tiny minority who struggle on in their traditional occupations of selling salt and *multani mitti*, cattle breeding and minor forest produce, the Banjara have largely turned to casual wage employment as labourers in agriculture, construction and stone mining.

The traditional craft of the Gadiya Lohars has been most affected by the spread of modern technology in agriculture and industry. Their coarse blacksmith services are no longer required. Their itinerant lifestyle excluded them from access to opportunities to upgrade their technical skills, leaving them with few occupational options. Bhopa, the wandering minstrels, also face a bleak future: the modern communication revolution has brought in new forms of entertainment, displacing their arts, even in remote villages. Increasingly, these various groups have been forced to seek low-paid, casual wage employment in overcrowded markets for unskilled labour in construction sites, mines, stone quarries, road building, agriculture and so on.

Nomads as citizens: low castes and others

The problems of the nomadic communities may have begun in the disruptions brought about by the colonial state, but they have not been mitigated in independent India, despite the fact that national independence brought with it the promise of equality for all citizens. This promise was embodied in the Fundamental Rights, Fundamental Duties and the Directive Principles of State Policy, spelt out in the Constitution of India. In addition, in recognition of their historical disadvantage, social, educational, cultural and employment safeguards were provided by the constitution to protect certain groups from further discrimination. These were the untouchable castes, classified for administrative purposes as scheduled castes, lower castes, classified as other backward classes, and the tribal groups, classified as scheduled tribes.

The Ministries of Social and Tribal Welfare within both the central and state governments have nodal responsibility for establishing programmes for the social and educational development of scheduled castes, scheduled tribes and other backward classes. Their efforts on behalf of marginalized groups have done little to address their marginalization because of the top-down, bureaucratic manner in which these efforts are conceived and implemented. In the case of nomads, however, the problem has been exacerbated by problems of 'misrecognition' (see p. 4).

Because of superficial similarities in the nomadic way of life, diverse communities with distinct livelihood practices and ethnonyms are grouped together and classified as one or other of the lists of officially recognized disadvantaged groups. In some cases, they are classified as scheduled castes or backward castes because they are seen to share the same social, educational and economic disadvantages. In others, they are classified as scheduled tribes because they are seen to have the 'primitive' traits, distinctive culture and geographical isolation associated with the tribal way of life. Indeed, the same nomadic communities may be classified differently in the different states in which they move. Thus the Banjara are included in the scheduled tribes list in Andhra Pradesh, Bihar, Orissa, and West Bengal, in the scheduled castes list in Delhi, Himachal Pradesh, Punjab, Karnataka and Tripura, and in the other backward classes list in Rajasthan, Gujarat, Madhya Pradesh and Uttar Pradesh.

Yet none of these classifications speak to the specificities of the nomadic way of life. Although inclusion on these lists entitles them to the associated affirmative actions and safeguards, the reality is that their way of life makes it difficult for them to access even the most basic rights and opportunities of citizens, let alone take advantage of any special provisions. Moreover, their way of life makes them the object of discrimination by the sedentary communities that once gave them shelter and made use of their services. They are manipulated by local power-brokers, who exploit their vulnerable status to deprive them of any forms of access they might otherwise have, and they are ignored by the state, whose officials reproduce many of the prejudices and biases of the wider society. Some of the different ways in which these processes of exclusion and marginalization are experienced by the nomadic communities with whom I interacted are reported in the following section.

The experiences of marginalization: reactions of the sedentary community

From colonial times, the peripatetic lifestyle of nomads has been regarded as 'backward'. Colonial legislation branded numerous categories of nomads, such as Banjara and Bawariya, as potential criminals. These stereotype persist: nomads are not merely seen as thieves and criminals, but as 'born' that way. As nomadic livelihoods are disrupted by the forces of development and change, nomads are being forced into a more sedentary way of life and alternative sources of livelihood.

Some have sought to camp on demarcated government land near or within villages. This has brought them into direct conflict with local communities, and old stereotypes have been given fresh life. As Suwa Bawariya told me:

> I live on a small portion of *siwai chak* [unassessed revenue] land. Villagers complained to *Tehsildar* [sector revenue official], who asked me to pay a penalty of R300 to the *Patwari* [grassroots village revenue and land records official]. I told him that if I had money I could have purchased a plot of land myself. He filed a complaint against me in the police station. I was jailed for three months.

A district official with whom I shared Suwa's bitterness was dismissive: 'The Bawariya are criminals; they are not to be trusted'.

Conflict over land was a recurring theme in the interviews. Nasiya Banjara, a woman from Bamanwas, told me:

> For nearly a year, the neighboring Meenas did not trouble us, thinking we would soon move on. When they found out that we meant to stay, they turned nasty. They stopped us from using village wells for water. They broke our pots when we approached the wells. One morning when we went to the well, we found human faeces floating in it.

Mana Bawariya from Malutana lamented:

> Villagers don't understand that we also need a place to live. Where will we go? The *Patwari* came yesterday. He asked me to leave the place. Villagers don't speak in front of me but have registered a complaint against me. I told the *Patwari*, let the villagers do what they want to do ... Kill me ... Throw me in the well or hang me up in the tree. Then they won't complain of my occupying their piece of land.

On some occasions, the reaction of the local community takes a violent form. Tara Bhopa in Akbarpur described to me one such violent incident that has instilled a sense of insecurity in his community. Despite having been in their present settlement for over two decades, they now fear for their lives:

> On 23 March 2002, about 40 to 50 Meos demolished our four huts. They erected a fence surrounding the demolished huts. They said that they want to build graveyard here. They challenged us saying that since you do not have a *patta* [title deed], you do not own land. Following this incident, Section 144 has been imposed in our habitat area. Police protection has been given to us. Now that it is a disputed area, we cannot even rebuild our huts until a court order comes in our favour.

Along with these various accounts, I was myself a witness to a blatant display of the power politics that nomadic communities are up against. When I was attending one of the administrative camps organized by the Rajasthan Government at Malutana, Alwar District, in October 2001, a band of Gadiya Lohar requested that they be allotted a piece of land to settle permanently. The Sub-Divisional Magistrate (SDM) asked the *Sarpanch* to allot land to them.[2] The *Sarpanch* allotted them a place near the cremation ground, which Gadiya Lohars refused. Later, after scanning the map of the village, *siwai chak* land was found. The SDM suggested that the Lohars could settle there. He also ordered that they be issued ration cards, which would entitle them to purchase government-subsidized grain and other essentials.

A group of villagers sprang up, protesting that they would not allow Gadiya Lohars to settle in their village, nor would they allow them to be issued with ration cards. They said that they were prepared to go to jail rather than let this happen, and threatened the Gadiya Lohars, the SDM and the *Sarpanch* with dire consequences. As the situation was getting out of control, the camp was brought to an end. It was later discovered that a group of powerful villagers had encroached upon the *siwai chak* land and had a vested interest in keeping the nomads out. They ultimately succeeded in evicting Lohars from Malutana. Humiliated and disheartened by this experience, the Lohars shifted to another location, but here too they are under pressure to leave as early as possible.

The experiences of the marginalized: the failures of the state

Much of the administration at the grassroots level in Rajasthan is paternalistic in style, and in many places, its attitude towards nomads does little to counter the discrimination they face within the community. State officials have, along with the local sedentary community, viewed the nomads' demand for land with title deeds with hostility.

Many believe that nomads are, and will remain, wanderers, and that attempts to help them settle are futile. Support for this belief relies on persistent references to efforts in the 1960s to provide housing to Lohars and Banjaras who, it is alleged, sold their plots or housing and moved away.

The officials also say that nomads cannot be settled wherever they demand to be settled. However, from the perspective of nomads, their requirements for land take diverse forms. For Gadiya Lohars, proximity to a market or roadside is essential for their livelihoods. For the Banjara and Bawariya, proximity to forests is preferred, while the Bhopa would like to live near or within villages. Refusal to respond to these needs by officials reflects the officials' own attitudes towards nomads rather than the availability of suitable land. As they put it: 'The question of choice does not arise'.

Nomads face resistance even when they seek to settle in isolated clusters of huts beyond the village limits. When I spoke to the *Sarpanch* of Thangazhi about the demand of Gadiya Lohars for land for permanent shelter, she said:

> We cannot let them stay here. We have given them this place temporarily. There is a girls' hostel here; we have to think of their security. We cannot trust them. They are rough and poor. They drink liquor and fight. They don't send their children to school. We suggested a place for them but they refused.

It is not only in relation to access to land that nomadic communities face little official response or sympathy. State primary health service personnel rarely concern themselves with the needs of such communities, and their children are bullied and harassed by their peers and teachers in local schools. They also find themselves excluded from various government programmes intended to address poverty and social injustice. The problem is not unique to nomads. The highly bureacratized structures of planning and service delivery at all levels of government have undermined the effectiveness of the programmes. Most have failed to show sensitivity to the needs of diverse target groups.

But the nomads have been at a particular disadvantage because there is little understanding of their way of life within the bureaucracy. In Bamanvas, a village in Thanagazi Block of Alwar district, Banjaras did not occupy free houses made available under Indira Awas Yojana, a government housing scheme for the poor, because they found the houses unsuitable to their lifestyles, since they are used to living in open spaces in forests, while the houses provided to them were small one-room dwellings. They also tend to miss out on special welfare schemes for scheduled castes, scheduled tribes, other backward classes and citizens who are below the poverty line, partly because of their own lack of awareness, but also because they have no authorized permanent residence and therefore lack formal identification, in the form of either a ration card or a voter identity card.

Nomads suspect, often rightly, that state officials and local leaders connive to prevent any benefits from government welfare schemes flowing to them. Tara Bhopa complained:

> We do not even come to know when the food quotas have arrived. We are entitled to 50kg of wheat but get only 25kg. We are helpless but do not want to protest. What if we lose the remaining? Where does all the food go if we are not receiving it? They are cheating us.

When this was brought to the notice of SDM Alwar, his response was: 'It is not only Bhopa who are getting 25kg wheat. All the poor suffer because of lack of awareness'. Suwa Bawariya, too, is sceptical of the intentions of the state officials and village elite. He criticizes the procedures of selecting families who are below the poverty line: 'Usually the *Sarpanch*, the schoolteacher and the rich village elite decide whose names should be included. Poor people have no say in this matter. For the sake of appearance, they select a few poor families and the rest goes to the people of their community'.

Collective action for rights and citizenship

Nomadic communities are generally too poor and too marginalized to exercise the capacity to mobilize on their own behalf and to counter the discrimination they face within society and from the state. For such groups, the role of an outside catalyst can provide a crucial impetus. MDS has played such a role with nomadic groups in Rajasthan. Through their interactions with MDS, nomadic communities are beginning to articulate their demands in the form of new rights claims. These include the right to property (specifically land with a title deed), the right to a settled life and the right to live with dignity. Land, in particular, is a critical need. They feel that title deeds to land will give them the documentation they require to access their entitlements and benefits, and to receive recognition and respect from agencies of the state and the community. Land also holds out the promise of a life with greater dignity. As Chaganram Banjara told me, for instance, land is necessary to bury dead family members decently: 'Villagers won't let us even cremate our dead in their cremation grounds. We need a place of our own'.

MDS supports the view that land is critical to the settlement and survival of nomads, and has actively promoted and facilitated nomads' occupation of government land. The slogan of their movement is *'Jo zamin sarkari hai, wo zamin hamari hai'* (the land that belongs to the government belongs to us). However, it only targets unclaimed and unassessed revenue land, and not private or disputed land, land allotted for projects or notified forest land.

The process of claiming land is organized through three categories of groups. One group, formed exclusively of men, searches for a suitable site and evaluates its safety, particularly in terms of surrounding villagers' attitudes. A women's group judges the quality of life offered by different potential sites. MDS itself explores the legal aspect, examining the feasibility of such an allocation. MDS has so far helped set up 25 settlements.

MDS has also set up non-formal education centres in nomads' settlements where villagers have not allowed nomad children to be enrolled in village schools. It has also assisted in setting up bore wells in the community settlements, and in providing maintenance equipment. The NGO has worked for the welfare and empowerment of nomadic women, facilitating their access to public health services and encouraging them to save and use banking services, and has generally involved them actively in their programmes.

MDS has also provided nomads with legal aid and direct legal services, such as protection from human rights violations, false criminal cases, illegal custody and detention, petitioning courts and government, getting bail and so on. MDS successfully filed a writ petition in the Rajasthan High Court against the district administration to provide civic amenities to the nomads. It has regularly interacted with the district bureaucracy to enable the nomads to access the public distribution system. Ration cards were issued to settled nomads in 1996. Nomads held a massive demonstration at Collectorate for their residential rights in 1997.[3] Residential rights for Banjaras at Bawanwas Chogan were finally issued in 1998.

Through the various forms of support it provides, MDS has sought to build up the organizational capacity of nomads. It has encouraged the formation of community forums for conflict resolution. Ghumantoo Vikas Panchayat, with two members (a male and a female) from each settlement, meets once a month.[4] It is also trying to facilitate the formation of a community-based organization, Ghumantoo Vikas Sanghatan.

MDS has also sought to keep nomads at the forefront of its campaigns to promote leadership. It has used public hearings, processions and media coverage to put pressure on the state to act. It has also lobbied for nomads, sending them in delegations to meet and talk with officials with their petitions and to take part in demonstrations and rallies. For instance, MDS organized a *padyatra* (foot march) in 1993 from Alwar to Jaipur to seek justice from the governor of the state. About 400 nomads participated, demanding their rights to settle. It filed a writ successfully in the Rajasthan High Court against the district administration to provide civic amenities to the nomads. And MDS has maintained a constant interaction with the Election Commission of India to provide nomads with their voting rights.[5] Nomads marched to demand their voting rights in 1994 and were granted them in 1995.

The MDS-led mobilization of nomads has made some difference in the attitudes of administration at local level. Officials have helped, although sporadically so far, to settle them in various areas and to provide them with ration cards, voting rights and so on. I observed this change in the attitude of officials when I met them in the context of the settlement of Gadiya Lohars in Karmseevaspura, Tapukada, in Alwar district. The district magistrate explained to me that the state agencies have taken steps to settle nomads in a prime industrial area, where earning a settled living would not be difficult. About 90 households have been given plots of land, along with title deeds of ownership. Rajveer, a Gadiya Lohar, expressed his jubilation:

> It's difficult to explain in words how we felt when we were finally allotted a piece of land to live. This was finally our own land. We spent the whole day and night feasting, dancing and singing ... We couldn't have imagined that one day we would be able to live in dignity like others.

It is not surprising that the support and advice of MDS have led many nomads to believe that the organization has brought them some dignity and self-respect. In fact, they depend on MDS for advice and assistance. Tara Bhopa said: 'Muktidhara issues letters to government officials for problems such as security from the villagers' harassment. Things start working. At least officials then listen to us.'

MDS interventions, however, have not always been smooth. Local state officials have resented MDS's, especially Ratan Katyayani's, confrontational stance. The officials accuse MDS of lack of accountability. Often, nomads associated with MDS have faced the wrath of state officials. Gadiya Lohars settled in Karmseevaspura, Tapukada, have since moved away from MDS because of the fear that continued association with them will alienate them from the powerful state bureaucracy and deprive them of any further benefits, especially concerning ownership of land.

Conclusion

The value given by nomads to new types of rights that are not expressly included in the constitution highlights, as other chapters note, the significance of struggle in defining a bottom-up construction of citizenship (see Introduction, p. 21ff). They are protesting against marginalization at the hands of the government. They are increasingly expressing a demand for inclusion in governance, while simultaneously challenging the nature of what it means to be included.

Yet the rights of the nomadic community have been secured only partially. There is still a significant gap between the rights they are entitled to and those they have secured. The study supported the point made in Kabeer (2003), that the specific strategies adopted by an organization will shape both the nature of what is achieved and the limitations on its achievements. Civil society interventions that are leader-centric and confrontational, rather than participatory and accountable, are likely to report short-run gains. An alternative approach would allow organizations like MDS to facilitate a more gradual and sustainable evolution of citizenship rights and agency among nomads by building bridges with both the settled society and the state. External lobbying and mobilization have advantages and can achieve certain piecemeal results, as we saw. But they cannot be a substitute for the nomads own capacity-building through their own community-based organizations, towards seeking and achieving an inclusive citizenship identity.

Let me conclude with one other observation. Nomads have been the object of a great deal of myth-making in India. These include negative myths that brand them as 'born criminals', unwilling to settle down and earn an honest living like members of the sedentary community, and positive myths that see their wanderings as an expression of their free spirit and their closeness to nature. In my encounters with nomads, I have learned that both sets of myths are misplaced. The nomadic way of life once expressed a way of living and earning a livelihood that was compatible with the way in which the larger society was organized. Nomads provided services to different communities, many of whom lived in such remote areas that they had no other access to such services. However, those days are gone. The changes brought about by population pressure, changing infrastructure, new technologies and by 'modernization' itself have made the nomadic way of life impossible to sustain. And, despite well-meant concerns about preserving their distinctive way of life and cultural identity, it is not at all clear whether this is what nomadic communities themselves want. They don't see a necessary contradiction between 'settling down' and their nomadic identity. When I raised this question with Nasiya Banjara, this was her answer:

> You live in houses in comfort. You move all over the place for your work, yet you have a place of your own. But we keep on wandering. Why? We need to have a place of our own. We too want to live in dignity. I am still a Banjara. I still follow our traditional practices. Where is the identity crisis?

Notes

1. The other was focused on tribal groups in the newly established state of Jharkand.
2. A *Sarpanch* is an elected head/chairperson of a village level local self-governing body called *panchayat*.
3. Collectorate is an administrative office of the district collector. A district collector is the highest administrative official (a bureaucrat) at district level.
4. Ghumantoo Vikas Panchayat (GVP) is the nomads' self-governing body for their development. MDS encouraged nomads to form GVPs where they can discuss ways to overcome their oppression. Two members – a male and a female – from each settlement attend GVP meetings at MDS campus. GVP meetings take place once a month, in order to review their experiences and take decisions for action in line with their self-deliberated priorities.
5. As residence is the only criterion for inclusion in the voter list, nomads did not have voting rights since they do not have a permanent address.

References

Kabeer, N. (2003) 'Making rights work for the poor: Nijera Kori and the construction of "collective capabilities" in rural Bangladesh', IDS Working Paper No. 200, Brighton: Institute of Development Studies

Kovoori, P. (1985) 'Seasonal migration and nomadism in western Rajasthan', Occasional Paper Series 11(5), Jaipur: Institute of Development Studies

Rao, A. and M. J. Casimir (eds) (2003) *Nomadism in South Asia*, New Delhi: Oxford University Press

Rights without citizenship? Participation, family and community in Rio de Janeiro

Joanna S. Wheeler

Over the past three decades, many things have changed in Brazil. Democracy has replaced a military dictatorship, and Cardoso's neo-liberal reforms have replaced hyperinflation and import substitution subsidies. However, despite some reductions in overall poverty rates, income and land distribution remain among the most unequal in the world. In the *favelas* (illegal land occupations) and housing projects of Rio de Janeiro, the number of urban poor has grown over the past 30 years to 40 per cent of the city's population (UNDP 2001). Drug trafficking groups now exert more control over low-income communities and *favelas* than any government. In the context of these dramatic changes, how have Rio de Janeiro's poor made use of notions of citizenship and rights? While certain rights are part of a basic language used by even the extremely poor and marginalized, traditional national democratic citizenship is failing to have meaning for the poor. This chapter will show how poor families in Rio de Janeiro are reinterpreting notions of citizenship on the basis of their experience of exclusion from formal political and economic structures.

The chapter draws on accounts of citizenship given by low-income families from different urban spaces, classes and races from within Rio de Janeiro: families from *favelas*, the housing projects and from the working class suburbs. By different urban spaces, I am referring to the stark spatial categories that characterize Rio de Janeiro. In addition to the ascribed class boundaries demarcated by the *Zona Sul* (traditional wealthy region), *Zona Norte* (industrialized working class area), *Zone Oeste* (newly rich, Miami-like region), and the *subúrbios* (working class allotments around the periphery), space in Rio de Janeiro is divided by degrees of legality. Although all *favelas* are technically illegal land occupations, some have clearer legal status than others. *Favelas* are interspersed throughout all three regions of the city, but concentrated in the *Zona Norte,* and as a result have greater legitimacy because there is little threat of removal there. By contrast, new *favelas* in the *Zona Oeste* are reminiscent of the shantytowns of the 1960s, with very precarious holds on the land and extremely poor conditions. These spatial categories have significant impacts on the lives of the poor in Rio de Janeiro (see Figure 6.1; for a more in-depth discussion see Wheeler 2001).

Data was collected through 40 open-ended interviews with extended families (three to four members of the same family from three generations) between September 2001 and March 2002. Questions focused on participants' perceptions of their citizenship, and participation in various aspects of city life. The following analysis also relies, as a secondary research source, on interviews with key community leaders, non-profit workers and members of the government.

Context

Hannah Arendt argues that 'the fundamental deprivation of human rights [and citizenship] is manifested first and above all *in the deprivation of a place in the world* [a political space] which makes opinions significant, and actions effective' (Jelin 1998, p. 405, emphasis added). A confluence of different factors in Rio de Janeiro has worked to dislodge the poor from their 'place in the world' and increase their distance from the political and economic mechanisms of power. First, despite increasing democratization in Brazil, extreme inequalities persist. The *2001 World Bank Development Report* gives Brazil's Gini coefficient as 0.60 – second only to Sierra Leone. For every year from 1970 to 1998, the richest 1 per cent of the population has received more income than the poorest 50 per cent of the population (Pães de Barros, Henriques and Mendonça 2000). And while the constitution of 1988 promises extensive rights and protections, the implementation of those rights has been slow to non-existent in many areas.

Second, neo-liberal reforms, as in much of Latin America, have been used to erode the boundary between public responsibilities and private roles. In particular, neo-liberal reforms have taxed the family structure, because as the state withdraws from social services, the family and social networks must fill the gap at a time when even fewer resources are available for those needs. The situation for women is particularly contradictory, because both growing financial pressures and the expectations behind neo-liberalism's 'market citizen' have forced more women to participate in remunerated work in the market economy (Bulbeck 1998, p. 99). In poor families, women's contributions make up to 38 per cent of the family's income (UNECLAC 1997). But there is no change in the distribution of household responsibilities: women are still responsible for childcare, cleaning, shopping and, in many cases, securing education and health care for the family. This problem is exacerbated in the case of single-mother households, which are dramatically on the rise in Brazil and Rio de Janeiro. Single mothers now head one in four households in Brazil (up from one in six in 1991) and earn an average US$246 per month in comparison to men's US$344 per month (IBGE: *Journal do Brasil* 2002, p. 18).

Finally, the power of drug trafficking groups in low-income communities is increasingly unqualified by any form of state intervention other than ineffectual and deadly raids by military police. Drug-traffic-related violence and the invasive power of drug mafias over poor communities in Rio de Janeiro are major factors in invalidating national democratic citizenship for the participants in this study. Drug traffickers are known as the *poder parallelo* (parallel power) because they control *favelas* and housing projects as if they were independent states and exercise all the powers of an autocratic government over the residents. The level of violence in some parts of the city peaked at 80 homicides per 100,000 people (equivalent to the levels of violence in Colombia and South Africa). From 1995 to 2000, the levels of violence declined somewhat (UNDP 2001), but in 2003 there was a significant resurgence, culminating in the bombing of city government buildings, bus burnings and army occupation of the streets during Carnival 2003. However, the violence in Rio de Janeiro, while endemic, is not homogeneous. It is, to use Holston and Appadurai's phrase, a 'city-specific violence of citizenship', meaning that it affects specific places and persons differently (2000, p. 16). The highest rates of violence are in *favelas* and poor neighbourhoods for Afro-Brazilians (*Zona Oeste* and *Zona Norte*) (see Figure 6.1) (UNDP 2001).

There, the violence is a combination of state-sponsored raids and battles with drug mafias (in 2001 over 900 civilians were killed by the police in Rio de Janeiro), and wars between competing factions and mafias of the drug trade (UNDP 2001). The extremely high level of violence in poor neighbourhoods due to the drug trade dramatically orders the daily lives of the residents of those communities. It is now unsafe to use public spaces like streets, bus stops and plazas after dark, and increasingly during the day. In one housing project involved in the study, one faction of traffickers took control of the local school and another of the local day care centre, and children were unable to attend

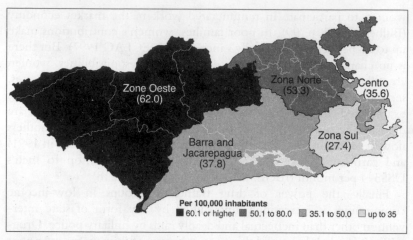

Per 100,000 inhabitants
■ 60.1 or higher ■ 50.1 to 80.0 ■ 35.1 to 50.0 □ up to 35

Figure 6.1: Homicide rate by area in Rio de Janeiro

either for over a month for fear of being caught in the crossfire between the warring groups. The overall result is *poder parallelo* and a growing irrelevance of formalized political rights for the poor:

> Democratic rights are compromised by other power circuits [including the military police, and the drug and gambling mafias] that obliterate the public dimension of citizenship, re-establishing violence and arbitrary power in the sphere of private relations, class, gender and ethnicity, thereby rendering the state increasingly ineffective.
> *Paoli and Telles 1998: 65*

In the face of extreme inequalities in income distribution, pressure for increasing economic participation through neo-liberal reforms and the erosion of the powers of the state by organized drug trafficking groups, the poor in Rio de Janeiro are increasingly distant from the means to influence political processes – and also increasingly disillusioned with notions of national democratic citizenship. As political and economic spheres are re-drawn by neo-liberal reforms and drug mafias, families in low-income communities are re-casting the boundaries between the private and their political and economic participation, and articulating new forms of citizenship linked to their everyday experiences.

The narrative of these new citizenships begins with another form of privatization of citizenship. While neo-liberal reforms erode the distinction between private and public responsibility, the participants in this study used the 'private', in the form of family and community, to engage with economic pressures – while protecting family and community priorities. These interviews highlighted how what is deemed the 'private' in liberal democratic theorizations of citizenship, and not what is public, is actually at the forefront of determining how citizenship is experienced (Castles and Davidson 2000, Chapter 1; Pateman and Gross 1987; Yuval-Davis 2000).

Formal citizenship and rights in Brazil

Over the past century in Brazil, there have been more than six constitutions and widely disparate forms of government, from populist authoritarianism under Getúlio Vargas, to military dictatorship, to formal democracy. The regime changes and subsequent constitutions have translated into shifting formal definitions of citizenship in Brazil. The current features of Brazilian citizenship began to emerge in the 1920s with a series of social movements calling for new forms of rights, such as the right to vote for women and the right to an education and a pension. The most powerful social movement during this period was organized labour, which made increasing demands for progressive labour laws. In 1930, populist governor Getúlio Vargas capitalized on existing social movements to gain national political power – and immediately abolished national, state and municipal legislatures on corruption charges. As a result of the power of the labour movement at that time, the 1934 Vargas Constitution established the right to education and encoded basic labour laws, including a 40-hour work week and the right to weekly leave.

The current constitution, ratified in 1988, marked the end of more than 20 years of military dictatorship, and expands considerably the number of rights and the concept of citizenship in Brazil set out by the 1934 Vargas Constitution. For the first time in Brazilian history, the illiterate were allowed to vote. The labour movement and other organized social protests suppressed during the dictatorship mobilized around the process of creating a new constitution, and ensured that the 1988 constitution defined Brazilian citizenship in broad terms:

> We the representatives of the Brazilian People, convened in the National Constituent Assembly to institute a democratic state for the purpose of ensuring the exercise of social and individual rights, liberty, security, well-being, development, equality and justice as supreme values of a fraternal, pluralist and unprejudiced society, founded on social harmony … this is a legal democratic state and is founded on sovereignty; citizenship; the dignity of the human person; the social values of labour and of free enterprise; and political pluralism.
>
> *Political Database of the Americas 2002*

The constitution also addressed Brazil's overall social structure:

> The economic order ... is intended to ensure everyone a life with dignity, in accordance with the dictates of social justice, with due regard for the following principles: national sovereignty; private property; the social function of property; free competition; consumer protection; environmental protection; reduction of regional and social differences; and the pursuit of full employment.
> *Political Database of the Americas 2002*

While some of the rights included in the 1988 constitution, such as the right to education and nationalized social security, had been established by the 1934 Vargas Constitution, the list of rights included in the 1988 constitution is unusual in its scope, far exceeding, for example, the American Bill of Rights. It includes the right to culture, sports, social security, education, health care, leisure, family planning and a healthy environment. Also included are sweeping labour rights, including a realistic minimum wage, paid maternity and paternity leave, retirement benefits and day care, among others (Kingstone 2000).

The influence of various social movements over the 1988 constitution shows that democracy, in comparison to dictatorship, has improved the rights and degrees of participation for some in Brazil. Because of the long history of organized labour and the success of the Vargas reforms, labour rights form part of the basic language of entitlements, even among the poor and marginalized in Rio de Janeiro. These labour rights also protect workers in the informal sector, such as domestic and service industry workers. The universal right to a 'thirteenth' month of salary for all workers in December, for example, is even enforced by taxi drivers, who double their fare rates for the entire month.

But this general assertion of progressive labour rights is paired with an equally pervasive sense of exclusion from the national democratic project of citizenship. In terms of the urban poor in Rio de Janeiro, the still-growing *favelas* and poor suburbs are clear signs that democracy has not dramatically improved access to society's resources. During the dictatorship, there were very active and effective *associações de moradores* (residents' associations) that organized within and between *favelas* around demands for access to basic services and infrastructure (Alvito and Zaluar 1998; Gay 1994). As democracy was implemented in Rio de Janeiro's city government, many leaders from *favelas* were incorporated into the new administration. This co-optation of community leaders combined with the rise in influence of drug trafficking mafias in Rio de Janeiro essentially to undermine the long-standing and powerful residents' associations. As a result, the poor in Rio de

Janeiro experience Brazil's new democracy from an even greater distance – mediated by the power of *Comando Vermelho* (the Red Command) and other trafficking groups. The rest of the chapter examines some aspects of this experience from the perspective of the participants in this study.

Privatizing politics

Participants were asked questions about their understanding of citizenship, their participation in politics and the most important forms such participation took. The results were particularly interesting, given a long history of populist regimes enforcing the notion of 'Brazilian-ness' as the basis of national identity. More recently, the country has passed through a very public process of debating and ratifying a new constitution which, as I noted, encodes extensive individual rights and privileges to its newly democratic citizens. Individual rights and formal democratic practices, such as signing petitions, joining political parties and participating in commissions, have been heavily promoted by the state and by organized social and political movements.

Yet none of the participants in the study referred to membership in a Brazilian nation when they defined citizenship. Nor did it appear that individual, rights-based citizenship as a category for understanding democratic practice had gained much purchase in Rio de Janeiro's *favelas*. Over 90 per cent of the participants reported having no trust in the national government. This distrust of the formal political structure goes deeper than any particular administration. In terms of the major changes in political regime in the past 20 years, very few could identify any major difference in their lives between dictatorship and democracy. One poor black woman, who lives in a city housing project, said that 'Brazil would be better off with a dictatorship. At least then things were working'. Another poor elderly woman from the suburbs identified 'more buses' as the major difference in her life between dictatorship and democracy.

In a plebiscite held in 1993, mandated by the 1988 constitution, Brazilians voted to choose a form of government. Only 66 per cent voted to maintain democracy (either as presidential or parliamentary), while 11 per cent voted for a monarchy and an additional 33 per cent voted for an 'other form of government'.[1] Several of the participants in this project said that they had voted against democracy for Brazil. One woman explained that she voted for the monarchy because she did not believe that the form of government would make any difference in her life, and 'a king or queen sounds more interesting than a president'. The refusal of several participants to take such a vote seriously, demonstrated by their choice of the highly improbable monarchy, is a symptom of deep disaffection from macro-level politics.

Several factors have contributed to the shift away from formal political and economic participation. The poor have not reaped the rewards of macro-economic reforms and do not have confidence in the effectiveness of formal democratic participation. Drug-related violence has further eroded the link between poor communities and formal democratic mechanisms. Evidence that they did not live in a just society was found in their accounts of daily confrontations with the evidence of injustice: police raids, overcrowded buses, inadequate schools, and crumbling and overcrowded health clinics.

In this context, formal democracy has little meaning for the residents of the *favelas*. Instead, they characterized their participation in family, community and city life as the most meaningful aspect of their political participation. They saw democratic practice as participation in a just society rather than in terms of voting, open elections and individual rights. So, while democracy and democratic impulses are important to poor women and men in Rio de Janeiro's *favelas*, they have redefined democratic practice in terms of their own values and beliefs. They have moved away from a notion of citizenship based on individual rights towards a notion that invokes collective responsibilities at the level of family and community. Examples of how this worked are presented below.

Recasting citizenship through the family

The market logic incarnated in Cardoso's neo-liberal reforms has been widely discussed in public discourse and heavily promoted by the state – including Rio de Janeiro's city government in the form of numerous micro-credit and funding programmes. However, residents in Rio de Janeiro's *favelas* face considerable economic exclusion. Almost every participant considered involvement in the market through employment to be essential, but the market logic of efficiency, competitiveness and individuality has been muted through interaction with notions of citizenship in *favelas*. Participants consistently placed their families and community at the centre of their market logic.[2] The family has become a key point of articulation between the market and individuals. The participants in this study on the whole did not approach the market as individuals but as members of families. Getting a job, taking loans, access to education and health care: all were mediated by family relations. This meant that certain aspects of market logic were promoted and others rejected.

This can be illustrated by the example of one of the participants, a woman who lived with her husband and son and over 40 members of her extended family in houses built on the family's property. The land was inherited from her great-grandfather, who emigrated from Portugal. Although her salary as a housekeeper in the city was essential income for the family, she wanted to continue to live with her family and so she commuted nearly five hours a day to the city centre. Several employers had offered her accommodation in the city during the week so she could avoid this lengthy and costly commute, but she refused. She used her salary to pay for daily household expenses, while her husband's salary went towards bills. When she had extra money, she transferred her son from a state-funded to a private school. She could have saved a considerable amount by living in Rio and avoiding transportation costs, but she refused to do this. When she became seriously ill, her mother and sister (also housekeepers in the city centre) filled in at her jobs so that she would not lose them. Her other sister stayed at home and provided childcare for the extended family's children, and also did the washing and cleaning. Although she could have made more money if she had got a job outside the home, she and her sisters believed it was more important for her to provide childcare and laundry services for the family.

Together, these women participated in the market: they used their family ties to secure jobs, health care, childcare and education for their children. While they participated in the market, they also rejected certain market demands. The family worked together to respond to crisis and uncertainty, fulfilling market demand for cheap day labour in the city, but using their connections in the city to guarantee other benefits. This strategy has affected family structure. Increasing numbers of women travel long distances for work, while men are more likely to find work nearer to the home (UNDP 2000). Since women are still responsible for household tasks, this puts an increasing strain on women to fulfil their work obligations. As a result, men are forced to take on a greater role in the home. Women's entry into the labour market has also increased their control over family finances, and women often opt to keep their children in school for longer than would have been possible if they were not working. In *favelas*, the family continues to be the space where integration into the market is negotiated.

Recasting citizenship through the community

The community has become another important site of citizenship practice. As one veteran community activist said in response to a question about his political participation:

I don't feel diminished because I live in a *favela* – each of us has tried to improve our own lives. All the intellectuals who came here, poor things, they never really understood anything because the changes you can make depend on the opportunities you take. [Governments] change and time passes and goes by, but who knows – tomorrow I might manage to do something else [to help the community].

In spite of pressure to participate in the formal economy and the new democratic structures of the Brazilian state, residents in low-income communities continue to contribute unremunerated labour into projects outside formal channels of political participation, by negotiating directly with those in control of housing projects and *favelas* (i.e. residents' associations controlled by drug-trafficking mafias).

This form of practice was evident in the example of one of the participants, a man who lived with his wife and two small children in a housing project ringed by *favelas*. He had committed considerable time and energy to community improvements. Although he had a job at the local university as a security guard, he had negotiated extended leave to carry out community development projects of his own design. Because the drug traffickers had taken control of the community where he lived and the local political structure, he had developed a form of community activism that carefully negotiated between the traffickers, other established local activists and his own family's well-being. He had claimed a piece of land in one of the *favelas* to construct a centre to address the problems he recognized in his community: lack of education, access to the job market and poor infrastructure.

Over the past six years, friends and family members had contributed labour and money to start construction on the centre. Every day he walked through the community to see who had time to help for a few hours. Every day children collected empty plastic bottles for the community centre's future recycling programme. Hundreds of bottles were stacked in one corner of the construction site. After six years, the first floor had yet to be completed. When there was no money or time, the project stopped until circumstances improved. He explained that the 'community centre is being built one bag of cement at a time, but it will be built'. The future centre would perform a wealth of functions: it would house a community association board, a recycling centre, language and information technology training courses, and a children's choir. He planned to name the centre after his daughter, because building it had 'taken the food out of her mouth, but it will make her life better'.

Participants in the research identified this form of activity as their most important form of political participation. Most had little or no interest in city-wide or state-wide politics. They consistently identified this community work as important to their own families, and they did not believe that the city government could ever do anything to address the problems in their community. At the community level, democratic impulses[3] in *favelas* are transformed into creative projects to improve specific aspects of the community. The major motivation for these projects, according to the participants in the study, was to build a better life for their children or their family. Citizenship is articulated at the level of the private. Political participation in low-income communities focuses on addressing the serious problems facing residents on a quotidian level: violence, lack of infrastructure, poverty and inadequate housing and education. National political discourse on democracy and individual rights is very distant by comparison.

Dignity and public services

Seventy-four per cent of the participants in this study identified dignity as citizenship's most important characteristic.[4] They made it clear that meaningful citizenship cannot exist without dignity. For the participants in this study, it was not their poverty or lack of rights that meant they had no dignity. Rather, it was the aggregation of everyday interactions and experiences, conflicts and triumphs that meant the difference between dignity and exclusion. As one woman said: 'Dignity is every-thing for a citizen – and we have no dignity. We are treated like cattle in the clinics, on the buses and in the shops. Only in rich neighbourhoods are people treated with dignity'.

An important aspect of dignity is related to access to public services. While such access may be guaranteed by Brazil's constitution as a right, it is the nature of that access that is most important to the poor. The erosion of health, education, housing and urban services over the past 30 years has compromised the dignity of the poor in everyday life. The participants in this study identified dignified access to these services as the most important characteristic of citizenship and the greatest lack in terms of their citizenship.

The end of the dictatorship coincided with a marked disintegration of many public services, because the new democratic government did not have the funds to make up for fifteen years of under-investment and neglect. The neo-liberal reforms of the Cardoso regime from 1996 to 2002 have further diminished the resources available for public services. The result is skeletal public education, and health care systems that have been abandoned by anyone with enough money to afford private services. The participants in this study went to great lengths to gain access to private health care and education. Most frequently, women working in domestic service jobs for the middle class used their employers to gain access to private health care and better education on behalf of their families. The daily struggle of the poor with the public health care system most clearly demonstrates how lack of dignified access to public services affects their lives.

The public health care system (*Sistema Único de Saúde Brasiliera*), which is supported by a heavy tax paid by employers, is woefully inadequate. Public hospitals do not have the resources to provide basic care. Currently, 40 per cent of the total population in Rio de Janeiro has resorted to private health coverage (UNDP 2001). For poor women, the most readily available form of health services is for prenatal care. Nonetheless, Brazil has the highest mortality rate among pregnant women in Latin America. The United Nations estimates that 200 women die in childbirth for every 100,000 children born (UNECLAC 1997). For all other types of health services, from family planning to hypertension, there are waits for appointments varying from months to years. In order to be seen by a doctor in a public hospital, ill people must start to form a line at 3 a.m. to get a ticket to join the waiting list for an appointment. Several participants travelled three hours across the entire city with their children to go to a public hospital that was rumoured to have a better paediatric service. But despite the clear problems in getting service in the public health care system, the major complaint of the participants was that at the public hospitals they felt as though they were treated as 'cattle' and 'not as a real person with dignity'. One interview with a poor black woman who lives in a housing project in the *Zona Norte* revealed that her former employer arranged an appointment for her in a private hospital after she had had no success getting treated for her hypertension in the public hospital. She commented that at the private hospital she was treated 'like a person' with 'politeness and respect', whereas at the public hospital the doctors and nurses were 'rude' and treated her 'like an animal'. Waiting in lines for inadequate service in public hospitals is tiring and discouraging, and what is most detrimental for the poor is the constant abasement that dealing with the public health care system requires.

Conclusion

The women and men who participated in this study did not define citizenship in terms of national identity, individual rights or formal democratic processes. Instead, they recast citizenship in terms of their families and communities in order to contest access to those of society's resources that have the most relevance to their daily lives.[5] This process of addressing their own communities' problems and reinforcing their sense of political community at a local level is the most important form of democratic practice, in their view. The women and men I interviewed redefined citizenship in their daily lives in three ways:

- As relating more to the 'private' than the public;
- In terms of a qualified political and economic participation that privileges their own families and communities;
- As dignity in their quotidian experiences.

The narrative of citizenship for the poor in Rio de Janeiro incorporates aspects of democratic and market logic, but recasts citizenship in terms of family and community structures, and participation with dignity in the city's life. In the absence of a meaningful discourse of citizenship at the macro political and economic levels for the participants in this study (the lack of a 'place in the world'), the place for the elaboration of citizenship is in the context of family and community. And this formulation of citizenship situates dignity in daily life at its centre.

Notes

I would like to thank Benjamin Junge at Emory University for his concise comments on an earlier version of this chapter, and apologize that I was not able to take up all his suggestions. I would also like to thank Evelina Dagnino, Alex Shankland and the other participants at the authors' workshop, June 2004, for their comments.

1. See http://conhecimentosgerais.hypermart.net. I would also like to acknowledge Carlos Pio of the Federal University of Brasilia for his correspondence regarding the plebiscite on governance.
2. For an example of how the family and community responded to market demands in Mexico, see Rocha (1994) and Rocha and Latapí (1991).
3. In terms of democratic impulses, the focus here is on forms of political participation that work for the good of some broader collectivity, rather than promoting representative governance, because that was the notion most commonly elaborated by the study's participants.
4. This focus among the poor on dignity as the central component of citizenship coincides with Evelina Dagnino's (1998) study on conceptions of citizenship amongst social activists in São Paulo. She asked about fifty social activists which of the following qualities is most important for democracy:
   - There are several political parties;
   - All have food and housing;
   - Whites, blacks, men, women, rich, and poor are all treated equally;
   - People can participate in unions and associations;
   - People can criticize and protest.
   Fifty-eight per cent of the sample chose the equal treatment of whites, blacks,

men, women, rich, and poor as the most important quality (p. 53). Dagnino goes on to note that a large majority of the poor and working class activists that she interviewed 'mentioned disrespect, discrimination, and prejudice as part of their daily experience in the city; referred to their status as "second-class citizens"; and complained of mistreatment because of their race or because they were not dressed well enough' (p. 55).

5. Ong (1996) makes a similar argument in reference to Asian immigrants to California.

References

Alvito, M. and A. Zaluar (1998) *Um século de Favela*, Rio de Janeiro: Fundação Getúlio Vargas

Bulbeck, C. (1998) *Re-orienting Western Feminisms: Women's Diversity in a Post-Colonial World*, Cambridge: Cambridge University Press

Castles, S. and A. Davidson (2000) *Citizenship and Migration: Globalization and the Politics of Belonging*, New York: Routledge

Dagnino, E. (1998) 'Culture, citizenship and democracy: Changing discourses and practices of the Latin American left', in S. Alvarez, E. Dagnino and A. Escobar (eds) *Cultures of Politics/Politics of Cultures: Re-visioning Latin American Social Movements*, Boulder, CO: Westview Press

Gay, R. (1994) *Popular Organization and Democracy in Rio de Janeiro*, Philadelphia: Temple University

Holston, J. and A. Appadurai (2000) 'Introduction: Cities and citizenship', in J. Holston (ed.) *Cities and Citizenship*, Durham, NC: Duke University Press

Jelin, E. (1998) 'Toward a culture of participation and citizenship: Challenges for a more equitable world', in S. Alvarez, E. Dagnino and A. Escobar (eds) *Cultures of Politics/Politics of Cultures: Re-visioning Latin American Social Movements*, Boulder, CO: Westview Press

Journal do Brasil, 8 March 2002

Kingstone, Peter (2000) *Key Events and Policy Changes in Brazil 1900–2000*, Hartford: University of Connecticut, mimeo

Ong, A. (1996) 'Cultural citizenship as subject-making: Immigrants negotiate racial and cultural boundaries in the United States', *Current Anthropology*, 37 (5), p. 737

Pães de Barros, R., R. Henriques and R. Mendonça (2000) *Desigualde e pobreza no Brasil: A estabilidade inaceitável*, Rio de Janeiro: IPEA

Paoli, M. C. and V. da S. Telles (1998) 'Social rights: Conflicts in contemporary Brazil', in S. Alvarez, E. Dagnino, and A. Escobar (eds) *Cultures of Politics/Politics of Cultures: Re-visioning Latin American Social Movements*, Boulder, CO: Westview Press

Pateman, C. and E. Gross (1987) *Feminist Challenges: Social and Political Theory*, Boston: Northeastern University Press

Political Database of the Americas (2002) *Brazilian Constitution of 1988*. www.georgetown.edu/pdba/Constitutions/Brazil/brazil.html (23 May 2002)

Rocha, M. G. de la (1994) *The Resources of Poverty: Women and Survival in a Mexican City*, Oxford: Blackwell

Rocha, M. G. de la and A. Escobar Latapí (1991) *Social Responses to Mexico's Economic Crisis of the 1980s*, San Diego: Center for US–Mexican Studies

United Nations Development Program (UNDP) (2000) *UNDP Poverty Report 2000*,

Washington, DC: United Nations

United Nations Development Program (UNDP) (2001) *Relatório de Desenvolvimento Humano do Rio de Janeiro 2001,* website: saturno.no.com.br/notitia/leitura: 2002

United Nations Economic Commission for Latin America and the Caribbean (UNECLAC) (1997) *Sustainable Development, Poverty and Gender, Latin America and the Caribbean: Working Toward the Year 2000,* Santiago, Chile: United Nations

Wheeler, J. (2001) 'The politics of being a citizen: Women and citizenship in Rio de Janeiro', thesis, University of Massachusetts, Amherst, MA

World Bank. (2001) *World Development Report: Attacking Poverty,* Oxford: Oxford University Press

Yuval-Davis, N. (2000) 'Citizenship, territoriality, and the gendered construction of difference', in E. Isen (ed.) *Democracy, Cititzenship and the City,* London: Routledge

Seven

Young people talking about citizenship in Britain

Ruth Lister
with Noel Smith, Sue Middleton, Lynne Cox

Introduction

'Vocabularies of citizenship' and their meanings vary according to social, political and cultural context, and reflect different historical legacies (Bussemaker and Voet 1998; Carens 2000; Saraceno 1997; Siim 2000). They are translated into 'lived citizenship': 'the meaning that citizenship actually has in people's lives and the ways in which people's social and cultural backgrounds and material circumstances affect their lives as citizens' (Hall and Williamson 1999, p. 2). Yet, 'very little is known about the realities of how different people understand themselves as citizens' (Jones and Gaventa 2002, p. 28). This conclusion, reached in a recent review of the citizenship literature, echoes the earlier observation in an empirical study by Conover et al. that much theoretical debate in the North about the meaning of citizenship is 'conducted in what is virtually an empirical void' (1991, p. 801). Although there have since been a few studies of how citizens themselves understand citizenship, compared with recent theoretical outpourings the empirical void is far from being filled.

This chapter reports findings from a three-year qualitative, longitudinal study of how young people in Britain negotiate the transitions to citizenship. One hundred and ten young people in the East Midlands town of Leicester, aged 16 to 17, 18 to 19 and 22 to 23 in 1999, were interviewed.[1] There was a gender balance and about one in eight was Asian, predominately of Indian-Hindu background (to reflect Leicester's main minority ethnic community). Given the salience of paid work to contemporary characterizations of citizenship, the group was stratified according to 'insider' and 'outsider' status as a proxy for social class. 'Insiders' conformed with a stereotypical model of the 'successful' young person as on the route through A-levels and university and into graduate-type employment; 'outsiders' fell well outside it, with few or no qualifications and a record of unemployment for most of the time since leaving school. By the third and final interview in 2001, 64 of the original group remained.[2]

The study needs to be understood in the context of the New Labour government's desire to strengthen citizenship, and of growing public concern about young people's relationship to citizenship in the face of perceived apathy and disengagement (Advisory Group on Citizenship 1998; Pearce and Hallgarten 2000). The study throws light on young people's understandings of citizenship and the extent to which they identify themselves and act as citizens. More specifically, the chapter looks at notions of 'first class' and 'second class' and 'good' and 'bad' citizenship, and at perceptions of rights and responsibilities. It concludes by comparing the young people's constructions of citizenship with those found in dominant theoretical and political models.

The meaning(s) of citizenship

Until recently, citizenship has not been a salient idea in the British political tradition. Few people therefore have a clear idea of what it means to be a citizen (Dean with Melrose 1999; Miller 2000; Speaker's Commission 1990). Not surprisingly, citizenship was not part of the everyday language of the young people in our study. Nevertheless, the idea resonated with their own attempts to make sense of their position in society. Five models of citizenship emerged. Moving from the most to the least articulated, these are as follows.

'Universal status'

At its most inclusive, everyone is understood to be a citizen by virtue of membership of the community or nation. In a 'thin' version, this reflected a view that 'citizen' means 'person'. This was the response given by a number of 'outsiders' in particular. For one, a 19-year-old white male, citizenship didn't 'mean owt', but he added that 'it's just a person at the end of the day – a citizen'. For another, a 19-year-old 'outsider' white female, 'it doesn't matter what they do, everybody's a citizen'.

A 'thicker' understanding drew on notions of 'belonging' – to either the local or national community. Two participants summed it up: 'Belonging. I think being part of something … a sense of belonging' (16-year-old 'insider' white female); 'citizenship is about being somewhere, belonging somewhere' (16-year-old 'outsider' Asian female). Overall, there were no obvious gender differences, but 'insiders' were more likely to subscribe to the universal status model and young Asians did so more consistently over the three years. However, in another study in the Economic and Social Research Council programme, African-Caribbean and Pakistani young people rejected the notion of citizenship as a universal status. Instead, 'many were convinced that citizenship was hierarchised and unequal' (Harris *et al.* 2001: 50).

'Respectable economic independence'

This model is embodied by a person who is in waged employment, pays taxes and has a family and their own house: 'the respectable economically independent citizen', associated with the economic and social status quo. As a 16-year-old 'outsider' white male put it: 'I think as soon as you're living in your own house, out working, paying your bills, that's when you're a citizen'. A 16-year-old 'insider' white male defined a citizen as being 'a working part of the country', which would mean 'when I've got a house, wife, kids, job going on'. The model underpinned understandings of 'first class' and 'second class' citizenship, discussed below. It effectively excludes many of the young people themselves in the short term because of age or dependence on their parents, and, in the longer term, some 'outsiders' because of anticipated unemployment and their generally disadvantaged labour market position. The young men were more likely to invoke this model; otherwise there were no clear patterns.

'Constructive social participation'

Here, citizenship denotes a constructive stance towards the community. This ranged from the more passive abiding by the law to the more active idea of citizenship as responsible practice – helping people and having a positive impact. A 22-year-old 'outsider' white female summed it up: 'A citizen is where you're helping in the community … You're helping people and you're trying to do your best. Trying to support where you are'. On this basis she considered that people 'who can't be assed to get off their beer bellies and help are not a citizen or anything. They don't care what happens around them'. A 16-year-old Asian male was one of a number of 'insiders' who talked about being responsible and contributing as part of a reciprocal relationship with the community or society: 'Being responsible; being mature about everything and again, not just taking, giving back… It's helping out in as many ways as you can'. This 'constructive social participation' model underpinned notions of 'good' citizenship discussed below. 'Outsiders' were rather more likely to subscribe to it than 'insiders', but there were no clear gender or ethnic differences. The model was also prominent in a recent national survey of school students (Kerr *et al.* 2003).

'Social-contractual'

A small number, particularly females, referred spontaneously to rights and/or responsibilities. An 'insider' white female, for instance, stated that citizenship means 'being a part of society and having rights and requirements of living within the law'. This represents one element of what Dean with Melrose (1999) identified as a 'social-contractual' citizenship discourse. An earlier American–British study of adults found that, in both countries, the majority subscribed to the social-contractual model (Conover *et al.* 1991).

'Right to a voice'

The right and genuine opportunity to have a say and be heard is at the heart of this model, which emerged from the responses of a small number of participants. As one 22-year-old 'outsider' white male explained: 'To feel a citizen, I'd say I should have a right to say what goes on'. A 16-year-old 'insider' Asian female talked about 'being able to help in decision-making ... just having your say in what's gonna happen'. A 16-year-old 'insider' white female thought she'd feel like a full citizen 'when people do respect you for your views and they listen to you'.

The five models were not mutually exclusive in that some young people subscribed to more than one, sometimes drawing on different models simultaneously. Overall, the 'universal' model dominated. However, over the three years of the study, it diminished in importance and the 'respectable economic independence' and 'constructive social participation' models, with their invocation of economic and civic responsibility, were articulated with increasing frequency.

To be a citizen?

The importance of identity to citizenship is increasingly being recognized in the citizenship literature (Isin and Wood 1999; Jones 1994; Jones and Gaventa 2002; Stevenson 2001; Turner 1997). Hall *et al.* observe that 'in the contemporary political and policy arena, much of the rhetoric of citizenship is about citizenship as an identity – encouraging young people in particular to think of themselves *as* citizens' (1998, p. 309, emphasis in original). Like other identities, citizenship identity is constructed and evolves, and it is possible to identify processes of differential citizenship identity formation (Hobson and Lindholm 1997). John Shotter underlines the difficulties involved:

> To be a citizen is not a simple matter of first as a child growing up to be a socially competent adult, and then simply walking out into the everyday world to take up one's rights and duties as a citizen. This is impossible. For ... it is a status which one must struggle to attain in the face of competing versions of what [it] is proper to struggle for.
> *1993, pp. 115–16*

National identity

One of the difficulties is the tendency to conflate citizenship and national identity (Fulbrook and Cesarani 1996). Alongside citizenship, national identity is a current preoccupation of British politicians, concerned to stimulate debate on what it means to be British – and also English – in a changing world and a devolved United Kingdom. In the study, participants, who had engaged readily with questions about citizenship, struggled when asked about nationality and national identity, and showed little enthusiasm for the topic. This echoed the difficulties Conover *et al.* (1991) reported among their British respondents.

White participants frequently used the terms British and English interchangeably, but for the most part found it difficult to articulate what they meant other than in comparison with other nationalities or in the context of British multiculturalism. The most common response was to associate nationality with country of birth, parental heritage and long-term residence. Culture (articulated in such terms as language, food, customs, history, humour, monarchy, the pound) tended to be a secondary theme. In terms of their own identification, responses ranged from a sense of significance and pride (sometimes expressed in relation to sport) through indifference to negativity.

In the case of a small number of white 'outsiders', discussion of nationality was tinged with hostility to Asian residents and asylum-seekers, who were perceived as receiving more help from the state than white people whose families had paid tax through the generations. Some also talked about cultural, religious and language differences. The majority, however, were more accepting. They thought it understandable that those of Asian background would want to be in touch with and have pride in their roots and culture, and one noted the ways in which people's roots are in any case 'all getting very global and mixed up'. The Asian participants themselves found it easier to talk about nationality, for it opened up discussion about the balance between, or compound of, British and Asian identities. Some described themselves simply as British, some as equally British and Indian, and others emphasized that they were as British as anyone else, referring to their Indian origin as 'just background'. The study by Harris *et al.* (2001) of African-Caribbean and Pakistani young people found more of a sense of 'not belonging'. This underlines the fact that young people in different minority ethnic groups do not relate to citizenship in a single, undifferentiated way.

Citizen identity

In all three waves of the research, over two-fifths of participants defined themselves unambiguously as citizens. This group included twice as many 'insiders' as 'outsiders', and more older and female participants. A further fifth who identified themselves as citizens at the third wave had earlier considered themselves either as partial citizens or not as citizens. Both 'outsiders' and females were over-represented in this group, and there was a clear age dynamic, with younger participants more likely to develop an identification with the status quo. Those who felt themselves to be partial citizens were more likely to be 'insiders' and male. The four participants who did not consider themselves to be citizens at the third wave were all older, white 'outsiders'. One of these, a 22-year-old white female, described herself as 'an insignificant little person' rather than a citizen and explained: 'I don't stand for anything. I haven't particularly achieved anything, so I don't feel like I'm a proper citizen'. Likewise, four out of the five who could not say whether they were citizens were white (younger) 'outsiders'. At each wave, 'outsiders' were less likely than 'insiders' to identify themselves as citizens. Ethnicity did not generally appear to be a distinguishing factor.

The extent to which the young people identified themselves as citizens reflected developments in their own lives, such as whether or not they had achieved waged employment and paid tax; been involved in their communities or undertaken voluntary work; or had voted. More subjective factors were also important. These included feelings about belonging, significance, respectful treatment, independence and whether they had had an effective say.

Different combinations of the models of citizenship described earlier underlay the young people's self-perceptions as citizens. Their assessment of changes in their sense of citizenship identity drew most frequently on the respectable economic independence model. This was followed by the constructive social participation model and then by the social-contractual and the right-to-a-voice models. Very few made reference to voting, but one 'insider' white female, eligible to vote for the first time, did so strongly:

I do feel a greater sense of being a citizen than I did... I can't stop talking about the whole voting thing, which is quite bad, but it's given me a sense of being a citizen, being a member of the wider society, and being able to count as something.

In some instances, citizenship did not appear an attainable status. One 19-year-old 'outsider' white female said that the word made her think of 'old people and people who are like lawyers and people like that. Lawyers and social workers and things like that. They're citizens – people who are so high up'.

'First' and 'second class' citizenship

The potentially exclusionary implications of the respectable economic independence model implied by this young woman were reflected also in responses to the notion of 'first' and 'second class' citizenship. First-class wave participants were asked what they thought of opinion polls which suggest that unemployed people are often made to feel like 'second class' citizens. There was considerable resistance to classifying people in this way. Nevertheless, the clear consensus was that unemployed people *are* regarded as second class citizens by society. A number of the 'outsiders' clearly saw the label as applying to them, and placed themselves at the bottom of a hierarchical image of society. 'Lower than everybody else' was a phrase used more than once:

It makes you feel like you *are* a second class citizen, 'cos you haven't got a job. I don't know what it means, but it makes you feel lower than everybody else. *(22-year-old white male)*

You feel – like everyone else has got more of a say than you. You're just last – at the bottom. *(19-year-old white female)*

Second class citizen, to me, means me really. *(19-year-old white male)*

The 'first class' citizen was overwhelmingly personified across groups by the educated home-owner, with a secure job, family and car – in other words, the embodiment of the respectable economic independence model and of the socio-economic status quo. Independence (from the state) and participation as workers and taxpayers were also the watchwords of 'first class' citizenship. Some typical examples of this exclusionary image, as articulated by 'outsiders', were:

Well a job, basically, ain't it, and decent house. If you've got a council flat and signing on or on Social, then you're a dosser, ain't you? *(16-year-old white female)*

Someone who's got a respectable job and a nice house and good children at private school. BUPA [private health insurance] and all that bollocks. (*22-year-old white male*)

'Good' and 'bad' citizenship

Understandings of 'good' and 'bad' citizenship (explored in the first two waves) stood in vivid contrast to those of 'first' and 'second class', drawing as they did on the constructive social participation model. This was epitomized in the observation of a 19-year-old 'insider' white female during the focus group held between the first and second waves:

> Money isn't always a good citizen. Sometimes the more money you've got, it seems as though you are a worse citizen... Whereas the working class person on their estate can't do enough for their neighbour; they're a very good citizen.

The good citizen

All but 13 of the 110 first-wave participants had ideas to offer as to what constitutes good citizenship. Most included a number of elements in their definition of good citizenship. The most common interpretation, offered by over two-thirds, involved a combination of the 'ordinarily' and 'extra' good (Conover *et al.* 1991): a considerate and caring attitude towards others and a constructive approach towards and active participation in the community. The latter emerged particularly strongly. Female participants were more likely to refer explicitly to constructive participation in 'community' or neighbourhood. Generally, frequent references were made to doing 'one's fair share in the community', sometimes in an organized way, and sometimes more informally, such as in 'looking out for' and 'helping' people in the neighbourhood. One 19-year-old 'outsider' white male explicitly emphasized the informal over the more formal:

> I wouldn't call a good citizen like the kind who goes out to do charity and trying to raise money. That's not my version of a good citizen. Mine's like they'll help you out. They'll lend you something if you need it, and that's the way I see a good citizen ... It's like your neighbours.

Bad citizens were defined as selfish, uncaring, lazy and lacking in respect. This was summed up by a 16-year-old 'insider' white male, who saw a bad citizen as:

> someone that's all take and no give, basically. Not participating in any way – just all for themselves ... when somebody cares more about getting

a car, or whatever, than what's going on with the people who are, say, homeless on their doorsteps, you know?

Whether or not someone shows 'respect' was a criterion used by a number of 'outsiders'. One, a 22-year-old white male, talked of the good citizen as someone with 'a bit of respect for his surroundings and ... respectful, polite. A bad citizen is someone who ain't got no respect for anybody... Smashing this and that up; couldn't give a toss about where he lives'. Another, a 19-year-old white female, argued that:

> People who have respect for each other and themselves are good citizens ... So I think good citizens are those that don't break the law, they respect, they have mutual respect for themselves and for people in their community and society. Whereas the bad ones are just, don't have any respect for anyone, not even themselves.

The importance that young people attach to respect when thinking about citizenship emerges from other research also (Harris *et al.* 2001; Kerr *et al.* 2003). One 'outsider' suggested, though, that respect was difficult when living in a poor environment. Here, respect was partly linked to not breaking the law. This reflected the second most common construction of the good and bad citizen overall: that of the law-abiding and non-disruptive versus the trouble-making citizen. A significant minority of first- and second-wave participants referred to abiding by the law or keeping out of trouble, although in most cases they referred also to other aspects of good citizenship. Political conceptions of good citizenship were less frequently articulated. In our study, only four, all female 'insiders', mentioned voting. This is consistent with a 1999 Institute for Citizenship/Natwest MORI survey, in which only 9 per cent chose voting as important to being a good citizen. A very small number in our study, mainly 'insiders', saw good citizenship in more active political or campaigning terms.

'Dissident citizenship'

Despite the link made with keeping within the law by a significant minority, a couple of 'insider' white males did question this from a political perspective, distinguishing between different kinds of law-breaking. Thus, one of them suggested that someone who broke the law in the name of animal rights could be a good citizen, while a car vandal would be a bad citizen. In the second wave, participants were asked whether it was ever justifiable or necessary for a citizen to break the law. Only 16 out of the 74 responded that it was never justifiable; 13 of these were 'outsiders' and the young Asians were disproportionately represented among this group. Most participants felt that citizenship status was not affected by certain illegal activities, such as minor traffic offences, use of cannabis, stealing food out of necessity and being part of a campaign.

A more specific question on whether it is ever justifiable or necessary for a citizen to break the law as part of a campaign or demonstration elicited a negative response from only nine participants. The most common justifications given were: the need to gain attention for an issue; the deservingness of the cause; the strength of feeling of the protesters; and the need to challenge an unfair law.

Holloway Sparks (1997, p. 75) has suggested the notion of 'dissident citizenship' to describe 'oppositional democratic practices', through which 'dissident citizens constitute alternative public spaces' to pursue non-violent protest outside the formal democratic channels. Such notions might help render citizenship a less oppressive notion for those who perceive it in terms of a status quo that excludes themselves. There was a sense, often not verbalized but expressed through tone, facial expression or atmosphere, that for some of the 'outsiders', questions about good citizenship and their own involvement in citizenship-related activities carried a potentially oppressive air (see also France 1998).

Voluntary work and good citizenship

In the first wave, the question of good citizenship was approached initially with reference to the UK government's promotion of volunteering as key to the development of 'responsible' or 'active' citizenship, particularly among young people. In the second wave, they were asked more generally about any connection they saw between voluntary work and good citizenship.

Of the 74 participants in the second wave, 50 believed in such a connection; a number though qualified this by emphasizing that it was neither an exclusive nor a necessary connection (an argument put also by those who opposed the idea). The two most frequently cited bases of such a connection were that both are about 'helping people' and about contributing to the community or society. In both instances, the young women and Asian participants were particularly likely to use such arguments. The small number of Asian participants in the second wave were also more willing to make the connection in the first place, but there were no obvious gender differences. 'Outsiders' were much less likely than 'insiders' to accept any connection.

There was less support in the first wave for the government's association of voluntary work with good citizenship. Some 'outsiders', such as this 16-year-old white female, also expressed a dislike of the idea of working without pay: 'No one's gonna get no medals to be a good citizen... I think you'd be silly actually doing something for nothing'. 'Insiders' who opposed the idea tended to raise questions of motivation or to argue that not doing voluntary work does not mean that one is a bad citizen. One, a 16-year-old white female, demonstrated a shrewd understanding of the politically dominant citizenship philosophy when she observed that previously citizenship 'was an automatic thing but it seems now that you gonna have to work for your status in a way'.

Rights and responsibilities

New Labour's promotion of voluntary work as active citizenship is one example of its repeated emphasis on the need for a 'fresh understanding of the rights and responsibilities of the citizen' (Brown 2000), with the accent on responsibilities and obligations over rights. The general presumption appears to be that set out in the Cantle Report: 'The rights *and – in particular – the responsibilities* of citizenship need to be more clearly established' (Cantle 2001, p. 20, emphasis added).[3] Yet, the young people we interviewed found it markedly more difficult to identify their rights than they did their responsibilities.

Responsibilities

In line with their views about good citizenship, the most frequently mentioned citizenship responsibility referred to 'being constructive'. This included notions of 'giving back to the community', being responsible and courteous, respecting others, behaving in a socially acceptable manner. A 16-year-old 'outsider' white female summed it up as 'whether it's through taxes or helping in the community, just giving back something to society'. An 18-year-old 'outsider' white male responded: 'Keep the country clean and that; help old people across the road, things like that. Being polite and courteous'.

Other responses referred to obeying the law; looking after oneself and one's family; being in work and paying tax; and voting. In the final wave, 'insiders' were about three times more likely than 'outsiders' to refer to employment and paying tax, and were twice as likely to refer to being constructive. 'Outsiders' were about three times more likely than 'insiders' to refer to looking after self or family. Female participants had a greater tendency to refer to obeying the law and to employment and paying tax, and older participants to being constructive. The small number of Asian participants were more likely to refer to obeying the law.

The contrast between 'outsiders' and 'insiders' has a degree of resonance with the starker finding of Harris *et al.* (2001), that African-Caribbean and Pakistani young people were only prepared to acknowledge obligations in relation to their own community, family and friends. However, the responses did not accord with those in Alan France's study in a deprived, working class community, which found that some young people's acceptance of citizen responsibilities in both the community and the labour market 'had been undermined by experiences of exclusion and exploitation' (1998, p. 108).

In contrast to the two studies just cited, when asked specifically about work obligations in earlier waves, the majority of 'outsiders' as well as 'insiders' signed up to the government's philosophy of paid work as a citizenship obligation, although sometimes with qualifications such as the state of the local labour market. Another qualification raised by some, most notably older 'outsider' white young women who had or were expecting children, was the presence of young children or pregnancy. When asked specifically in the second wave whether waged employment or parenting is more important to society, about half of both the young men and women answered the latter, and most of the others felt they were of equal importance. Some articulated views that reflected the position of a number of feminist citizenship theorists, that care should be acknowledged as an expression of citizenship responsibility alongside paid work (Knijn and Kremer 1997; Lister 2003; Sevenhuijsen 1998). For example, a 16-year-old 'insider' white female responded:

> I do see the value of working, I really do. But I think I'm going to have to side with a really positive, important role – to stay at home and raise the children. You're at home with them, and teaching them things: how to grow up to be good citizens.

Some participants, in particular both Asian and white 'insider' younger women, referred explicitly or implicitly to an underlying responsibility to be self-reliant and independent. In line with their general views about citizenship responsibilities, 'outsiders' were more likely to define paid work responsibility in relation to themselves and their families, whereas 'insiders' tended to talk more of a responsibility to the wider society, sometimes in addition to themselves and their families. A small group, mainly of 16-year-old 'outsiders', did not see employment as a responsibility and rejected the idea as coercive. One 16-year-old white male, for instance, rejected the idea as 'a load of rubbish ... just pushing you to get a job, you know what I mean. Just trying to get you down so you say "Sod this! I'm getting a job; don't want none of this stick"'.

The other area of particular concern to British politicians at present is voting, in the wake of the unprecedented low turn-out in the 2001 General Election, especially among young people. Very few participants referred spontaneously to voting as a citizenship obligation. In the first wave, of 52 participants specifically asked, 12 were in favour and 34 opposed to the idea of voting as a social obligation, with the rest unsure. All but one of those in favour were 'insiders'; nine were female and none was Asian. The most forcefully put argument against voting as an obligation was, in fact, premised on a notion of responsibility that serves to problematize a simple equation of voting and sense of civic responsibility. A number of the young people believed strongly that it was more irresponsible to vote in ignorance – without knowledge of the candidates or issues at hand – than not to vote at all. A 16-year-old Asian female 'insider', still at school, who held the view that voting is important because 'one vote can make a full difference', believed strongly that the responsible citizen should 'not just vote for the hell of voting'. She suggested that 'if I was a bad citizen, I'd go to a voting poll and just tick any names. Not knowing what I was ticking – that would make me a bad citizen'. Such beliefs need to be read in the context of the acknowledgement by a number of participants, both 'insiders' and 'outsiders', of their lack of political knowledge both in terms of what the parties stand for and the mechanics of voting.

Rights

As noted, the young people were less fluent in the language of rights than in that of responsibilities.[4] When asked specifically about this in the third wave, around half struggled to identify their rights. Sixteen of these (of whom fifteen were white 'outsiders') were unable to do so at all. In contrast, only one participant was unable to identify any responsibilities. Roughly a quarter of the remaining participants referred to political and social rights respectively, the former in relation to the vote and the latter in relation to social benefits, housing, health care and education.

Two thirds referred to civil rights, such as freedom of speech, movement and worship, and freedom from discrimination. This included nine of the ten remaining Asian participants. One of them, an 18-year-old 'outsider' male, spoke of 'freedom of speech; to be counted as equal; just to be treated equally really, like any other British citizen should be treated'. None of the 'outsiders' referred to social rights. Several participants (mainly 'insiders') also referred to employment as a right. The findings contrast with those of Conover et al. (1991), who remarked on the primacy given by British respondents to social rights of citizenship and their relative disregard of civil rights (see also Dean with Melrose 1999; Dwyer 2000).

With regard more specifically to the right to social security, only a minority believed that they had an unconditional right to benefit, when questioned in the first wave. This small group referred to their right as a British citizen and/or the taxes paid by their parents or themselves. The majority, though, linked social rights with responsibilities, talking of benefit receipt as a conditional right, the most common condition specified being active job-seeking. A number questioned the fairness of taking money from people who are working and paying tax, without putting something back.

Others expressed some ambivalence about their own position. A 16-year-old 'outsider' white male, for example, spoke of a right to benefit in the face of the government's failure to supply jobs. Yet he also felt that in a way he didn't have a right because:

It's the taxpayer's money that we're having, ain't it? When they pay tax it's coming towards us and we're just sitting on our arses all day and doing nothing. And in that way I don't think we deserve it, but like I say, I don't think we'd be able to survive without.

While, on the whole, opinions did not differ significantly between 'insiders' and 'outsiders', the most noticeable group to hold a distinct view was some older 'outsider' white women who had or were expecting children. They believed that lone mothers with young children or expectant mothers should have an unconditional right to benefit.

Young people as citizens

Current political debate about young people's citizenship tends to focus on what young people do not do, creating an image of young people as deficient citizens (Eden and Roker 2002). When the focus shifts to what young people do do, a rather different picture emerges. In the present study, the great majority of young people had engaged at some time in some form of constructive social participation. There were a number of elements to this: formal, organized voluntary work; informal voluntary work (such as regularly helping elderly neighbours); informal political action (such as demonstrations) designed to bring about or prevent change; activities with political implications although not explicitly political (for example, involvement in a Hindu society that served to promoted inter-cultural relations); awareness-raising (for instance, challenging racism in conversation); altruistic acts (such as donating blood or giving to charity); and general social participation contributing to the strengthening of social capital (including reciprocal neighbourliness and membership of community or sports organizations).

Levels (although not patterns) of participation were similar among 'insiders' and 'outsiders'. Around half (more among 'insiders') had participated in formal voluntary work; nearly a quarter (more among 'outsiders') had experience of informal voluntary work. About a quarter (mainly 'insiders' and female 'outsiders') had some experience of informal political action (beyond signing petitions). Although the distinction was not sharp, 'insiders' were more likely to engage in less active, more global or national forms of action in comparison with 'outsiders' who were more likely to engage in more active, local forms (such as a demonstration to prevent the closure of a youth club).

With regard to formal political engagement, there was considerable fluidity in attitudes towards using the vote over the three years of our study. When it came to the 2001 General Election, about half voted. Although 'insiders' were twice as likely to have voted as 'outsiders', the differential had almost disappeared among the oldest participants. 'Insiders' and young women were more likely to give reasons for voting that reflected a sense of civic duty. Six (five of whom were female) said they were motivated to vote by the knowledge that the vote had been fought for. The main substantive reasons given for not voting among the other 33 referred to a perception of politics as boring or irrelevant; critical attitudes towards formal politics and politicians or the efficacy of voting; and lack of political literacy.

Conclusion

Young people take seriously the question of their relationship to the wider society. The overriding impression received from in-depth discussions on the meanings of citizenship is of a highly responsible group. The common assumptions of politicians that rights have been over-emphasized at the expense of responsibilities, and that young people, in particular, need to be made aware of their citizenship responsibilities, are not borne out by the study. Indeed, the young people found it much more difficult to talk about rights than responsi-bilities, and when they did identify rights they were more likely to be civil than political or social rights. Few saw social security rights as unconditional. The young people also tended to place a high premium on constructive social participation in the local community, and many of them had engaged in such participation. It represented, for many of them, the essence of good citizenship and was one of two more responsibility-based models that emerged as prominent from general discussions of the meanings of citizenship. The most dominant model was, however, a less active one rooted in membership of the community or nation. Few thought about citizenship in social-contractual terms.

Together, these elements indicate that of the three main citizenship models developed in the literature, it is the communitarian model to which the young people were most likely to subscribe (Bussemaker and Voet 1998; Delanty 2000). They also displayed a belief in at least some 'civic virtues' (Dagger 1997) and the importance to citizenship of civility and respect (McKinnon 2000) and giving to the community (Heater 1990). Liberal, rights-based and civic republican, political, participation-based models did not figure prominently in their discussions. This suggests that they may have taken on board political messages about active citizenship and about responsibilities over rights (though not the related social-contractual model propounded by New Labour) that have become increasingly dominant over the past couple of decades in the UK.

Similarly, the young people's image of the first class citizen is redolent of the successful citizen promoted by Thatcherism and to a degree under New Labour: economically independent, with money, their own home and a family. For some of those classified as 'outsiders', this meant that they themselves identified with the label of 'second class citizen', below everyone else. The respectable economic independence model of citizenship that underpinned such understandings, became more dominant during the course of the research. Its potentially divisive and exclusionary nature stands in tension with the more inclusive, universal, membership model, which was most dominant overall. It also stands in contradiction to T. H. Marshall's (1950) classic definition of citizenship as bestowing equal status on all full members of a national community. Instead of challenging class divisions, the respectable economic independence model of citizenship reinforces them.

This points to how everyday understandings of citizenship can have both inclusionary and exclusionary implications. Also, the ways in which individuals frequently drew on a number of models simultaneously to make sense of citizenship and their own identities as citizens suggests that the 'lived citizenship' of young people needs to be understood in fluid terms, cutting across fixed theoretical categories. Such findings pose a challenge for both the theorization and the politics of citizenship.

Notes

1. The study was funded by the Economic and Social Research Council (project L134 25 1039). References to the young people's ages all give their age at the time of the first wave. An earlier version of the chapter appeared in *Citizenship Studies* 7 (2) (2003), http://www.tandf.co.uk and in M. Barry (ed.) (2004) *Youth Policy and Social Inclusion*, Routledge. I am grateful to the publishers for permission to use the material.
2. Apart from the above-average attrition of 'outsiders', anticipated in the construction of the original sample, the final group broadly reflected the balance of the original. The analysis refers to the 64 who participated in all three waves, except where questions were confined to the first and/or second waves. In addition to the three qualitative interviews, a short, factual questionnaire was administered at recruitment stage and a focus group of some of the participants was held after the first wave to help inform questioning in subsequent waves.
3. The Cantle Report was commissioned by the government following disturbances in a number of northern towns.
4. A MORI poll found that two-thirds of 15–24-year-olds felt they knew little about their rights as citizens compared with half who felt the same about their responsibilities (Wolchover 2002).

References

Advisory Group on Citizenship (1998) *Education for Citizenship and the Teaching of Democracy in Schools*, London: Qualifications and Curriculum Authority

Brown, G. (2000) James Meade Lecture, 8 May, London

Bussemaker, J. and R. Voet (1998) 'Citizenship and gender, theoretical approaches and historical legacies', *Critical Social Policy*, 18(3), pp. 277–307

Cantle, T. (2001) *Community Cohesion: A Report of the Independent Review Team*, London: Home Office

Carens, J. H. (2000) *Culture, Citizenship and Community*, Oxford: Oxford University Press

Conover, P. J., I. M. Crewe, D. D. Searing (1991) 'The nature of citizenship in the United States and Great Britain: Empirical comments on theoretical themes', *Journal of Politics*, 53(3): 800–32

Dagger, R. (1997) *Civic Virtues: Rights, Citizenship and Republican Liberalism*, New York and Oxford: Oxford University Press

Dean, H. with M. Melrose (1999) *Poverty, Riches and Social Citizenship*, Basingstoke: Macmillan

Delanty, G. (2000) *Citizenship in a Global Age*, Buckingham: Open University Press

Dwyer, P. (2000) *Welfare Rights and Responsibilities: Contesting Social Citizenship*, Bristol: Policy Press

Eden, K. and D. Roker (2002) *'...Doing Something': Young People as Social Actors*, Leicester: Youth Work Press

France, A. (1998) '"Why should we care?" Young people, citizenship and questions of social responsibility', *Journal of Youth Studies*, 1 (1), pp. 97–111

Fulbrook, M. and D. Cesarani (1996) 'Conclusion', in D. Cesarani and M. Fulbrook (eds) *Citizenship, Nationality and Migration in Europe*, London: Routledge

Hall, T. and Williamson, H. (1999) *Citizenship and Community*, Leicester: Youth Work Press

Hall, T., H. Williamson and A. Coffey (1998) 'Conceptualizing citizenship: Young people and the transition to adulthood', *Journal of Education Policy*, 13 (3), pp. 301–15

Harris, C., Roach, P., Thiara, R., Amory, D. and Yusuf, R. (2001) *Emergent Citizens? African Caribbean and Pakistani Young People in Bradford and Birmingham*, Birmingham: University of Birmingham

Heater, D. (1990) *Citizenship*, London and New York: Longman

Hobson, B. and M. Lindholm (1997) 'Collective identities, women's power resources, and the making of welfare states', *Theory and Society*, 26, pp. 475–508

Isin, E. F. and P. K. Wood (1999) *Citizenship and Identity*, London: Sage

Jones, E. and J. Gaventa (2002) *Concepts of Citizenship: A Review*, Brighton: Institute for Development Studies

Jones, K. B. (1994) 'Identity, action and locale: Thinking about citizenship, civic action and feminism', *Social Politics*, 1 (3), pp. 256–70

Kerr, D., E. Cleaver, E. Ireland. and S. Blenkinsop (2003) *Citizenship Education Longitudinal Study First Cross-Sectional Survey 2001–2002*, London: Department for Education and Skills

Knijn, T. and M. Kremer (1997) 'Gender and the caring dimension of welfare states: Towards inclusive citizenship', *Social Politics*, 4 (3), pp. 328–61

Lister, R. (2003) *Citizenship: Feminist Perspectives*, 2nd edition, Basingstoke: Palgrave

McKinnon, C. (2000) 'Civil citizens' in C. McKinnon and I. Hampsher-Monk (eds) *The Demands of Citizenship*, London and New York: Continuum

Marshall, T. H. (1950) *Citizenship and Social Class*, Cambridge: Cambridge University Press

Miller, D. (2000) 'Citizenship: What does it mean and why is it important?' in N. Pearce and J. Hallgarten (eds) *Tomorrow's Citizens: Critical Debates in Citizenship and Education*, London: Institute for Public Policy Research

Pearce, N. and J. Hallgarten (eds) (2000) *Tomorrow's Citizens: Critical Debates in Citizenship and Education*, London: Institute for Public Policy Research

Saraceno, C. (1997) 'Reply: Citizenship is context-specific', *International Labor and Working-Class History*, 52, pp. 27–34

Sevenhuijsen, S. (1998) *Citizenship and the Ethics of Care*, London and New York: Routledge

Shotter, J. (1993) 'Psychology and citizenship: Identity and belonging', in B. S. Turner (ed.) *Citizenship and Social Theory*, London: Sage

Siim, B. (2000) *Gender and Citizenship*, Cambridge: Cambridge University Press

Sparks, H. (1997) 'Dissident citizenship, democratic theory, political courage and activist women', *Hypatia*, 12(4), pp. 54–110

Speaker's Commission (1990) *Encouraging Citizenship: Report of the Commission on Citizenship*, London: HMS0

Stevenson, N. (ed.) (2001) *Culture and Citizenship*, London: Sage

Turner, B. S. (1997) 'Citizenship studies: A general theory', *Citizenship Studies*, 1 (1), pp. 5–18

Wolchover, J. (2002) 'Today's lesson: Citizenship for beginners', *The Independent*, 18 April

Rights and citizenship of indigenous women in Chiapas: a history of struggles, fears and hopes

Carlos Cortez Ruiz

Introduction

The Zapatista rebellion began in 1994 in the state of Chiapas in the south of Mexico, and called into question social practices and government policies, as well as the basic premises of the neo-liberal model. At the same time as it challenged the position of indigenous people as citizens in Mexico, the rebellion gave momentum to an indigenous women's movement that is demanding respect for the rights and dignity of indigenous women and for new forms of sovereignty. This chapter discusses how this movement has led to changes in the lives of indigenous women in Chiapas. Drawing on the daily experiences of women, it identifies the fundamental elements of the struggles that motivate them. It also explores the fears that these women have had to overcome, and the hopes that maintain their struggle. The changes that are emerging as a result of this movement are complex, and are deepening as they are perpetuated across a range of experiences.

The emergence of the Zapatista movement and the struggle for indigenous women's rights

The situation of indigenous people in Mexico is an extremely difficult one. They represent around 10 per cent of the national population and live largely in rural areas. They make up the poorest section of the population in Mexico. Chiapas is one of the states with the highest proportions of Indians in its population. However, indigenous women suffer additional disadvantages. Gender inequalities within their communities are greater than in the rest of society, and exclusion, violence and oppression are common features of their daily life. While their exclusion has social and cultural roots, it is reinforced by legal or political practices. Their subordinate status is manifest in a range of different practices, from violence within the home – often associated with male alcoholism – to their exclusion from basic services, such as health and education.

Indigenous women's struggles for their rights therefore cut across different spheres of life and imply the transformation of power relations at all levels, from the family to the nation. Various factors have facilitated these struggles, including the shift from subsistence production to market-orientated production (which provides women with an additional income), increasing participation in organized groups, and, of course, social movements, such as those organized by indigenous women related to the Zapatista movement. For indigenous women, the Zapatista movement has led to a heightened awareness of their rights and of possibilities for social and cultural transformations that would allow them to realize both their right to difference as indigenous women and their right to equality as human beings.

The demand for indigenous rights came onto the agenda in 1974, when the Indigenous Congress, held in San Cristobal de las Casas, Chiapas, condemned unequivocally the situation of indigenous people. However, it was not until 2001 that representatives of indigenous people were able to present their demands in the National Congress. Between these years, as the struggle for indigenous rights began to gather momentum, a number of different organizations offered their support for women within these communities. Since the 1970s, for instance, organizations of artisan women and peasants have been among those who have contributed to the women's movement in Chiapas. Parallel to their efforts, non-governmental organizations (NGOs), and political, academic and religious activists began work with a gender perspective on reproductive health, civil and human rights, and campaigns against violence. The participation of different actors, such as social organizations, NGOs and the Catholic Church, helped indigenous women to organize. The roles of these actors have been very important over the past three decades in demanding changes in the situation of indigenous women.

In January 1994, the Zapatistas emerged to claim from Mexican society political changes for its indigenous population. After a short time in talks, from 1995 to 2000 the government responded with a 'low intensity war' against the movement, considering the problem to be a military rather than a political one. The demands of indigenous women were submerged by the militarization of public spaces and by the violence against them. However, the repression did not hinder the growth of indigenous groups as social actors demanding changes in the cultural, political and social arenas. Actually, the principal demand is the implementation of the San Andres Agreement by the Mexican government. While these demands addressed different priorities (such as health, education, collective rights), they were united in their attempts to raise awareness, build social organizations and define an independent political agenda ('Declaración política de la sociedad civil...' in *Revista Chiapas*, 1999, p. 237).

With the change in government, the Zapatistas made a mobilization to present their demands for national political change at the Mexican National Congress in 2001. However, it was their demand for a Revolutionary Law for Women that gave concrete representation to the struggle of indigenous women and translated it into a political agenda. Commandante Esther, a member of the Zapatista political leadership, gave a speech at the National Congress that announced the demands of indigenous women as part of the general agenda of the Zapatistas (Congreso Nacional Indígena 1996, p. 181). She emphasized that she was speaking not only as a Zapatista but also as an indigenous woman.

This moment was central to the indigenous women's movement because it was the first time that the demands of their struggle were articulated and presented at the National Congress. More than any other aspect of the Zapatista agenda, women's demands implied the need for Mexican society to embrace the principle of multiculturalism (Villoro 1998). The speech also highlighted some of the new dimensions that the indigenous women's movement was bringing to political life. What Commandante Esther asked for in her speech was the 'amendment of the national constitution in light of the feelings, values and relations of everyday life'.[1]

However, the rich, multi-dimensional politics that developed out of the analysis of the subordination of indigenous women was reduced in the proposal for constitutional reform on indigenous rights to the phrase 'men and women are equal'. Nevertheless, while constitutional change fell well short of what had been hoped for, important changes took place at the local level. For example, local education efforts, regional organizations and communitarian assemblies all began to focus on indigenous women's experiences. And in remote and isolated areas, there has been a movement to increase awareness and articulate a vision of rights that will create new spaces of participation by indigenous women (Cornwall and Schattan 2004).

The everyday realities of indigenous women

The indigenous communities in Chiapas live principally in the mountainous regions and in the rainforests.[2] Within the former communities, indigenous women live in more traditional ways. They contribute to agricultural production and work as artisans. Women in the rainforest region have begun to alter their way of dressing and their cultural perspectives, they contribute to agricultural production, but their work as artisans is becoming less important. They find it easier to seek employment or study in urban areas. Despite these differences, however, indigenous women from different parts of Chiapas share many aspects of subordination. Daily life for indigenous people in general, and for women in particular, is very difficult. Much of it is taken up with work. Women's tasks within the family begin at an early age. One woman told us: 'I was seven years old when my mother taught me how to cook and to weave. I did not want to weave because I preferred to play. When I was nine or ten years old I began to work in the fields, carried firewood and was doing everything' *(Francisca, an indigenous Tzotzil from the heights region [AC*[3]*])*.

This woman, Francisca, described a typical day:

> As I have children, I get up very early, sometimes at three-thirty. I prepare *tortillas* until around six, and then if my husband is going to work [in the fields] early I prepare his breakfast. When he goes, I begin to wash or I begin to weave. Around three or four in the afternoon ... I prepare my meals. Sometimes I sleep at half-past eleven. When my children go to sleep, around eight, I begin to work [on handicrafts]. That is because during the day I don't work on handicrafts because I have a lot of things to do. That is why I get up very early ... I have to work because my husband works in the field, so we will have maize and beans and we don't have to buy these. Men work in agriculture but they have to look for other jobs where they are paid cash. So they look for one or two days' additional work a week, and so immigration to look for work in other places is growing.

Domestic violence is commonplace in the lives of indigenous women. Francisca also explained how violence has affected her life:

> My father used to drink and to hit us, and yell at us. He used to shout and hit my mother. There were ten siblings in my family and my father did not buy us any clothes, or even any soap. My mother had to take care of everything, and she suffered a lot. When I was a child I suffered a lot because my father used to hit us. We were afraid of my father and afraid that he would hit my mother. When we learned to weave, we helped my

mother support our little brothers. With the extra money my sisters and I earned we bought maize and some clothes. But my father began to get angry because he wanted the money that my mother earned through the sale of our handicrafts. But my mother refused because the money was ours.

When my sisters and I were married, my mother told us that my father shouted at her and that he tried to hit to her... My sisters and I began to talk about what to do, and decided that it was not possible to continue like this, and that we would put my father in jail if he did that again... We told him this and he got very angry, but he has never hit my mother again.

Women also experience violence when they attempt to participate at the community level. As one woman explained:

> If a woman speaks [in public], the men tell that she must be silent. Even the authorities don't let women speak their opinions. I experienced this myself because I wanted to participate in the communitarian assembly and the men wouldn't accept this. They shouted: 'How can she be allowed to speak? Take away the microphone, she is crazy or maybe she just wants a husband'. That happened, and the authority didn't do anything... That is why women don't participate in the community ... that is what is happening.
>
> (Hilda, an indigenous Tzeltal, artisan from the heights region [AE])

The problem of land access is one of the most significant for indigenous people. For decades, the possibility of settling in the rainforest was an option for young people, but now there are restrictions on settling new tracts of rainforest. As one young woman from the rainforest told us: 'There is not enough land, and new generations will have a lot of problems getting land. The youngest generation is looking to the Zapatistas for the possibility to get access to land. Until now, it has not been possible'. (Herminia, an indigenous Tzeltal, communitarian teacher from the rainforest region [AE])

Women do not have the right to own land,[4] leaving them dependent on male family members. As one woman explained:

> I do not have land, only a little space where I live. But I have no land for agriculture. Here, men have more rights than women. My father had land, but as I am a woman nothing was left to me. The land was for my brothers. I had no right to land, only this space where I live. If a woman's husband dies, she will not inherit the land, so where will she get her food?
>
> (Petrona, indigenous Tzeltal, artisan from the heights [AE])

In recent years, a number of social, economic and cultural changes have affected women's lives within the indigenous community, including changes in family relations, ideas about women's participation, the significance of the work they do and ideas about cooperatives. One of the most important changes is the increase in the economic value of women's handicrafts. While agricultural production remains oriented towards self-consumption rather than the market, handicrafts are generating additional income for families.

In terms of the most important needs within the community, one indigenous woman said:

> We need health, education ... jobs. The health services are very bad, without medicines. The doctors treat indigenous people badly... The education is inadequate, teachers treat children badly, they don't listen... In general, there is no accountability for the way doctors and teachers behave.
>
> *(Hilda, indigenous Tzeltal, artisan from the heights [AE])*

Making rights real for indigenous women

Over the last decade, demands for the rights of indigenous people, and social movements in support of these demands, have gained momentum within society. The key political demand of the Zapatista movement for constitutional reform to promote 'indigenous cultural and political rights' is linked to political reform at the state level. These demands have implications for social relations and the hierarchies of control they embody at all levels of society.[5] They clearly also have implications for gender relations.

From a general perspective, they are designed to guarantee the social, cultural and political rights of indigenous women (Huenchuan Navarro 2003). At the local level, they are designed to develop alternatives means of income generation for families. Different actors have contributed to attempts to build women's awareness of their own rights and their ability to realize them. While these changes are important, additional efforts are necessary to realize women's rights to health care, social organization and security. These are being addressed by cooperatives of women artisans.

One member of an artisan cooperative explained:

> We joined this organization because we wanted to have peace in our lives. When we joined this organization, we found direction. First, we went to the assembly and our forces were growing and growing. Then we began to join with other women partners to inform them about the

information that we got in the meetings where we participated. That was the way we began to organize other women. And then we began to understand the importance of being organized... We are not isolated in seeking for change. Women have organized to claim their rights, to participate, and now that women are organized, men accept our right to participate. We consolidate our advances, and we have created our own spaces because we were well organized. Then we began to look for ways to sell our handicrafts and how to demand better payment for our work... [At the local level] women now participate in the assembly... There are woman that participate in the meetings and take part in public demonstrations.

(Eleuteria, indigenous Tzeltal, artisan from the heights [AE])

The artisan organizations helped empower women by transforming individual and private problems into public and collective ones. The most important outcome has been that women are now acting collectively to find their own solutions and construct alternative forms of family, community and social relations. The artisan organizations offer hope that a different future is possible. As one woman said:

For me, the workshops are very important because we can express our opinions and come to agreements. We can think and take advantage of all the experiences of different women who come from different places and different regions. That is why such meetings are very important, because we can share experiences and ideas. It is important because we are learning about women's rights; about the rights and responsibilities that we have in the family, the society and in the church.

(Luvia, indigenous Zoque from the heights region [AE])

Women's participation also occurs in other spaces and around other problems, including subsistence agriculture, the commercialization of handicrafts and access to health care and education. One health practitioner described these changes:

We are realizing that they are not going to crush us. On the contrary, they will be wary of us. We are clear that we have rights that they have not recognized in the past, but now we know the consequences of this ignorance and why they never educated us about this before. Why did they never educate us about our rights? Because we as women did not even have the right to go out of our homes. But now we can go out and share with other women what we know about our rights, and in these meetings we can make advances and move forward.

It is very important for women to mobilize around their reproductive health:

If I go alone, I cannot do anything; nobody will take me into account. But if we are a group of partners, they have will have to listen to us because we are many. Our rights as women are important because in this moment it is like waking up from a dream. Before, nobody told us anything about women's rights. But we have learned that we have the right to speak, to demand our rights. Why? Because we are learning that we have the same rights that men have.

(Guadalupe, health practitioner from the rainforest region [AE])

Young people play a very important role both within the Zapatista movement as well as within indigenous women's organizational efforts. In the case of women, an important factor has been that more young women are able to read and write. During the past decade, different educational approaches have been developed by social organizations and by the Zapatistas' autonomous municipalities. Multicultural and bilingual education has been given added emphasis. Herminia, a young teacher in an independent educational programme, explained the importance of this approach:

Children must learn their mother language because their parents are *Tzeltales*, and so the children must learn this... They can also learn Spanish, and if they learn both languages, *Tzeltal* and Spanish, they can recognize their rights as indigenous people, but they can also get work and continue their studies.

The process of women's participation in different spaces around different problems provides a means for them to express their own vision of their rights, both as Mexican citizens and as indigenous women. It also expresses a conception of development that is grounded in local priorities. Their organizations address a wide range of issues. Some groups are engaged in advocacy for basic human rights, including social and cultural rights. These demands imply the direct responsibility of the state to provide adequately for social needs. Other groups are engaged in advocacy to defend indigenous culture, giving rise to a national debate about cultural rights and their relationship to other rights.

The controversy about individual and collective rights is directly related to indigenous women and their rights. It is clear that women's conception of their cultural and social rights has collective dimensions. For example, cultural rights are related to collective demands around language, collective interests and land. But other social rights that are conventionally understood as individual have a collective significance for indigenous women, so that when they speak of them, they are speaking as members of a collective rather than as individuals (Kabeer 2002). This perspective is not accepted by the wider Zapatista movement and is one of the central points of divergence over legal reform.

Women's fears and resistance to change

For thousands of indigenous women in Chiapas and across Mexico, the Zapatista rebellion has expanded the meaning of rights and the possibilities for organizing to bring about social change. But it has required them to overcome some of their fears. These fears include: rejection by the community; domestic violence; abandonment by their family; changing values, traditions and practices. They also fear, paradoxically, that they will not be able to bring about change, given the unfavourable conditions they face.

The efforts of different organizations seeking to promote the rights of indigenous women to health and education, as well as their cultural and political rights, have not followed a simple linear trajectory. There have been important advances, but there has also been stiff resistance to change from various sectors. The struggle to realize rights implies changes in power relations at different levels. Accordingly, resistance to change has emerged from many of these levels.

Women first encounter problems and resistance within the family:

> Sometimes young women want to work, but their parents won't let them go out to study or to work, even if they have finished secondary school. Their parents continue refusing their rights as women. They don't let them participate or go elsewhere to work. [Those are the main problems, but] sometimes their parents don't let them get married, and that is a woman's right. *(Herminia)*

Women also face resistance within the community – they are often dismissed as 'crazy' when they try to speak out. However, the strongest resistance they have faced is from those within the government. Many individuals have used their position to benefit themselves at the expense of the indigenous communities, and have used fear to protect their position. Political repression against the Zapatista movement was at its peak from 1995 to 2000. During this period, the national and state governments rejected a political solution in favour of a military one. This involved the creation of paramilitary forces under the control of the government and resulted in repression.

It was not only the Zapatistas who were affected by this policy. Anyone considered to be allied to them was also repressed – and this included the cooperatives. As one artisan commented:

It is hard to be in a cooperative, because cooperatives have had problems even before 1994... [In the previous years], the heads of the cooperative were persecuted in order to restrict women's participation. When the Zapatista rebellion emerged, they accused cooperatives of being Zapatistas, which was a hard problem for an organization such as the cooperative.

They didn't want us to be organized. They wanted to instil fear by threatening us, following us and insulting us in the streets. There have been problems ever since the armed forces turned up. In 1997, under the accusation of being Zapatistas, a partner and I were knocked down on the street and severely threatened. That made us afraid. [That is what they wanted], to instil fear and to prevent us from participating. By provoking fear, they wanted us not to organize ourselves in a cooperative. We confronted all these problems. It was very difficult for us ... but we didn't leave the cooperative.

It is very hard to be threatened, but we must not let them control us easily. Women give us courage. We have to continue working and participating in meetings. This is the way we have continued to work, both in the cooperative and outside. We do not have to be afraid of problems. *(Rosalinda, indigenous Tzeltal, artisan from the heights [AE])*

Hope

Clearly, the Zapatista movement has been an important force in giving meaning and expression to indigenous women's citizenship. It has given new meanings to organizational spaces that existed before, such as artisans' cooperatives, and it has created new organizational spaces where women are able to participate alongside men, such as autonomous municipalities. Through these different forms of participation, women have struggled to find a voice, generate awareness and construct alternatives in the areas of health, production and education, amongst others.

The process of change has been a complex one, with some advances but also many drawbacks. Nonetheless, there is sufficient evidence to suggest that the lives of indigenous women are being transformed. From the family and the community to autonomous municipalities, cooperatives and social organizations, women have a more important role in the demand for their rights, in setting up their priorities and in creating their own alternatives.

Different elements have helped to bring about these changes, but the fundamental one is hope. The Zapatista movement and the Revolutionary Law for Women have generated hope in people, and particularly in women – hope for change, for a different future and for a better life for the next generation, free from violence and benefiting from education. Hope is what has sustained the struggle of women for their particular rights as indigenous women and for their universal rights as human beings.

During 2001, an exercise with young education practitioners from different communities took place in order to reflect upon the interests of the communities and to express these through a mural.[6] The project took place in the municipality of San Andrés Sacamchen, in the rebel region, at the Aguascalientes Cultural Centre II, Oventik.[7] Most of the residents of this region are *Tzotziles*, but at school there are also *Tzeltales*. The Cultural Centre is linked to different autonomous municipalities and to hundreds of communities through their social services, such as health and education. A secondary school, Escuela Secundaria Rebelde Autónoma Zapatista (ESRAZ), functions in the centre, with around 80 young men and women enrolled who are training to be educational practitioners in their communities.

A group formed by students from ESRAZ and people from the communities participated in the construction of the mural. Through a participative process, the group visited the different communities to consult on its content. The design of the mural and its actual painting were the result of collective work and reflection. The proposals that emerged from this process revealed their vision for the future. They included:

- approval of the Indigenous Law, endorsement of the San Andrés Agreements and acknowledgment of autonomous municipalities;
- respect for the rights of indigenous people; recognition of their cultures and their right to decide how to live, work and use their natural resources;
- housing, food education and work for all; free meals and books for students; the happiness of children;
- 'no' to poverty, personal interests and indigenous division;
- democracy; a life in peace and partnership; peace, freedom and justice.

The young women who worked as educational practitioners in their communities emphasized the importance of the incorporation of the rights of indigenous women in the mural:

> Through the painting of the mural we expressed our right to decide. We want to decide by ourselves and have nobody decide for us... All of us

have rights; indigenous women have rights. I am a woman and I have the right to speak, to democracy and justice, to participate and to work. We don't want governmental impositions; we want to organize ourselves. We want justice, we want democracy. We want an education truly related to our history; to recover our culture. We want a new type of education: our own indigenous education. We don't want the education that the government gives.

We refer to the eleven Zapatista demands: we want education, food, housing, autonomy to decide for ourselves, freedom, dignity; we don't want the government to continue oppressing us... We want nourishment. In the midst of all the richness that there is here, we do not have a place to live and we do not have any food... We have rights. Rights are not just for rich people. Indigenous women and men have rights too: a right to justice and democracy, to participate and to organize ourselves in the way we want.

(Student at ESRAZ, preparing to be an education communitarian practitioner)

On the issue of women's rights, one student explained:

We can talk and decide by ourselves. We can decide how many children we want to have because nobody, not even our husbands, can impose on us how many children to have. It will allow us to participate and to have responsibilities at the organization and in our struggles... We have a right to a healthy life... We have the right to study, because a lot of times this right is neglected... We demand the accomplishment of this right ... the right to organize ourselves. *(Student at ESRAZ)*

The revolutionary law is very important, especially for women, since it involves women's rights. I think that maybe not all the points concerning their rights will be accomplished. To achieve all that is very difficult. In my view, if this is to be achieved, it is necessary to educate the children in another way. Now that there is education for women, something may change. Women now go to school, to basic school and even secondary school, but there are still too few ... Marriage has changed too. At least now young women can decide if they are going to get married, when and with whom. Yes, the situation has changed a little. I think that there will be a time when we, as young women, at least will have the right to decide what we want to do with our lives: whether we want to study or have different responsibilities. I have seen in our cooperative that there are young women that participate. *(Rosalinda)*

In recent years, even the poorest indigenous women from Chiapas have been able to speak out and present their demands, and have, to some extent, influenced policy. They are constructing their own vision of development based on their rights. This can be interpreted as a process of citizenship construction. Through their participation, indigenous women are promoting change and guaranteeing their social, political and cultural rights. Their struggles are grounded in their conviction of their 'right to have rights'. Indigenous women can be seen as political actors, creating their own history in a particular territory and in a multicultural nation. Individual and collective empowerment is the outcome of their participation and actions in different spaces. Many obstacles still need to be overcome, but new pathways are being created all the time.

Notes

1. Congreso Nacional Indígena, *La Voz de las Mujeres*, Mexico, 8 October 1996.
2. The heights region includes mainly the municipalities of San Cristóbal, Chamula, Tenejapa, Larrainzar and Zinacantan, but also others like Guaquitepec and Chilon. The rainforest region includes the municipalities of Ocosingo, Las Margaritas, Altamirano, Palenque, Marques de Comillas. It is principally in these regions that the Zapatista movement has influence.
3. The testimonies in this chapter are taken from interviews conducted by Adriana Estrada (AE) and Amaranta Cornejo (AC), and are part of the 'Human Development in Chiapas' research programme, coordinated by the author.
4. Mexican legislation does not limit women's right to land, but within the community, widows have no right to land.
5. This analysis of social movements in Chiapas is based on Melucci's approach to social movements. This author reviews traditional approaches to collective action and proposes discussion of identities, the history of social movements, social links and symbolic–cultural elements to understand the social action.
6. This exercise was coordinated by Professor Sergio Valdes, Universidad Autónoma Metropolitana. He is a member of the 'Human Development in Chiapas' research programme.
7. As this chapter was being finished, the leadership of the Zapatistas decided to dissolve the Aguascalientes Cultural Centre, and create instead four Good Government Assemblies (*Juntas de Buen Gobierno*), where the 30 autonomous municipalities created during the last few years were to be coordinated to drive the project of autonomy.

References

Congreso Nacional Indígena (1996) 'La voz de las mujeres', *Cuadernos Agrarios*, 13, October
Cornwall, A. and Schattan, V. (eds) (2004) *New Democratic Spaces? The politics and dynamics of institutionalised participation,* IDS Bulletin, 35 (2)
'Declaración política de la sociedad civil en su encuentro con el EZLN' (1999), *Revista Chiapas*, 7, México: Ed. ERA
Huenchuan Navarro, S. (2003) *Saberes con Rostro de Mujer: Mujeres Indígenas, Conocimientos y Derechos*, México: Modernmujer

Kabeer, N. (2002) *Citizenship and the boundaries of the acknowledged community: Identity, affiliation and exclusion*, Brighton: Institute of Development Studies

Melucci, A. (1999) *Acción Colectiva, vida cotidiana y democracia*, México: El Colegio de México

Villoro, L. (1998) *Estado Plural, Pluralidad de Culturas*, México: UNAM

Citizenship and Struggle

Nine

'We all have rights, but …' Contesting concepts of citizenship in Brazil

Evelina Dagnino

Introduction

During the past two decades, the notion of citizenship has become increasingly recurrent in the political vocabulary in Latin America, as well as in other parts of the world. In Latin America, its emergence has been linked to the experiences of social movements during the late 1970s and 1980s, reinforced by efforts toward democratization, especially in those countries with authoritarian regimes.

In Brazil, the notion of citizenship has been increasingly adopted since the late 1980s and 1990s by popular movements, excluded sectors, trade unions and left parties as a central element in their political strategies. Since then, it has spread as a common reference among a variety of social movements, such as those of women, blacks and ethnic minorities, homosexuals, retired and senior citizens, consumers, environmentalists, urban and rural workers and those organized in the large cities around urban issues such as housing, health, education, unemployment, violence, etc. (Alvarez, Dagnino and Escobar 1998; Foweraker 1995). These movements, organized around different demands, found in the reference to citizenship not only a useful tool in their specific struggles but also a powerful articulating link among them. The general claim for equal rights, embedded in the predominant conception of citizenship, was then extended and specified according to the different claims at stake. As part of this process of redefining citizenship, a strong emphasis was put on its cultural dimension, incorporating contemporary concerns with subjectivities, identities and the right to difference. Thus, the building of a new citizenship was to be seen as reaching far beyond the acquisition of legal rights, since it would require the constitution of active social subjects who would define what they consider to be their rights and struggle for their recognition. Such a cultural emphasis asserted the need for a radical transformation of cultural practices that reproduce inequality and exclusion throughout society.

As a result of its growing influence, the notion of citizenship soon became an object of dispute. In the last decade it has been appropriated and re-signified by dominant sectors and by the state to include a variety of meanings. Hence, under neo-liberal inspiration, citizenship began to be understood and promoted as mere individual integration into the market. At the same time, and as part of the same process of structural adjustments, consolidated rights are being progressively withdrawn from workers throughout Latin America. In a correlative development, philanthrophical projects from the so-called third sector, which convey their own version of citizenship, have been expanding in numbers and scope in an attempt to address poverty and exclusion.

Today, the different dimensions of citizenship, and disputes over its various appropriations and definitions, largely constitute the grounds of political struggle in Latin America. Such a dispute reflects the trajectory followed by the confrontation between a democratizing, participatory project to extend citizenship and the neo-liberal offensive to curtail the possibilities it contained. In what follows, I will examine these different versions of citizenship as they have emerged in the Brazilian context of the last decades. In addition, I will discuss how these recent versions relate to two previous conceptions of citizenship that have shaped Brazilian historical formation and continue to be active today: *cidadania regulada* (regulated citizenship) (Santos 1979) and *cidadania concedida* (citizenship by concession) (Carvalho 1991; Sales 1994).

Citizenship became a prominent notion in the past two decades because it was recognized as a crucial weapon, not only in the struggle against social and economic exclusion and inequality but – most importantly – in the widening of dominant conceptions of politics itself. Thus, the redefinition of citizenship undertaken by social movement sectors intended, in the first place, to confront the existing boundaries of what is to be defined as the political arena: its participants, institutions, processes, agenda and scope (Alvarez, Dagnino and Escobar 1998). Contrasting with previous conceptions of citizenship (conceived of as strategies of the dominant classes and the state for the gradual and limited political incorporation of excluded sectors towards a greater social integration, or as a legal and political condition necessary to the installation of capitalism), this was a strategy of the non-citizens, a political project of the excluded – a citizenship 'from below'.

In order to understand the full meaning of this redefinition of citizenship, it is important to examine previous dominant conceptions of citizenship in Brazil and the historical context in which they emerged, as this redefinition and the particular directions it assumed were part of a struggle to confront and break up those earlier conceptions and the practices they promoted.

A brief history of citizenship in Brazil

Since the abolition of slavery in 1888 and the proclamation of the republic in 1889, Brazilian political history has been shaped by three important events. First, the revolution of 1930 inaugurated a process of conservative modernization, in which the state came to play a fundamental role in the installation of industrial capitalism and in the organization of society itself. From 1930 to 1945, under the leadership of Getúlio Vargas, a truly national, authoritarian, centralized and interventionist state constituted the leading force behind national development. Relations between the state and civil society were structured along corporatist lines, and the political organization of social sectors was put under state tutelage and control, setting the basis for the populist arrangement that predominated from 1946, when the democratic regime was re-established, to 1964.

Second, the period of authoritarian military rule, which followed the 1964 *coup d'état*, restricted civil liberties and democratic institutions, repressing the political expression of opposing social sectors.

Third, the transition to democracy, roughly comprising the period between the mid-1970s and late 1980s, was marked by the gradual strengthening of civil society and by the emergence of different social movements. By forming an opposition to the military regime, they tried to establish new parameters for the relations between state and civil society and the re-establishment of democracy. The constitution of 1988, which expresses not only the formal re-establishment of democracy but also significant steps towards its deepening, was a result of the struggle of those forces. These steps included an extension of rights and, most importantly, several mechanisms for the direct participation of civil society, which will be discussed later.

In the following year, Fernando Collor defeated Luís Inácio Lula da Silva, the labour leader and founder in 1980 of the Partido dos Trabalhadores (PT, Workers Party), and became president after an election that epitomized the struggle between two different political projects (which continued in the years to follow). His government, which lasted from 1990 to 1992, when he was impeached for corruption, began the implementation of neo-liberal structural adjustment, and this was continued by his successor, Fernando Henrique Cardoso. It was in the context of these expanding neo-liberal measures that the main debates during the 1990s began to revolve around different visions of democracy and citizenship. The election of Luís Inácio Lula da Silva in October 2002 was perceived as a victory against the neo-liberal forces. But his government has still to prove it.[1]

Santos (1979) coined the expression '*cidadania regulada*' to designate what was the first relatively wide and systematic recognition of social rights by the state in Brazilian history, through the Consolidation of Labour Laws in 1943 under Vargas's authoritarian regime. However, this recognition did not have a universal character but was restricted to workers. Moreover, only those workers in professions recognized and regulated by the state were entitled to social rights.[2] Finally, and most importantly, only workers belonging to unions recognized and regulated (that is to say, controlled) by the state were entitled to social rights. Such a version of citizenship – a masterpiece of ambiguity, we could say – ingeniously intertwined the recognition of social rights and the political existence of workers and their organizations, on the one hand, with state political control over unions and workers on the other. Thanks to this ambiguity, it constituted one of the pillars of the populist arrangement that presided over Brazilian politics until 1964. In addition, it promoted an exclusionary view of citizenship – as a condition strictly related to labour – that is still very much alive in Brazilian society.[3]

Although one can see signs of it in what was just described, the conception of citizenship as a concession (*cidadania concedida*) is found by Sales (1994) to have its roots in a more remote past. Seen as emerging from the rule of large landowners (*latifundiários*), whose private power within their rural domains was converted into political power in the Brazilian state and society after the Republican advent at the end of the nineteenth century, this view of citizenship is an attempt to account for what is, in fact, an absence of citizenship. Such a view of citizenship relies on a conception of rights mediated by power relations of rule and submission, transferred from the private domain to the public, civil domain. Rights are conceived of as favours, as 'gifts' from the powerful, in what Sales calls 'a culture of gift' ('*cultura da dádiva*'). The maxim, as put by Sales, 'In Brasil either you give orders or you plead' (*No Brasil ou bem se manda ou bem se pede*), expresses an authoritarian, oligarchic conception of politics, characterized by favouritism, clientelism and various tutelage mechanisms. In it, the lack of distinction between the private and public realms obstructs the emergence of a notion of rights *as* rights, and stimulates a conception of rights as favours. It is in this sense that *cidadania concedida* can be seen as, in fact, a peculiar 'absence' of citizenship. This peculiarity relies on the fact that rights are not recognized as rights, but rather as gifts, favours from those who have the power to concede them. The concept, rooted in Brazilian culture, expresses the resistance of social authoritarianism, which continues to obstruct the political organization of the excluded while simultaneously enlarging the political autonomy of the elites.

Contemporary struggles over citizenship

The concern of Brazilian social movements to affirm a right to have rights is clearly related to extreme levels of poverty and exclusion, but also to the pervasive *social authoritarianism* that underpins the unequal and hierarchical organization of relations within the larger society. Class, race and gender differences constitute the main bases for the extreme social stratification that has historically pervaded our culture, hierarchically positioning different categories of people in their respective 'places' in society. Thus, for excluded sectors, the political implications of the cultural meanings embedded in social practices are part of their daily life. As part of the authoritarian, hierarchical social ordering of Latin American societies, to be poor means not only economic, material deprivation, but also submission to cultural rules that convey a complete lack of recognition of poor people as subjects-bearers of rights. In what Telles (1994) calls the 'incivility' embedded in that tradition, poverty is a sign of inferiority, a way of being in which individuals are unable to exercise their rights. This cultural deprivation imposed by the absolute absence of rights – which ultimately expresses itself as a suppression of human dignity – becomes then constitutive of material deprivation and political exclusion.

Recognition of this cultural social authoritarianism as a dimension of exclusion, additional to economic inequality and political subordination, has constituted a significant element in the struggle to redefine citizenship. First, it has made clear that the struggle for rights – above all, for the right to have rights – had to be a political struggle against a pervasive culture of social authoritarianism. This set the grounds for urban popular movements to establish a connection between culture and politics that became embedded in their collective action. The experience of the *Assembléia do Povo* (People's Assembly), a *favelado*[4] movement in Campinas, state of S. Paulo, organized from 1979 to the early 1980s, shows this connection. At the beginning of their struggle for the 'right to the use of the land', *favelados* knew they would have to struggle first for their very right to have rights. Thus, their first public initiative was to ask the media to publicize the results of their own survey of the *favelas,* in order to show the city that they were not idle people, those who are marginalized or prostitutes (the popular stereotypes of the *favelados*), but decent, working citizens who should be seen as bearers of rights.[5]

The connection between culture and politics has been a fundamental element in establishing the basis for articulation between the urban popular movements and other social movements – some more obviously cultural, such as those of minority ethnic people, women, gay people and ecology movements – in their search for more egalitarian relations at all levels. This has helped to demarcate a distinctive, enlarged view of democracy. The concern with rights and citizenship grew to constitute the core of a common ethical–political field, where a large part of those movements and other sectors of society were able to share their struggles and mutually reinforce them. For instance, the emergence of the *Sindicato Cidadão* (Citizen Trade Unions) in the early 1990s indicates the recognition of that concern within the Brazilian labour movement (Rodrigues 1997), which was traditionally inclined to more strict, class-based conceptions.

Second, the recognition of the cultural dimension of politics led to a broadening of the scope of citizenship beyond incorporation into the political system in the restricted sense of the formal/legal acquisition of rights. The struggle for citizenship was presented as a *project for a new sociability:* a more egalitarian framework for social relations at all levels; new rules for living together in society and for the negotiation of conflict; a new sense of public order and public responsibility; a new social contract. A more egalitarian framework for social relations at all levels implies the recognition of the 'other' as a subject-bearer of valid interests and legitimate rights. It also implies the constitution of a public dimension of society, where rights can be consolidated as public parameters for interlocution, for debate on and negotiation of conflicts, making possible the reconfiguration of the ethical dimension of social life. Such a project unsettles not only social authoritarianism as the basic mode of social ordering in Brazilian society, but also more recent neo-liberal discourses, which erect private interest as the measure for everything, obstructing the possibilities for an ethical dimension of social life (Telles 1994).

This understanding of citizenship implies that it is no longer confined within the limits of the relationship with the state: the recognition of rights should not only regulate relationships between the state and the individual, but has to be established within society itself, as the parameter governing social relations at all levels. Such a political strategy implies moral and intellectual reform, a fresh process of social learning, a building up of new kinds of social relations. This implies the constitution of citizens as active social subjects. For society as a whole, it requires learning to live on different terms with these emergent citizens, who refuse to remain in the place socially and culturally defined for them.

This may be more evident in the struggles of social movements such as, for instance, women, black people or gay people, since a significant part of their struggle is directed towards fighting discrimination and prejudice embedded within the social relations of their daily life. But it is also clear, as the *Assembléia do Povo*'s first public initiative shows, in popular movements whose 'material' claims, such as housing, health, education, transportation, sewage, etc., are directed towards the state.

Third, the notion of rights is no longer limited to legal provisions, to access to previously defined rights or the effective implementation of abstract, formal rights. It also includes the invention or creation of *new* rights, which emerge from specific struggles and their concrete practices. In this sense, the very determination of the meaning of rights, and the assertion of something as a right, are themselves objects of political struggle. The rights to autonomy over one's own body, to environmental protection, to housing, are examples (intentionally very different) of this creation of new rights. Moreover, this redefinition comes to include not only the right to *equality*, but also the right to *difference*, which deepens and broadens the right to equality.[6]

Participants in social movements, both of popular sectors organized around claims such as housing, water, sewage, education and health, and those of a wider character, such as women, black people and ecology movements, have emphasized the constitution of active social subjects – the ability to become political agents – as the crucial dimension of citizenship. In some definitions, citizenship is even thought of as *consisting of this very process*. Thus, consciousness, agency and the capacity to struggle are seen by them as evidence of their citizenship, even if other rights are absent. Among 51 civil society activists we interviewed in Campinas, S. Paulo, in 1993, such a view was a distinctive feature in the answers of members of those movements and of workers' unions, and formed a contrast to the views of members of middle class and entrepreneurs' organizations. Answering the same question ('Why do you consider yourself a citizen?'), the latter emphasized the fact that they 'fulfill their duties' and 'have rights', whereas the middle class activists stressed their 'position in society', derived from their professional activities. By contrast, while the large majority of participants of social movements and workers' unions' members did not consider themselves to be *treated* as citizens, they did consider themselves to *be* citizens, primarily because they struggled for their rights (Dagnino, Teixeira, Silva and Ferlim 1998, pp. 40–1).

The role of the social movements of the 1970s and 1980s in shaping this redefinition of citizenship obviously reflected their own struggle and was rooted in its practices. If they drew on the previous history of rights as ensured by *regulated citizenship*,[7] they also rejected many aspects of this history. They rejected the conception of the state and the power embedded in it. They also rejected the control and tutelage of the political organization of popular sectors by the state, political parties and politicians that had for so long sustained populism. And they further rejected the culture of favours, which created clientelistic relations with these political actors, and had outlived populism as the predominant political arrangement in the relationship between the civil and the political society. The redefined conception of rights and citizenship expressed a reaction against previous notions of rights either as favours or the objects of bargains with the powerful. This struggle for rights – also influenced by the human rights movements that emerged in the 1970s in the struggle against the authoritarian military regime – carried with it not only claims for equality, but also the negation of a dominant political culture.

The *Assembléia do Povo*: on becoming citizens

I had followed closely the experience of the *Assembléia do Povo*, but it was only after many years that I realized how much it exemplified the emergence of new meanings of citizenship. When I decided to write about it, I went back to one of its leaders, D. Marlene, to research her history. It was then I understood how these new meanings of citizenship reflected the life experiences of those who had been oppressed by social authoritarianism. Along with thousands of other Brazilians who had migrated from the countryside into the towns, D. Marlene had moved into the *favela* in the early 1970s. Her struggle began when she started to go on her own to City Hall to demand the installation of running water. The answer she got was that *favelas* were on the city's land, which 'belonged to the Mayor', and that running water could not be installed there. She recalled her reaction to that explanation:

> What Mayor's land are you talking about? If that was the Mayor's land, he would be living there with us, he would be a *favelado* himself! That is

the land of poor people like us, who do not have a decent salary... If you have the right to drink a glass of water from a faucet, we have it too. We are citizens like you; we are human beings like you.
Dagnino 1994b, p. 74

And she explained to me:

You have to look closely at the city government: it owns nothing. Nothing. Neither the Mayor nor anybody there owns anything; when they enter there they do not become owners, they become employees of the people. Everybody has the right to claim what they want and they have the duty to answer, if it is right, if it is wrong, but they must answer... Because they [the people in City Hall] didn't have anything. The strength they had came from the people, it was not theirs.
Dagnino 1994b, pp. 75–6

After hearing D. Marlene's account of the gender discrimination she had faced all her life, I asked her if she had not been afraid of speaking out in public. She answered:

'Will you speak?' they asked me. Of course I will speak, my grief is here inside me, this pain in my chest, my feelings, my life! And our rights? We all have rights, all of us have rights. It is not only me, it is not only half a dozen, all have equal rights. But rights are different. Rights are equal but they are very divided [meaning unequal but maybe also separate]; the division is very big: power, money, beauty, houses. Whereas some have everything, others have nothing. And all are workers, salaries are very divided but all are professionals. You do not have to think that a bricklayer has to receive less than a teacher, a garbage collector less than a doctor.
Dagnino 1994b, p. 82

While her ideas were far from being shared by the large majority of popular sectors in Brazil, they were able to gain her a significant leadership position within the *Assembléia do Povo*. D. Marlene was eventually nominated by the movement to run for the City Council in the 1982 municipal election as one of the candidates of the then newborn *Partido dos Trabalhadores*. In spite of an impressive number of votes, she wasn't elected. But the movement's decision to participate in institutional politics signals an additional dimension of the redefinition of citizenship that needs to be noted.

This additional dimension transcends a central reference in the liberal concept of citizenship: the claim to access, inclusion, membership, belonging to an already-given political system. What is at stake in struggles for citizenship in Brazil is more than the right to be included as a full member of society; it is the right to participate in the very definition of that society and its political system, to define what we want to be members of. The direct participation of civil society and social movements in state decisions constitutes one of the most crucial aspects in the redefinition of citizenship, because it conveys a potential for radical transformation in the structure of power relations of Latin American societies. Recent political practices inspired by this redefined notion of citizenship include the participatory budgets[8] introduced in the cities governed by the *Partido dos Trabalhadores*, where popular sectors and their organizations have opened up space for the democratic control of the state through the effective participation of citizens in power. Such practices help to visualize future possibilities. Initiated in Porto Alegre in the south of Brazil in 1989, participatory budgets have been conducted in around 100 other cities in the country[9] and are being considered as models to be implemented in countries like Mexico, Uruguay, Bolivia, Argentina, Peru, Ecuador and others. Also inspired by this notion of citizenship, the struggle of social movements and other sectors of civil society ensured the inclusion of mechanisms of direct and participatory democracy in the Brazilian Constitution of 1988, known as the Citizen Constitution. Among them, there was the establishment of management councils for public policy (*Conselhos Gestores de Políticas Públicas*), with membership equally divided between civil society and government, at city, state, and federal levels, to develop policies on issues related to health, children and adolescents, social services, women and so on.

The rise of neo-liberal versions of citizenship

The participation of civil society in the extension of citizenship spread all over Latin America in the last decade, under the slogan of *participación ciudadana*. In recent years, however, this concept has been appropriated and reinterpreted by the state as part of its strategy for the implementation of neo-liberal structural adjustment. There is thus a perverse confluence between, on the one hand, participation as part of a project constructed around the extension of citizenship and the deepening of democracy, and on the other hand, participation associated with the project of a reconfiguration of the state that requires the shrinking of its social responsibilities and its progressive exemption from the role of guarantor of rights. The perversity of this confluence reflects the fact that, although pointing in opposite and even antagonistic directions, *both projects require an active, proactive civil society.* Recent research focusing on the different spaces for participation by civil society existing today in

Brazil found more than a few examples of this perverse confluence (Dagnino 2002). It is evident in the frustration of many representatives of civil society within the *Conselhos Gestores*, and members of social movements and non-governmental organizations (NGOs) who have engaged in partnerships with state sectors for the implementation of public policies. Responding to calls to participate that used a familiar discourse, such as the importance of civil society engagement and the extension of citizenship, these people soon found that their role was very different from what they had expected, as was the actual meaning that lay behind this familiar rhetoric.

A particularly important aspect of the perverse confluence is precisely the notion of citizenship, which is now being redefined again through a series of discursive shifts to make it suitable for use by neo-liberal forces. This new redefinition, part of the struggle between different political projects, attests to the symbolical power of citizenship, and the mobilizing capacity it has demonstrated in organizing subaltern sectors around democratizing projects. The need to neutralize these features of citizenship, while trying to retain its symbolical power, has made its appropriation by neo-liberal forces necessary.

Neo-liberal redefinitions of citizenship rely upon a set of basic procedures. Some of them recuperate the traditional liberal conception of citizenship; others are innovative and address new elements of contemporary political and social configurations in Latin America. First, there is a reduction of the collective meaning entailed in the social movements' definition of citizenship to a strictly individualistic understanding. Second, neo-liberal discourses establish an alluring connection between citizenship and the market. To be a citizen comes to mean individual integration into the market as consumer and producer. This seems to be the basic principle implicit in a vast number of projects to enable people to 'acquire citizenship'; that is to say, learning how to initiate micro-enterprises, how to become qualified for the few jobs still on offer, and so on. In a context where the state progressively withdraws from its role as guarantor of rights, the market is offered as a surrogate arena of citizenship. The drive to eliminate social and labour rights in the name of 'free' negotiation between workers and employers and the 'flexibilization' of labour, is a well-known aspect of the neo-liberal agenda. As a result, rights ensured in the Brazilian Constitution since the 1940s are now being eliminated, on the grounds that they constitute obstacles to the free operation of market forces and hence restrict economic development and modernization.

Such a rationale transforms bearers of rights – citizens – into the new villains of the nation, privileged enemies of the political reforms intended to shrink state responsibilities. Thus a peculiar inversion is taking place: the recognition of rights, seen in the recent past as an indicator of modernity, is now becoming a symbol of 'backwardness', an 'anachronism' that hinders the modernizing potential of the market (Telles 2001). Here we find one of the decisive arguments legitimizing the construction of the market as the surrogate instance of citizenship: the market becomes the incarnation of modernizing virtues and the sole route for the Latin American dream, inclusion into the First World.

An additional procedure in the building of neo-liberal versions of citizenship is evident in social policies to eradicate poverty and in-equality. A large part of the struggles around the demand for equal rights and the extension of citizenship focused on the definition of such policies. Moreover, the participation of social movements and other sectors of civil society was a fundamental claim in struggles for citizen-ship, because they hoped this would contribute to the formulation of social policies that ensured universal rights for all. However, with the advancement of the neo-liberal project and the reduction of the role of the state, those policies are increasingly being formulated as strictly emergency measures directed at specific sections of society whose conditions for survival are at extreme risk. The targets of these policies are not seen as citizens entitled to rights, but as 'needy' recipients of public or private charity.

A number of consequences derive from this, all with important implications for contestations over different conceptions of citizenship. One consequence is the displacement of issues such as poverty and inequality. These issues are being withdrawn from their proper place in the arena of public politics, alongside concerns with justice, equality and citizenship, and assigned to the domain of technical or philanthropic management.

Moreover, the idea of collective solidarity that underlies the classical reference to rights and citizenship is now being replaced by an emphasis on solidarity as a strictly private moral responsibility. This understanding of citizenship is dominant in the action of entrepreneurial foundations, the so-called Third Sector, which multiplied their numbers in countries like Brazil over the past decade. Characterized by a constitutive ambiguity between market-oriented interests to maximize their profits through their public image and what is referred to as 'social responsibility', these foundations have contributed to the discourse of citizenship rooted in a moral individual solidarity. As with state sectors under the influence of neo-liberal forces, this discourse is marked by the absence of any reference to universal rights or to political under-standings of the causes of poverty and inequality.

Such re-significations of citizenship and solidarity block out their political dimension and erase references to public responsibility and public interests – the hard-won fruits of the recent democratizing struggles. The favoured allocation of social services now occupies the place formerly held by rights and citizenship, and institutional channels for claiming rights have been replaced by appeals to the goodwill and competence of the relevant sectors. More dramatically, the very formulation of rights and their enunciation as a public question is becoming increasingly impossible to realize (Telles 2001). The symbolic efficacy of rights in the building of an egalitarian society is thus being dismissed, and the consequence has been a reinforcement of an already powerful privatism as the dominant code orienting social relations.

A second set of consequences relates to the idea of participation by civil society, an idea that constituted the core of the democratizing project of social movements and progressive sectors of society. During its ascendance, this project was able to ensure the creation of public spaces for citizen participation, including spaces associated with the formulation of public policies. With the advance of neo-liberal forces, the notion of participation has also been appropriated and re-signified. While the neo-liberal agenda requires the participation of civil society, it is in order for civil society organizations to assume functions and responsibilities associated with the provision of services formerly considered duties of the state. The effective sharing of the power of decision, i.e. a full exercise of citizenship as conceived of by democratizing forces, is being carried out in most of the cases within the limits of a framework presided over by the dominant neo-liberal project.

The relations between the state and NGOs exemplify the perverse confluence we have referred to. Endowed with technical competence and social insertion, considered 'reliable' interlocutors among the various possible interlocutors in civil society, NGOs are frequently perceived as ideal partners by sectors of the state engaged in 'privatizing' their responsibilities. A parallel tendency within government is the 'criminalization' of those social movements that have remained organized and combative, such as the Landless Movement (MST) and some trade unions. These dual tendencies have been reinforced by the mass media and international financing agencies, and have resulted in the growing identification of 'civil society' with the NGOs or as a synonym for the third sector. 'Civil society' is thus reduced to those sectors that demonstrate 'acceptable' behaviour, according to government standards or to what one analyst referred to as 'the five-star civil society' (Silva 2001).

Conclusion

Attempts to reconfigure civil society and to redefine participation in Latin America are intimately connected with the emergence of neo-liberal versions of citizenship. Their central aim appears to be the de-politicization of these concepts, both of which have been central references in the struggle to democratize society. As such, these efforts represent a counter-offensive to the gains made by that struggle in expanding the boundaries of the political arena. The emergence of the third sector as a surrogate for civil society is particularly expressive of this attempt to implement a 'minimalist' conception of politics, and to nullify the extension of public spaces for political deliberation opened up by democratizing struggles.

The perverse confluence of discourses around participation has produced a minefield, where sectors of civil society, including NGOs not supportive of the neoliberal project, feel deceived when, motivated by an apparently shared discourse of citizenship, they get involved in joint actions with state sectors committed to that project. A number of social movements have shared this reaction and face a dilemma as to future action. They can either reject any further joint action, or else be extremely selective about such collaboration, paying careful consideration to the balance of forces present within these spaces and the concrete possibilities opened by them (Dagnino 2002). What is clear is that, despite an apparently shared discourse, what is at stake in these collaborations is the advancement or retreat of very different political projects and very different conceptions of citizenship.

Notes

1. In December 2003 an amendment to the Constitution that reduces the social rights of public servants, proposed by the government, was approved by the Congress.
2. Gradually, new professions have been included, but exclusions remained for decades, such as that of rural workers, whose social rights were recognized only in 1964, or domestic labourers, who are still not fully entitled to social rights.
3. Up to this day, when stopped by the police, Brazilians show their 'worker's card' (*carteira de trabalho*) in order to prove that they are 'decent citizens'.
4. *Favelados:* poor people living in shantytowns, the *favelas*.
5. The survey showed that people living in the *favelas* held regular jobs. For an account of the *Assembléia do Povo*, see Dagnino (1994b, pp. 69–84).
6. For a discussion on citizenship and the connections between the right to difference and the right to equality, see Dagnino (1994a).
7. It is not by chance that Getúlio Vargas, also known as the 'Father of the Poor', is still a powerful positive reference in the memory of Brazilian popular sectors.
8. For participatory budget processes, see Abers (1998); Avritzer (2002); Baierle

(1998); Fedozzi (1997); Santos (1998).
9. Because of their success, participatory budgets have been adopted recently by other parties in Brazil. Some of them clearly have strictly electoral purposes.

References

Abers, R. (1998) 'From clientelism to cooperation: Local government, participatory policy, and civic organizing in Porto Alegre, Brazil', *Politics & Society*, 26, p. 4, December

Alvarez, S. E., E. Dagnino, A. Escobar (eds) (1998) *Cultures of Politics/Politics of Cultures: Revisioning Latin American Social Movements*, Boulder, CO: Westview Press

Avritzer, L. (2002) *Democracy and Public Spaces in Latin America*, Princeton: University of Princeton Press

Baierle, S. (1998) 'The explosion of experience', in S. E. Alvarez, E. Dagnino, A. Escobar (eds) *Cultures of Politics/Politics of Cultures: Revisioning Latin American Social Movements*, Boulder, CO: Westview Press

Carvalho, J. M. de (1991) *Os Bestializados*, S.Paulo: Companhia das Letras

Dagnino, E. (1994a) 'Os movimentos sociais e a emergência de uma nova noção de cidadania', in E. Dagnino (ed.) *Os Anos 90: Política e Sociedade no Brasil*, São Paulo: Brasiliense

Dagnino, E. (1994b) 'On becoming a citizen: The story of D. Marlene', R. Benmayor and A. Skotnes (eds) *International Yearbook of Oral History and Life Stories*, Oxford: Oxford University Press

Dagnino, E. (ed.) (2002) *Sociedade Civil e Espaços Públicos no Brasil*, S.Paulo: Paz e Terra

Dagnino, E., A. C. C. Teixeira, D. R. da Silva and U. Ferlim (1998) 'Cultura democrática e cidadania', *Opinião Pública*, V (1), November

Fedozzi, L. (1997) *Orçamento Participativo – Reflexões Sobre a Experiência de Porto Alegre*, Porto Alegre: Tomo Editorial/FASE

Foweraker, J. (1995) *Theorizing Social Movements*, London: Pluto Press

Rodrigues, I. J. (1997) *Sindicalismo e Política: A Trajetória da CUT*, S. Paulo: Scritta/FAPESP

Sales, T. (1994) 'Raízes da desigualdade social na cultura Brasileira', *Revista Brasileira de Ciências Sociais* (ANPOCS), 25

Santos, B. de Souza (1998) 'Participatory budgeting in Porto Alegre: Toward a redistributive democracy', *Politics and Society*, 26(4)

Santos, W. G. dos (1979) *Cidadania e Justiça*, Rio de Janeiro: Campus

Silva, C. A. (2001) Oral comment in a debate transcribed in 'Os movimentos sociais, a sociedade civil e o "terceiro setor" na América Latina: Reflexões teóricas e novas perspectivas' in E. Dagnino and S. E. Alvarez (eds) *Primeira Versão* 98, October

Telles, V. da Silva (1994) 'A sociedade civil e a construção de um espaço público', in E. Dagnino (ed.) *Os Anos 90: Política e Sociedade no Brasil*, São Paulo: Brasiliense

Telles, V. da Silva (2001) *Pobreza e Cidadania*, S. Paulo: Editora 34

Bodies as sites of struggle: Naripokkho and the movement for women's rights in Bangladesh

Shireen P. Huq

Introduction

Women in Bangladesh suffer both an unequal legal status with regard to many important rights and an inferior position with regard to cultural beliefs and practices. This situation is aggravated further by what appears to be a lack of social and political will to deliver justice on violations that women routinely suffer, and, on the part of women themselves, by a lack of knowledge, confidence and skills to challenge such situations. The most frequent violations that women suffer in Bangladesh have to do, first, with their personal status and cultural identity as females – they are frequently treated as minors with few rights but disproportionate responsibilities – and, second, with their legal status as unequal citizens, because of which they are routinely and systematically the recipients of lesser resources, opportunities and rights.

Attempts to challenge women's subordination in Bangladesh reflect a number of different forces. Bangladesh's independence in 1971, a few years prior to the United Nations International Year of Women, meant that, from the outset, policy interest in 'women's issues' tended to be subsumed within the rubric of 'women and development', in particular women's contribution to production and a preoccupation with family planning. The interest in women's issues among even progressive political parties tended to be rhetorical and limited in scope, these limitations arising out of their own adherence to middle class norms of gender propriety.

This chapter deals with the experiences of Naripokkho,[1] a women's organization that seeks to carve out an autonomous space for feminist politics in Bangladesh that is neither driven by the women and development agenda nor subsumed within a male-dominated party politics. This has allowed the organization to bring onto the public agenda various new, often controversial, issues that emerge out of the organization's commitment to link the personal experiences of women to a political analysis of their subordination. One of the issues, one that constitutes a continuous and central thread in its activism is related to women's bodies as a site of oppression. This chapter will deal with the reasons why this politics emerged and the form it has taken.

The founding of Naripokkho

A number of us, all women who were engaged in one way or another with the situation of rural women in Bangladesh, had come together in 1980 to try to forge a collective identity from wherein we could intervene on the woman question. We wished to pursue, both professionally and politically, our vision of social change and women's emancipation. The choices we had made in our personal lives reflected our desire and our determination to be free and different from what was destined for women in Bangladesh.

Naripokkho was founded as a result of that collective desire. The catalyst was a three-day workshop on women and development, organized in 1983 by the Asian Cultural Forum on Development (ACFOD), that brought together 33 women development workers from non-governmental organizations (NGOs) all over the country. They came to the workshop expecting to make, and listen to, the usual presentations about their organizations: how many women 'beneficiaries' they were reaching, what kind of income generation programmes they were supporting, and so on. However, a number of us felt that there were ample opportunities to talk about what development NGOs were doing about 'poor and disadvantaged women', but few or none to talk about the women employed to reach them.

Despite initial resistance to the idea of talking about 'ourselves', I was able to use my influence as one of the facilitators to help transform the workshop into a first-person discussion of the life and experiences of the women who were attending: the women *in* development work. Who were these women? How did they end up in jobs that represented a dramatic and often unacceptable break with tradition?[2] What life circumstances had led to the choice of a job or a career that required women to be visible and mobile in unprecedented ways? Frontline female development workers, going from village to village, many on bicycles, were considered by some as pariahs and a bad omen. They represented a significant departure from the   ' ɔrm of remaining within the confines of one's home and at best venturing out into 'accepted' female occupations, such as teaching in schools. What did these women face that their male colleagues did not? What problems and challenges did they face in the villages they worked in? What problems and challenges did they face within the organizations that employed them? These questions had never been addressed.

The workshop allowed us to reflect on a number of questions that touched on our personal experiences: our first memories of being discriminated against as females; the circumstances that had led us to opt for a role different from those destined for the majority of women in Bangladesh; and the problems we faced in our personal and professional lives that male colleagues did not. We had no idea of the intensity of the sense of injustice that lay beneath the surface, ready to explode. Many women had *literally* never spoken about themselves before. A few still could not say the words, and simply cried. Others could not stop speaking, describing events and situations that testified to how deep, how widespread and how constant the experience of discrimination was, and how poignant and long-lasting the pain it inflicted.

Charting new territory: the first 'small steps'

By the end of the workshop, we were clear that we did not want this process of discovery to end and that we wanted to stay connected. The genesis of Naripokkho was thus in the realization of the links between personal experience and societal discrimination, and this formed an important dimension of its organizational strategy from the outset. The seeds of the organization were laid at a workshop, and workshops have remained an important way in which the organization has sought to achieve its goals.[3]

The discussions at our workshops have evolved over the years to encompass a number of different issues. One set of discussions, which stems from the questions we set ourselves at that first workshop, focuses on women's observations and experiences of gender discrimination at home and at work, and what these might have in common with those of the women who were targeted as beneficiaries by the development NGOs that employed them. This helps both to establish the grounds for a personal engagement with the issues of discrimination, violence and injustice, and to form the basis for identification with 'others'. This has become a significant feature of Naripokkho's strategy for change – *a first person engagement in the movement for change and the emergence of a collective 'we'*.

A second set of discussions focuses on the position and treatment of women in law. The first workshop had revealed how little women knew about their legal rights and how little they understood about discrimination in the content of the law itself. Personal law in Bangladesh, as in India, is governed by religion. This means that religious rather than civil law governs such areas as marriage, the dissolution of marriage, custody and guardianship of children, and inheritance. Given that all religions discriminate against women, women from different religious communities not only enjoy different rights from each other but also have fewer rights than men in their communities. Legal discrimination thus formalizes and justifies customary inequality.

These discussions have a subversive potential. They open women's eyes to the injustices encoded in law and suggest that litigation and courts cannot always be relied on for justice. This was a revelation for many, who until then had thought the only problem women faced in relation to the law was lack of access to the judicial system. These discussions have brought out the important distinction between 'law' and 'justice' *(ain o nyaybichar)*; a distinction that enabled us subsequently to evaluate everything from the point of view of *nyaybichar and nyajjota* (justice and fairness).

And finally, the workshop discussions focus on women's bodies, providing a safe space in which women are able to share some of the more private and intimate aspects of their 'embodied' experiences of deprivation and discrimination, and re-examine their personal lives. Understanding and appreciating their bodies, unravelling their attitudes to their own bodies and sexuality, and analysing how others have treated them, have been an important part of this re-examination. These discussions have clarified how much of the discrimination, ill treatment and violence women suffer is connected to the ways in which their bodies, their sexuality, their reproductive roles and their health are perceived, valued and constructed by their families, their colleagues and by society at large.

These discussions have also revealed how little so many women in Bangladesh know about or understand their bodies, and how little they acknowledge their sexuality and sexual needs. The discovery by some women of where their uterus was located was a revelation! For others, it was the idea of sexual pleasure that proved to be revolutionary! The opportunity to talk about these aspects of their lives opened the floodgates to other more private areas of suffering. In some cases, women described unwanted sexual advances by men taking advantage of their vulnerability in particular situations. In other cases, they spoke of rejection, often in hurtful and abusive terms, by their husbands when they expressed their desire for sexual pleasure. One woman said that she had been married for seven years and did not know that women could have orgasms. Another described how her husband had thrown her off the bed, shouting '*Aami ki bajaarer meyelok ghorey anchi naki?*' ('Have I brought home a woman from the brothel?')[4] The common refrain during these discussions has been 'the pleasure is not for us to have, it is always for them to take'. The issue of sexuality has become central to our discourse on rights and freedoms, and women from the brothels have become our sisters in struggle.

What has transpired in these workshops has helped to determine who we have become as an organization. First of all, from the start, we opted for a strategy that stressed process over blueprint, and a process that entailed continuous learning and clarification based on the participation of women and the sharing of first-hand experiences. We wanted engagement on the basis of personal identification with the issues. As a result, every issue that we have taken up has a basis in the reality of our lives and of women's lives more generally. We say that 'we speak *about* ourselves and we speak *for* ourselves'.

Secondly, our concern with various aspects of women's self-determination – their right to freedom of speech and movement, to freedom from violence, to control over their bodies and their sexuality, and so on – meant that we were, in effect, redefining ideas about *personhood* as they related, in the first instance, to women, and by extension to men. The first understanding of rights for most of the women we work with comes from the recognition of discrimination, and with it the understanding of discrimination as injustice. The right not to be discriminated against – that is, the right to non-discrimination – was then our starting point; the basis on which we demanded equality and justice. Our experience of discrimination as *women* led us to demand fair treatment and respect for our dignity as *human beings,* and only thereafter to claim our rights and entitlements as *citizens*. It was only through the process of seeking redress for unfair treatment and discrimination, demanding changes in the law and cultural behaviour, and requiring accountability from the state, that we became aware of ourselves as citizens and bearers of rights.

And finally, given our approach, it was inevitable that a concern with 'body politics' would be an important theme in Naripokkho's work. The centrality of women's bodies in the countless trivial, as well as significant, instances of oppression that have been recounted in our workshops, was striking. Over time, the connection between these instances and the processes by which male power over women is maintained and reproduced in Bangladesh has become increasingly clear, and we have come to realize how profoundly our bodies affect every aspect of our being, experience and consciousness as women.

Bangladesh has long been characterized by the dramatic absence of women in public spaces. Women were not visible in the streets, on public transport or in markets. In rural areas, women rarely ventured beyond the boundaries of their *bari*,[5] and in towns and cities women stayed away from streets and parks. Although this scenario has changed considerably in the past two decades, the norm continues to relegate women to the 'shelter' of the family and the home; their enforced dependence on men for both protection and provision reinforces their cultural devaluation.

We are socialized into 'becoming women' on the basis of a combination of Islamic strictures and Bengali cultural norms of gender propriety whereby we are not to be seen or heard. We are expected to speak quietly, to keep our eyes downcast, to cover ourselves in the presence of strange men and to eat when everyone else has eaten. Despite constitutional provisions and policy declarations regarding the advancement of women, and the entry in recent years of large numbers of women into the formal workforce, societal norms continue to value women primarily as bearers of children – or, rather, sons – even though many have died from too early, too frequent and too many pregnancies.

Although economic pressures have forced women to defy social, and often family, expectations, and take up work in public space, it is assumed that only women without male provision or protection do this. A woman outside the boundaries of her family and home is therefore either destitute – an object of pity – or immoral – an object of shame. And yet, despite this stress on the protection of women and their confinement to the 'safety' of the domestic sphere, we have found that violence against women appears to be a part of everyday life, within the domestic sphere and outside it: wife beating, dowry deaths, assaults, rapes and, more recently, *fatwa*-related violence and acid attacks, are common. Consequently, although Naripokkho has been active on a variety of issues and on a number of different fronts, body politics has remained a continuous thread in its work.

The 'politics of the body' in Naripokkho's agenda

Making violence against women visible

Not surprisingly, the first issue around which Naripokkho mobilized, and one that continues to dominate our agenda, is that of violence against women. Not only was this was woven into the everyday experiences of the women who came together in the workshops, but also more generally: fear about their personal safety acts as a crippling constraint on what women can be and do in Bangladesh.

Our standpoint on violence has evolved partly as a critique of the way the issue has been handled by the mainstream women's movement, and partly as a response to the specific instances that have come onto our agenda. The mass rape of women by the Pakistan army during Bangladesh's independence war in 1971 continues to be referred to by our politicians, intellectuals and public leaders as 'the loss of honour' of Bangladeshi women rather than as a war crime. We challenged this interpretation. If 'loss of honour' was at all an issue, then surely it was that of the rapist. The *raison d'être* for protest on the issue of rape should surely be the necessity to shame the rapists. However, the idea that women are the repositories of family, community and national honour is a deep-rooted one. It continues to dominate the political discourse about the national struggle for independence. And it leads communities to congratulate themselves upon successfully forcing the rapist to marry his victim! This practice is common, especially in rural communities, and is seen as the only way of recouping lost honour.

Naripokkho's first involvement in a campaign on the issue of violence against women was in 1985, when the then military government had imposed a temporary ban on all political activities. Denied their usual source of news, journalists filled the front pages with reports of crimes, including violence against women, that previously had been relegated to obscure sections of their papers. Opposition groups saw this as an opportunity to mobilize public opinion against the ruling regime. By choosing to focus on violence in terms of women's safety in public space, it was able to define the issue as a law and order problem and cast it in terms of the failure of the government to maintain law and order. The fact that the majority of the violence reported in the media occurred within the home and had been perpetrated by family members offered little possibility for political capital. Thus the issue of domestic violence was ignored.[6]

At about the same time that year, newspaper reports of the sale into prostitution and subsequent death of a ten-year-old girl named Shabmeher sparked off unprecedented public anger. In the same week, newspapers reported the rape of a five-year-old girl. The fact that both these incidents represented the violation of 'innocent minors' evoked unprecedented sympathy, even among those who appeared to have become immune to the daily reports of violence against women all over the country. A high-profile campaign against violence against women was mounted by various women's organizations and other social groups, convened by Bangladesh Mahila Parishad, the largest women's organization in the country. Naripokkho was invited to join the eighteen-member National Steering Committee.

Naripokkho's concern with women's safety and security, our belief that violence against women was a product of systemic discrimination rather than a purely individual act, and our conviction that women had to be both visible and audible in the fight against violence if they were to transcend their status as passive victims led us initially to become involved in this campaign, and also explain our subsequent decision to leave it. From the outset we found ourselves at odds with the politics and strategy that animated the campaign organizers, in particular their reluctance to take on board the issue of domestic violence and their desire to promote 'important men' as patrons of the campaign in a bid to give it social acceptability and defuse any 'feminist' connotations.

We were not happy with this framing of what is a critical issue for the women's movement. The focus on law and order as the fundamental problem was, in our view, born out of a partisan politics that sought to use the campaign to mobilize against the government in power. It reflected neither an analysis of the patriarchal power relations that permitted, condoned and even encouraged various forms of violence against women, both within the home and in the public domain, nor any intention of building a serious campaign against such violence. We welcomed the support of men, but not their leadership or patronage. We wanted the public face of the campaign to be female, and we wanted the campaign to project the image of women fighting back. We suggested that the campaign highlight positive programmes that contributed to reducing women's economic dependence. We also proposed the promotion of martial arts training for girls so they could defend themselves rather than wait passively for male protection. The slogan we mobilized our members around was '*nari nirjaton rukhbo shobey, haath achey hatiar hobey*' ('we will fight violence against women, our hands will be our weapons').

We also wanted to give space in the campaign to survivors of violence. Our proposal to have one such survivor speak at one of the main public meetings organized by the committee was turned down in favour of their chosen 'important' men. We did manage, however, through 'guerrilla action', to bring someone who had experienced such violence on stage and have her speak.[7] We felt that it was important to give those who were perceived as 'victims' the opportunity to take back control over their lives through such engagement in public action. However, our attempt to include the issue of domestic violence in the campaign agenda met with strong opposition, and we were effectively silenced.

The abrupt collapse of the campaign with the lifting of the government's ban on political activities confirmed to us that it had merely been a stick to beat the government with at a time when other sticks had been banned. This made us keenly aware of the use, and misuse, of women's issues to further partisan interests, and wary from an early stage about coalition politics. We have, since then, stayed clear of coalitions, and instead opted to work with others in alliances formed on the basis of shared stands on particular issues.

Action on acid violence

For reasons not fully understood, amongst the many different forms of violence against women in Bangladesh is the deliberate use of acid as a weapon. While this is not the most common form of violence, it is significant both because there is a much higher incidence of such attacks in Bangladesh than anywhere else in the world, and because of the horrific physical and psychological damage they can inflict. Given the importance of appearance to women's chances in life, and to their chances of marriage – long considered the only acceptable destiny for women in Bangladesh – the psychological damage can be particularly devastating.

In 1995, a journalist following up on the case of Nurun Nahar, a young girl who had been attacked by a rejected suitor, first drew Naripokkho's attention to the devastating effects of acid violence. Naripokkho mobilized government action to ensure that Nurun Nahar received appropriate medical treatment, and that those responsible for the attack were prosecuted. Above all, Naripokkho provided her with the emotional support she so badly needed not to give up on life.

In 1997, Naripokkho organized the first workshop of acid survivors. A total of nine young girls from different parts of the country and their mothers were invited to participate in the workshop. We were determined to avoid any media sensationalization of this event, so we decided not to inform the press about it. Instead, we focused our energies on arranging meetings with the Ministers of Health and Family Welfare, Home Affairs, Women's Affairs and Law, Justice and Parliamentary Affairs. We needed government action to ensure that these girls and others like them received appropriate medical treatment and police investigation of the crime and prosecution of perpetrators was taken seriously. We also arranged a meeting with UNICEF to take on board what was largely (at that time) a form of violence targeting young girls.[8] These meetings succeeded in bringing home to ministers and government officials the severe consequences of this crime, and motivated them to make declarations about the serious nature of it and their intention to take stern action. UNICEF followed this up by supporting an initiative to set up the Bangladesh Acid Survivors Foundation in 1998, to provide support for acid survivors in the form of medical treatment, prosecution and rehabilitation.

Our encounter with acid survivors on this first occasion taught us a number of important lessons. First of all, our attention had been on the girls themselves, and on their mothers, because we thought they were the ones who suffered most from the attack itself and from dealing with its aftermath. However, at a meeting held at the start of the workshop to introduce the survivors and their families to members of Naripokkho, we found that many fathers and brothers had also come. We had not thought of inviting them at all.

As we went around the room introducing ourselves, some of the girls broke down, saying they wished they had died instead of having to live with the consequences of the attack. One girl in particular said she wanted to die because she could not stand the pain this had inflicted on her mother and her family. At this point, we were startled by a heart-rending cry from one of the young men, a brother. He broke into what can only be described as inconsolable weeping. Then the older man sitting next to him, a father, started crying. Soon we were all crying. Why hadn't we thought of the pain that fathers and brothers suffered? We understood then that our most important allies in the fight against violence against women were the fathers and brothers of women who had suffered.

The second thing that took us by surprise was when some of the family members asked that we organize a meeting of the acid survivors with the press. While we had been bending over backward to avoid giving the media any opportunity for sensationalism, one of the fathers told us firmly, 'People need to see and know what kind of damage acid attacks can cause'. On the last day of the workshop, we organized a meeting with selected journalists who were known to us and who we felt would be sensitive. We also invited the Secretary of the Ministry of Women's Affairs.

At this meeting, the girls presented on a flip chart what they had identified during the workshop as the causes and consequences of such attacks, what their needs were, what they wanted to achieve and what they dreamed for themselves. It was front-page news the next day, and apart from one newspaper that actually printed a photograph of one of the girls at the flip chart, all the other papers carried close-ups of their badly disfigured faces. We had not been able to prevent the sensationalism we had feared. From then on it was a snowball effect: special features, television, CNN, ABC and so on. We tried wherever possible to inject our real and serious concerns about all forms of violence against women, but violence against women was too common an occurrence. The acid story, by contrast, had shock value.

Our focus in the workshop was to make these girls want to live again, and to know that there is a lot to live for. On their last evening with us, the Theatre Centre for Social Development – a theatre group that has been a friend and partner for Naripokkho through the years – organized an evening of entertainment. A drag show was followed by music, and a makeshift dance floor helped to transform these girls, who had become used to hiding behind veils and holding back from living, into young teenyboppers having fun. Selina's mother beamed as she watched her daughter, who had not spoken since the attack six months prior to the workshop, laugh and begin to speak a few words. Empowerment for these women has meant the journey from victim to survivor, and then from survivor to activist. We wanted not only to let the survivors find their voices but also to bring them into the movement against violence against women. The torchlight procession organized by Naripokkho on the eve of International Women's Day in 1998 was led by Bina, Nurun Nahar and Jhorna, victims who had made the journey to activists and no longer covered their faces.

Advocacy around services for women

The work with acid survivors saw an expansion of Naripokkho's activism from protest to advocacy. We lobbied the government for better services for women who had suffered violence, and for changes in both the policies and institutional arrangements through which services were delivered and justice administered. We began a new project called 'Monitoring State Interventions to Combat Violence Against Women' in 1999; this has regularly monitored all 22 police stations in Dhaka Metropolitan area, the two major public hospitals (emergency, gynaecology, burns and forensic medicine departments) and the special court which tries all cases involving violence against women.

At quarterly meetings with service providers, findings from the monitoring are presented in a spirit of dialogue. Representatives from these institutions, together with Naripokkho, prepare recommendations for improvements, and the dialogue is sustained on the basis of trust. Naripokkho's commitment to constructive engagement with the problems has meant an unwritten agreement on our part not to publicize these findings in the media. It has also helped that we present this work as action research rather than as 'monitoring'. Most service providers put forward lack of resources as the major problem. While the resources issue is often a real one, and we do offer to lobby to address it, we also try to get providers to focus on their own behaviour and attitudes (identified by violence survivors as a primary problem).

Naripokkho has also been active around women's health and reproductive rights. The urgency attached to population control in the country had led to the imposition on family planning providers of numerical targets, a practice fraught with potential for abuse. In 1987, one of our members reported the death of a woman from tetanus infection following a sterilization operation in a Model Family Planning Clinic. Closer investigation revealed that the woman had actually approached the clinic for an abortion. The clinic staff decided she was a good candidate for sterilization and did not want to miss the opportunity of increasing their performance figures. Instead of giving her the anti-tetanus serum with her abortion, which would take a number of days to take effect and require her to come back for the sterilization, they decided to operate there and then.

This incident raised serious questions regarding the government's preoccupation with numerical targets over women's right to choose and the safe delivery of services. In 1989, we documented abuse in the Norplant[9] programme: doctors were reported to be refusing to remove the implant when women complained of side-effects. Our concerns around safe contraception, reproductive rights and sexual freedom have come to be clustered around the theme 'shorir amaar shiddhanto amaar' ('my body, my decision').

In 1996, Naripokkho took up the issue of the accountability of health service providers to women on an experimental basis, in connection with monitoring the government's commitment to the Programme of Action of the International Conference on Population and Development (ICPD). Health constitutes a key arena of women's suffering, and represents the end results of discrimination, violence and inequality. Naripokkho sought to activate the Upazila Health Advisory Committee, set up by the government to monitor and improve health services at local level. This committee, composed of a cross-section of society, public representatives and government functionaries, proved to be effective in bringing about improvements, once activated.

Solidarity with sex workers

The rights of sex workers is another aspect of our politics of the body. Sex workers occupy an uneasy marginal status in Bangladeshi society. In a culture that is built on the repression of women's sexuality, confinement to the home, and marriage as women's ultimate destiny, sex workers appear to defy every precept of 'normal' Bengali womanhood.

Although treated in the popular press as victims, they often appear to enjoy a peculiar autonomy denied to other women: they mix freely with men, they speak their minds assertively on television, they live on their own earnings, have children outside marriage and bring them up without male guardians, and even, occasionally, declare an active sexuality. Sex workers have appeared periodically in the media over the past decade because of attempts by the government or self-motivated groups of citizens to demolish brothels and evict their occupants.

The first threat of eviction that Naripokkho associated itself with was that of Tanbazaar in 1991. Although this threat was successfully resisted, six years later the Kandupatti brothel in old Dhaka was attacked and its residents were evicted by the hired musclemen of local vested interests. The most recent attempt took place in 1999, when the government evicted sex workers and their children from a complex of brothels, over a century old, located in the Tanbazaar and Nimtoli areas of Narayanganj. This action was met by an unprecedented mobilization of development NGOs and human rights organizations to defend the rights of sex workers. For the first time in the country's history, a major public debate took place in the newspapers over the meaning of sex work and the status of sex workers. All the major dailies carried news and features on the topic for nearly a month after the eviction.

The mobilization was led by Naripokkho and led to the formation of Shonghoti, a broad-based human rights alliance protesting the government actions and demanding that sex workers be respected as citizens. Eighty-six organizations of various types joined Shonghoti. They provided active support in mobilizing protests against the unlawful eviction, as well as assistance for those rendered homeless. The formation of Shonghoti marks a new chapter in the struggle for women's rights as human rights in Bangladesh. However, the successful alliance-building effort of 1999 had a 10-year history behind it, involving various attempts at brothel evictions and Naripokkho's encounter and *porichiti*[10] with sex workers.

The public response to sex work has conventionally taken two forms: moral condemnation of 'loose' women, or moral benevolence towards 'hapless' victims. In 1991, women from Tanbazaar had themselves attempted to claim their rights as citizens, as workers and as women, and condemned attempts to evict them as violations of these rights. Their voice at that time, however, was drowned by the dominant discourses of moral outrage and benevolence. In the ensuing ten years, however, their assertion of their citizenship has been heard several times; finally in 1999 it found a place both within the struggle for universal human rights and women's emancipation, as well as in the public discourse on prostitution.

Recognition of the human rights of all, including women engaged in prostitution, brought the issue of work and what constitutes work to the centre of the public debate. This has been a thorny issue for many, including Shonghoti members. Even as we declared unequivocal support for upholding the rights of women in prostitution, we were arguing over some basic questions amongst ourselves. Can sex be considered work? If sex in prostitution is work, then is sex in marriage work as well? If sex in prostitution is not work, then what is it? Naripokkho's strategy in trying to hold together this unprecedented mobilization of a diverse range of organizations was to deliberately avoid public discussion of these issues. It was felt that public debate on this complex issue carried the danger of prompting simplistic public stands and unnecessary polarization. Instead, we focused our campaigning on the human rights of sex workers, their status as citizens, the rights of citizenship and the obligations of the state.

Talking to sex workers, however, has left us in no doubt that for them sex *is* work, sometimes pleasurable, more often not. Moreover, it is work that offers higher returns for their labour than many other work opportunities available to poor women with no assets of their own.

And finally ... working on ourselves

Public claiming of rights, and accountability, are important aspects of the assertion of women's citizenship in a culture where women are defined as dependants, politically, culturally and economically, and where they are expected to accept their position without protest. However, while a great deal of our energy as an organization has been devoted to body politics in the public domain, we have also accepted from the outset that our own bodies were implicated in this politics in particular ways.

Our beginnings in the shared life experiences of women working in development NGOs focused our subsequent work in particular ways, and helped to bring a different dimension into the politics of gender in development, based on the concrete experiences of discrimination, inequality and resistance of women development workers themselves. This raises uncomfortable issues around the 'culture' and body politics of development organizations, including issues of sexual harassment, recognition of women's reproductive and caring responsibilities, and issues of physical security. Naripokkho has brought discussion of these issues, previously relegated to the realm of the personal – and hence the private – into the realm of the professional – hence public – domain, raising them as matters that NGOs had to address within their own organizational structures: a process not always welcomed by the organizations in question.

We have also used our workshops to think through the politics of our own bodies. We try to provide participants with a variety of skills that will strengthen their self-confidence in the public domain, such as chairing sessions (a function normally monopolized by men), taking responsibility for devising cultural events and producing a daily 'wallpaper' bulletin. Above all, we use workshops to give them a place to be themselves – the selves they have not been allowed to be. They write and draw whatever they wish on the wallpaper provided. The cultural sessions provide them with a space to sing, dance, recite poetry and generally express the imaginative side of themselves. The idea of 'play' does not feature much in women's lives in Bangladesh, and in many parts of the country they are not permitted to sing and dance. Allowing themselves to throw off their inhibitions, to let their bodies move as they wish and not worry about how their saris fall is an exhilarating experience for many of the women, who have been brought up since childhood to take up as little space in the world as possible.

These workshops have produced over time a body of testimonies that provide us with the knowledge, anger and conviction to fight 'for women', as well as with the hope, energy and inspiration to do so in a way that remains true to our collective voice. Looking back on over two decades of activism, we find that our interactions with each other, our willingness to stand out against mainstream ideas about women's politics, our determination to counter cultural ascriptions of passivity to women – the *bhadramahila*[11] paradigm that mainstream women's organizations continue to operate within – have given us an energy that makes us appear bold and uninhibited to the wider public. This public perception was brought to our attention by journalists covering our movement against the 8th Amendment to the Constitution, which sought to make Islam the state religion. They commented on the speed with which we took our first procession down from Shahid Minar to the Press Club. What they did not know, however, was that this was not entirely intentional. Because of our inexperience with banners, we had not cut holes in them for the wind to pass through, so they caught the wind and the procession sailed through the streets of Dhaka at an amazing speed. The predominant image of Naripokkho members since then has been one of women 'with saris worn high and no make-up', moving with an agility out of keeping with the customary decorous walk expected of women.

Although we are perceived as a threat to the established paradigm of how women should behave, we have also invoked a reluctant admiration. Our energy, our apparent audacity, our *'damn care bhaab'* ('couldn't give a damn attitude') have been described by many of our friends and colleagues outside the movement as possessing a certain appeal – *'bhalo lagey kintu bhoyo lagey'* ('attractive but dangerous'). The causes we take up and the politics we bring to them have reinforced this public image. In particular, our decision to take up the cause of the 'bazaar women', a despised social group living on the margins of society but apparently exercising some degree of autonomy in their lives, appears as yet another example, to those who disapprove of us, of our willingness to flout convention and align ourselves with women who deserve pity or condemnation perhaps, but certainly not the solidarity one extends to one's own kind.

Notes

I wish to express my gratitude to Professor Naila Kabeer and Professor John Gaventa at the Institute of Development Studies, Sussex, for insisting that activists can write and not giving up on me, and especially to Naila for insisting that the Naripokkho story needed to be heard and helping to pull out a coherent piece from the longer 'stream of consciousness' narrative I had embarked on.

1. Naripokkho means 'pro women'.
2. There has been a considerable expansion in the scale – and visibility – of female employment since that workshop. The erosion of male incomes, the rising cost of living, the pressure on women to contribute to household income and the emergence of new opportunities for them to do so – particularly in the export-oriented garment industry, but also within the NGO sector itself – have all led to a far more visible involvement by women in paid work.
3. We often observe that Naripokkho began as it meant to go on: by challenging externally determined agendas to create a space for women to find their own voice.
4. There are two revealing equations at work here. There is the explicit equation between the behaviour of a wife wanting sexual pleasure and that of a prostitute. The second equation is implicit in the colloquial use of the term *'bajaarer meyelok'*, which literally means 'woman from the marketplace', to describe women in prostitution. In other words, women who go out to work (enter the market place) can only be selling sexual services.
5. The 'bari' is the shared compound in which members of an extended family reside, usually in independent houses.
6. In fact, Naripokkho's study on violence against women, conducted during 1995–7, found that 60 per cent of the women interviewed across all classes had experienced conjugal violence, and that 63 per cent of violence-related injuries requiring hospitalization occurred within the home.
7. We had the support of a leading woman lawyer in Bangladesh who was a speaker at this meeting, and who at the end of her speech invited the survivor to come on stage and address the auditorium. It was not possible at this point for the organizers to intercept her.

8. Acid is now used as a weapon for vengeance in all kinds of enmity arising out of marital discord and dowry demands, family feuds and land disputes and the number of male victims is on the increase.
9. Norplant is a contraceptive implant, which has to be surgically placed and removed.
10. The Bangla word *porichiti* can mean both 'acquaintance' and 'identity'. Interestingly for Naripokkho, it was both an acquaintance and identification with sex workers.
11 The *bhadramahila* is the equivalent of the Victorian gentlewoman. Historically the term refers to the women of the *bhadrolok* class (gentry), a Western-educated urban middle class whose emergence in mid-nineteenth-century Kolkata was characterized by a break with the feudal class.

Eleven

'Growing' citizenship from the grassroots: Nijera Kori and social mobilization in Bangladesh

Naila Kabeer

Formal definitions and lived experiences of citizenship in Bangladesh

The constitution of Bangladesh is committed to uphold certain universal human rights, including the right to life and personal liberty, privacy, equality and non-discrimination, and freedom of movement, religion, expression, thought and conscience, and property. It also contains fundamental principles of state policy that address the need for the state to ensure the availability of food, shelter, employment, health and education for all its citizens. Though non-justiciable, the constitution provides that these principles should be fundamental to the governance of Bangladesh, applied in its laws, and a guide to constitutional and legal interpretation.

The reality, however, bears very little relation to these constitutional provisions. It is characterized instead by corruption and clientelism. The state does not merely fail to protect the rights of citizens, it actively contributes to their violation. The legal system offers uncertain recourse to justice: cases can be dismissed, prolonged or delayed for the right price. Extensive control over the allocation of resources by state officials has given rise to rent-seeking and corruption. There is widespread reliance at every level of society on membership of social networks and the ability to pull strings to get anything done. The poor and marginalized are either excluded from these networks or can only participate on terms that deprive them of independent voice and agency. The pervasiveness of these patron–client relationships serves to fragment and disunite such groups, and prevents the emergence of horizontal, class-based solidarities that could be mobilized to defend and promote their interests.

The non-governmental organization (NGO) sector, which emerged in Bangladesh in the aftermath of its war of independence in 1971, was partly a response to these institutional deficiencies. It has expanded rapidly in recent decades, not least because of funds made available by international donors seeking to implement a neo-liberal agenda of reducing the role of the state. There are around 22,000 NGOs in Bangladesh today. 80 per cent of its villages have some form of NGO presence, and around 35 per cent of the country's population directly benefit from their activities (Thornton *et al.* 2000). In a country of 130 million people, this suggests an astonishing outreach.

Most NGOs have certain characteristics in common. They are partly or wholly reliant on foreign funding, they see their mission as working with the poor, and they tend to rely on group-based activities to achieve their goals. In addition, over the years they have increasingly engaged in some form of service delivery. The provision of micro-finance services dominates because its stress on building micro-entrepreneurship fits neatly into the neo-liberal vision of a market-based society. However, NGOs are also involved in the delivery of health, education, safety net programmes, low-cost housing and so on.

My focus in this chapter is on Nijera Kori (NK), an organization that is an exception to this general rule in that it has determinedly refused to engage in any form of service delivery. Instead, it concentrates entirely on building up the collective capabilities of the poor to demand their rights. The chapter will draw on both secondary studies as well as primary fieldwork[1] in order to examine NK's vision, goals and activities, and what these imply for the understanding and practice of citizenship within its constituency.

Nijera Kori's vision, goals and strategy

NK has been involved since 1980 with the working poor in a number of districts in Bangladesh.[2] It defines its constituency as those men and women who have no assets of their own but must sell their physical labour, or its products, to earn a living. Early documents spelt out what it saw as the key factors that led to the disenfranchisement of this constituency (see, for instance, Ahmed 1982).

- In *economic* terms, they had to sell their labour to meet their basic needs, but had little control over the terms and conditions on which this labour was sold. Consequently, they often earned barely enough to feed themselves and their families.
- In *social* terms, their reliance on patron–client relationships served to

fragment them along vertical lines and prevent the emergence of horizontal, class-based alliances that could challenge these hierarchical structures. Their capacity for agency was further suppressed by norms, beliefs and ideologies that explain and justify their poverty and marginalization as the product of fate, fault or failure, and by practices that kept them ignorant of their basic rights.

• In *political* terms, they were denied voice in the collective structures of decision-making through which rules were made and resources distributed within the society. This was true in relation to decision-making forums such as the *shalish*, the informal body responsible for resolving conflicts and dispensing justice. It was true at the level of local government, which was responsible for the delivery of state programmes, many intended explicitly for the poor. And it went without saying that it was also true in relation to national processes of decision-making.

From the outset, therefore, NK has defined the problem of poverty not simply in terms of lack of resources but also in terms of lack of voice, agency and organization; as the manifestation not simply of individual deprivation, but also of underlying structural inequities. This explains the holistic nature of its vision of social change: 'To establish an exploitation-free society by changing the present system of social exploitation with the aim of emancipation of working class people' (Annual Report 1998–9).

It also explains the holistic nature of its strategy for change. NK believes that the struggle for social transformation has to be carried out in all spheres of life and at all levels of society, starting with the individual and extending to the local, the national and, where relevant, the international. And it explains key aspects of NK's strategy for change: the purposive construction of social relations that reflect horizontal alliances of the poor and that displace the vertical patron–client relations that have kept the poor fragmented and isolated for so long. Consequently, it seeks to nurture the values of solidarity, self-reliance and collective action, rather than those of individual prosperity, personal advancement and competition associated with the neo-liberal vision of social change.

It is this reasoning that has led NK consistently and firmly to reject any form of service delivery role and to remain one of the few NGOs in the country to resist the widespread 'turn to micro-credit' evident in the NGO sector since the mid-1980s. It fears that such a role could create new forms of dependency between NGOs and their constituencies, diverting the energies of both from the larger goals of transforming society and democratizing the state.

In short, in a climate that is characterized by a flourishing culture of corruption and clientilism, NK's strategy can be described as one of 'growing citizenship from the grassroots'. It is sowing the seeds of an alternative culture of rights, first in the consciousness of its marginalized constituency, then in their relationships with each other and finally in their relationships with the rest of society. At the heart of this strategy is a process of group formation – groups created not for administrative convenience or as social collateral for micro-finance services (as with most other NGOs), but as the basic units of new sets of social relationships between the poor and marginalized, and the foundations for the longer-term transformation of society.

Currently, NK has a total of 8,622 groups around the country, which translates into over 180,000 members, of whom half are women (Annual Report 2002). The groups meet on a weekly basis, contribute to a collective savings fund (intended to reduce their dependence on moneylenders or patrons), elect members to take on organizational responsibilities, and participate in various forms of training. As groups mature, they become more independent of NK, calling their own meetings, initiating their own collective actions and acting as local-level leaders for the wider community. NK remains involved in providing support for activities that cover larger areas and require mediation and advocacy at local, regional and national levels.

Transforming consciousness

As noted earlier, ideological factors play an important role in NK's analysis of the disenfranchisement of the poor in Bangladesh. The problem of 'collective inaction' is seen as a reflection of poor people's resignation in the face of what appear to be the invincible forces ranged against them, and their unwillingness to challenge these forces and risk what little security they might have. In addition, of course, many simply do not know, or believe, that they have any rights. For poor rural women in particular, whose devalued sense of personhood reflects the intersecting asymmetries of class and gender ideologies, the sense of powerlessness is often deep-rooted.

Despite its highly structuralist analysis of injustice, therefore, NK's strategy for social change takes the individual as its starting point. Training plays a central role in this process. It provides members with information about their rights and entitlements, and gives them the opportunity to reflect on and analyse their individual situations and how these relate to wider social inequalities. It gives them exposure to various theoretical explanations of these problems – which locate them in the deep structures of class, gender and social organization – and it discusses news and events that illustrate how these structures are manifested in other parts of the world.

NK also attaches great importance to cultural dimensions of training, and has staff with specific responsibility for developing its cultural materials – songs, theatre, stories and role play. This is not only because cultural activities liven up its training courses, but also because, as one trainer pointed out, they constitute an essential element in NK's vision of social transformation: 'We want to create a different kind of person. And to be a different kind of person, you need a different kind of culture'.

Some of this change was evident from our interviews with members of NK groups. They talked about the way in which poverty had constrained their capacity for voice and agency in the past:

> Poor people were afraid to be united at that time. They were worried because they had no money, no assets. They didn't have the perspective that would have allowed them to unite. They didn't even have that little bit of courage that you must have in order to do something like that. They were afraid because they thought that if they challenged someone who was rich, they would lose out later because the rich would not help them out. They were scared. And they faced pressure from all directions. And as long as they were afraid like that, there was nothing that they could do.

> Before we did not protest even when there was a lot of injustice and oppression within the village. We were afraid of the chairmen, the village leaders, the members of the councils. We could not even see any reason to protest. After all, they were our leaders; we used to honour them. We used to think to argue with the chairman was to commit an offence.

The changes they described as a result of their association with NK reflected both the training they had received about their rights as well as its organizational practices:

> Now the difference is that those who are powerful in society, those who have money, they can no longer do things in the same way that they used to. A poor person now has a different understanding of things, of themselves and what they can do. And because of that, the rich cannot put pressure on the poor in the way that they used to. The laws that were there before, they are still the same laws. But we didn't know about them, we didn't understand what they all meant. And because of that, they could easily just force something on us. In my father's day, my father was a farmer, he was not educated ... but now, I have some education so

I understand more about society than he did. And because of that, maybe, if someone tries to trick us, blame us for something or treat us unjustly, we can protest.

Those people who were silent then now give speeches in meetings, processions and conferences. Where we have always seen that ministers and MPs are the ones who always stand on the stage and deliver speeches, now a landless person is standing in that place and giving a speech.

Now we can talk to the chairman; not only the chairman, we also face the *upazilla* [administrative unit] administration, the TNO,[3] police station and so on. Earlier we did not even know what a TNO was. Now we talk to the TNO and if there is any injustice, we protest, we *gherao* [surround in protest], we bring out processions. Before we did not have a chance to see their faces; now we sit beside them in a chair. Through our protest we hope to change society.

Some of the changes described by women members were often more dramatic than those of men because of the greater constraints they had faced:

Before we even feared talking in front of our husbands, nowadays we do not even fear talking with the magistrate.
Ali et al. *1998, p. 46*

Earlier, before we joined Nijera Kori, we were afraid. We didn't even leave our *para* [neighbourhood]. Now it is completely different, we move everywhere. We even travel to Comilla [for court cases], we don't care any longer. Before joining, I felt like an orphan, but not any longer. The group's unity gives me strength. Now people reckon with me, respect me.
Christensen 1999, p. 70

The women we interviewed also testified to the changes that had taken place in their beliefs and attitudes:

In the past, women in this area were confined to the home. Now they have learnt to fight the *jotedars* [landlords]. It is not possible to fight hunger sitting at home. My first right from society and from the state is a place to live. If I have a safe and secure place to live, I would be able to manage, to look after myself. But society does not give me this simple right. In addition, I have rights as a woman. I believe that men and women are equal, that having to stay within the home is against women's rights. If the prime minister of the country can be a woman and she is able to run the country, then why do we have to stay at home?

Building solidarity

Changes in individual definitions of selfhood were bound up for members of NK groups with recognition of a collective identity based on the shared interests of the poor and marginalized. NK uses a variety of means to actively reinforce this sense of identity among its group members. The starting point for group formation is the joint savings programme, which not only serves to reduce their dependence on the wealthy to tide them over in times of crisis, but also forms the basis of various kinds of collective activity. Members decide how much they will contribute each week, who will manage the funds and how they will be used.

In general, they are encouraged to think of collective rather than individual uses for their funds: the collective leasing of land or purchase of technology for use or rent. In addition, groups use their funds to support each other in various ways. Our interviews came across several examples of group funds being used to tide an individual member through a period of crisis or to meet expenses incurred during participation in social movements: for instance, helping out the families of members who have been arrested or sharing their litigation expenses; rebuilding the house of a member that had been burnt by the henchmen of a local landlord during conflicts over land (see also Khan and Khan 2000). Group members also raised donations from the local community to mount various campaigns and protests.

The effectiveness of the process of building group solidarity is evident from the way in which group members talked about each other and about their relationship with the staff of NK:

> When we five women stand together, then no man can get away with misbehaving with us. Because we have solidarity among ourselves, we will catch him and question him as to his misbehaviour. If it is one woman, anyone can insult her without fear. It is the same for men. If poor men stay united, no one will be able to get away with deceiving or insulting them.

> Many of us in this group knew each other before. We live in the same village. But since our association as a group, our attitudes have changed. Before we used not to share each others' problems. But now we have got united, each one's problem influences the other … we all take care of each other.

> Before, people used to lose everything by going into debt. But now we try and make ends meet through our own efforts. The basis of all our activities is to be united under the same umbrella. Nijera Kori provides us with that umbrella. The organization has brought us close to each other.

A recent review of NGOs in Bangladesh noted striking differences between the groups formed by social mobilization organizations and those formed by organizations engaged in financial service delivery (Thornton *et al.* 2000). Groups formed by micro-finance organizations were found to be made up of members from differing social, economic and political backgrounds and to have differing lengths of membership. Their members appeared to have very limited contact with each other or with the organization's staff outside of the weekly meetings. Meetings were focused primarily on the collection and distribution of money, and often referred to as 'collection meetings' by NGO staff and group members: 'During the actual *samity* [group] meetings, members arrive at different times, make whatever transactions they have to and leave. There is no need to sit together since there is nothing really to discuss' (p. 11).

This was in considerable contrast to experiences of those groups – NK groups were the example cited – that had been organized around the goal of social mobilization: 'Most of these *samities* [groups] had recorded minutes of their meetings and the range of issues discussed was very wide… The *samity* may also meet outside of the established timings if circumstances require. In these types of *samities*, the role of the fieldworkers is very distinct. The fieldworker is not a "collector", but a brother or sister, and their main role is one of advising and supporting the *samity*' (p. 11). As a result, members of *samities* organized by bodies like NK 'have a stronger sense of belonging to the group, and a greater set of common goals and values. For many the *samity* has become a central reference point in their lives'.

My own discussions with a group of NK women, some of whom also belonged to Grameen Bank micro-credit groups, provided an opportunity to explore what these different forms of NGO membership meant to the women in question. I asked them why they chose to belong to both Grameen Bank and Nijera Kori groups, given that this required them to attend *two* sets of group meetings a week and that there were no obvious material benefits from NK membership. This elicited the following responses:

> We are all poor people. For us to get hold of 3,000 or 4,000 *takas* at one time is not easy. That is why we are members of Grameen Bank. If we get a loan of 5,000 *takas*, we can then go and get some material to work our looms. We can go and buy thread … and we can make a good profit… With Nijera Kori, we have savings when we need it … and we are united. No one can stop us. If someone comes to beat one of us, we all sort out the matter together. Grameen would not do this for us. They

just give us loans and take them back. That is what they are concerned about.

With Grameen Bank, it is like this: my relationship to them is based on the loans. Even if someone has died in your family, you have to pay the instalment. That is the agreement you reach with them when you join. They say, 'Even if you have a dead body in the house, you have to pay the instalment. On that basis, if you are willing to take the loan, then you take it.' But as to how we might change our ideas, how we can be given a way to improve ourselves, this is not something that they do. With Nijera Kori ... they don't give us money but they give us good advice: how we can improve our lives, or what will be good for us in order to create a better future for ourselves. We were ignorant before; now we have become wise.

Being in a Grameen *samity* brings you one kind of benefit, and you get something else from being a member of Nijera Kori. NK gives you knowledge. Say if my husband throws me out, if he threatens me with divorce ... then I will come to the *samity*. Then they will definitely do something to help me, definitely they will. And these ideas were not part of our thinking... If someone comes to the Nijera Kori *samity*, and informs people about some injustice like this, they will protest. Grameen people will not do that. With them the relationship is based on loans.

Mobilizing around rights: economic, social and political

The transformation of individual consciousness, the strengthening of analytical capacity and the construction of relationships based on horizontal forms of solidarity are the foundations on which NK members are able to engage in collective action to challenge the manifestations of social injustice in their lives. As can be seen from Table 11.1 (on p. 191), their collective actions straddle different spheres and combine strategies of co-operation and contestation, depending on the issue.

Economic mobilization

Although NK does not provide any direct material resources to its group members, it does mobilize to fight for resources to which they are entitled. In areas where there is a considerable amount of *khas* (unclaimed) land to which the landless have a legal entitlement, struggles around land rights have been a key focus of NK group activity. The confusing plethora of legislation surrounding land rights in Bangladesh has allowed local power-holders not only to evade legislation aimed at curtailing the size of their holdings, but also to seize government *khas* land and water bodies to which the landless are legally entitled. With economic liberalization, and the emergence of the industrial farming of shrimps for export as a profitable new activity, local entrepreneurs have also become active in the illegal occupation of *khas* land, often using violent means, with a view to transforming it from agricultural use to shrimp farming. The threat presented by this new industry to the livelihoods and rights of the poor, and to an already fragile environment, has taken NK from collective action at the local level to participation in global efforts to mobilize against industrial shrimp production.

Elsewhere in the country, the focus of collective action has been on fairer wages and working conditions. The leverage that individual wage labourers can bring to bear on their employers varies considerably across the country. In more prosperous areas, where alternative avenues of employment are available, group members have been able to mobilize the support of non-members in their struggle to raise wages paid during the slack season by organizing boycotts during the busy season (Ali *et al.* 1998; Christensen 1999). Where, however, there are few local opportunities, so that men from landless households have to migrate outside for work, the capacity to negotiate over wages is extremely limited.

Struggles over remuneration take a different form when they relate to entitlements in the context of state-provided safety-net measures. Here, NK groups appear to have been more consistently successful in ensuring fair treatment. By holding demonstrations, 'gheraoing' responsible officials and going on strike, NK members have been able to obtain their due as well as to negotiate increased rates of remuneration.

Attempts to claim their entitlements have brought NK members into direct confrontation with local elites. According to NK organizers, while rural elites continue to rely on armed *lathials* (muscle-men) to undermine the collective struggles of the poor, they are increasingly resorting to the use of false litigation and police harassment to achieve the same ends. As a result, at any one time, there can be up to ten false cases lodged against an NK group member. This has made legal activism an important corollary of NK's struggles over resources. The costs associated with fighting these cases and providing support for families are met through contributions from NK's budget and from members' group savings. NK has also built networks of supporters among concerned journalists, lawyers, students and others within the local district towns where it works. These provide advice and support, and draw public attention to what is going on.

Table 11.1: Collective action by NK groups (1998–2000)

Issues involved	By Divisions				
	Khulna	Dhaka	Rajshahi	Ch'gong	Total
Gender issues (dowry, divorce, polygamy, rape, kidnapping and assault); resistance to fundamentalist forces and the issue of *fatwas* which attack women's rights.	49	37	148	56	290
Movements against corruption in local government: corrupt legal practices, decisions which undermine the interests of the landless, misappropriation of wheat from food for work and food for education programmes, false cases.	26	17	62	20	125
Establishment of rights over local resources, including *khas* land, water reservoirs, regaining possession of disposed land, etc.	30	26	58	203	317
Environmental issues: resistance to spread of saline shrimp culture; excessive use of chemical fertilizer and pesticides.	52	28	8	13	101
Resistance to attacks and harassment by local power holders, including eviction of the landless, illegal harvesting of their paddy, burning their houses, physical assault etc.	76	36	69	44	225
Protesting micro-credit malpractice	6	7	17	8	38
Fundamentalists/ *Fatwabaz*.	6	6	10	14	36
Wage-related struggles.	22	13	22	26	83
Total	267	170	394	384	1215

Source: NK Annual Reports

Social mobilization

Collective action around social issues concerns attempts to bring about change in the sphere of family, community and civil society. Gender-related violations of rights constitute the most frequent cause of collective action after economic struggles. These include such practices as verbal marital repudiation, polygamy, child marriage, dowry and violence against women. Where such violations occur within families of group members, they are addressed through group action such as threat of ostracism or group adjudication. Where they occur outside the group, members resort to protests and campaigns, as well as legal action or the threat of it.

Evidence from Ali *et al.* (1998) suggests that NK members reported lower likelihood of marriages with dowry, fewer polygamous marriages and a greater likelihood of legal divorce as opposed to verbal repudiation. They also note that NK women were more likely to take action against violations of their rights than non-members: pressuring rural elites to ensure that women's rights were respected during *shalish* (village tribunal) hearings; filing cases with courts of law; and public mobilization and signature campaigns to ensure fair trials and so on. According to one of the women we interviewed, their group activism around gender violence may have served to curtail its incidence. The fact that NK groups were prepared to demonstrate to demand justice for incidents of violence that had occurred in other districts warned those contemplating such acts to be careful: 'They will know that we are protesting about incidents in faraway places; they are getting proof that our organization is strong; as such, they won't have the same courage as before to commit such acts'.

NK's activism on gender issues has brought its members into direct conflict with local mullahs, who use *fatwas* (religious pronouncements) as weapons of social control. Since mullahs rely on village elites for their livelihoods, their pronouncements are rarely impartial. *Fatwas* usually concern issues of morality and tend to be directed against women, although they may also implicate men. Here again, NK training and group activities have helped their members to challenge the (mis)use of religious authority to uphold class and gender privilege. NK members believe that local religious leaders have become more circumspect in their interpretation of religious law in areas where NK groups are active because they know they are dealing with a more informed population. Group members, in turn, know that not everything that the mullahs claim in the name of religion has the sanction of religious texts (Netherlands Ministry of Foreign Affairs 1998).

NK groups have also challenged the impartiality of the *shalish*, which is often used by the powerful sections of village society to discipline, punish and dispossess the weak. NK members are now often invited to participate in *shalishes* to represent the interests of the poor. In many villages, they have set up their own *shalishes* to settle disputes, thus creating a parallel structure of jurisdiction. In one of the areas studied by Christensen (1999), around 90 per cent of *shalishes* were organised by NK groups, suggesting that confidence in the NK *shalish* procedure to dispense justice extended considerably beyond its group members. The NK *shalish* often overturned the verdict of the village *shalish* or came to the aid of those who had been unfairly treated (Khan and Khan 2000).

NK group action to assert their entitlement to legally-set wage norms on government food-for-work programmes can be seen as part of a wider movement on the part of the organization to hold the public sector accountable to its poorer constituency. My field interviews with NK group members suggested that they were aware not only of their *rights* as citizens, but also of their *contributions* as citizens. They saw the variety of indirect taxes and tolls that they had to pay – to purchase certain essential goods, to use bridges and public highways, to sell their wares in the market-place – as their contribution to the public budget and the basis on which they could demand their entitlements, as well as greater accountability on the part of government servants.

The demand for greater accountability has led NK groups to organize against those who are officially responsible for ensuring service delivery. Case studies of such actions can be found in most studies or reports on NK, and also came up during my brief period of fieldwork. They included a campaign against a local hospital that had not given proper treatment to a member; a refusal to pay the illicit fees routinely charged by health officials; a demand for compensation from the railway department for land that had been acquired to build railways; successful pressure on a local administration to locate cyclone shelters within easy reach of the landless; and group monitoring of the distribution of vulnerable group feeding cards and other relief programmes administered by local government (Ali *et al.* 1998; Khan and Khan 2000; Rao and Hashemi 1999).

Political mobilization

While much of what NK does is political in nature, actual participation in the formal political domain was not a priority in its early years. However, this has changed as the initiation of a limited process of decentralization offers more opportunities at the local level. NK has increased the number of group members it fields as candidates in areas where it is strong, while it actively mobilizes support for pro-poor candidates, regardless of their party affiliations, in other areas. It has used its political clout wherever possible to demand that those running for local and national elections explain the policies they stand for.

Political awareness appears to be higher among NK members. Ali *et al.* (1998) found that NK members were less likely to have voted in the national elections according to the *mattaabars'* (rural elite) wishes and more likely to have voted along political party lines. NK women were less likely to vote according to husbands' wishes than non-NK women, particularly in local elections. They were also more likely to have engaged in political mobilization than non-NK women. NK group members I interviewed offered the fact that they no longer 'sold' their votes as an indicator of their greater political awareness.

In their case study of local election politics in one district in Bangladesh, Westergaard and Hossain (2002) found that NK members were approached for their support by many candidates from middle-income groups, suggesting that the poor were becoming a local power factor to be reckoned with. This, as much as the number of seats they won, was a measure of their effectiveness as a political force. The authors concluded that clientelist relations of domination were weakening in the area as a result of the exploitation of new political opportunities by advocacy NGOs like NK, and the emergent political agency of mobilized groups of the poor (p. 229).

Growing citizenship from the grassroots: NK as agent of social change in Bangladesh

NK positions itself as an agent of social change in Bangladesh, challenging deep-rooted inequalities within the wider society through the provision of intangible resources, such as information, ideas and knowledge, which build the 'collective capabilities' of the poor: their ability to mobilize as rights-bearing citizens on their own behalf. The unevenness of its impact reflects the contradictory nature of the environment it is operating in. On the one hand, it is dealing with extremely resilient structures of constraint, which have an in-built tendency to reproduce themselves. Wood (2000), for instance, has suggested that these structures constitute a 'prison', whose inmates must accept the prevailing rules in order to survive, despite the fact that these rules perpetuate the arbitrary and inequitable nature of the social order.

On the other hand, however, there have been a number of changes in the institutional environment of Bangladesh that have been conducive to the project of social mobilization. Economic growth in recent years has been accompanied by a gradual decline in poverty but a fairly rapid rise in levels of social development and a diversification of

economic opportunities. One result of this is that poor people are no longer as dependent for work on a few powerful landlords as they used to be. Nor are they dependent on them for credit, partly because of their improved earning capacity and partly because of the proliferation of micro-credit organizations. Migration as a source of livelihood has also taken them out of the orbit of local power structures.

These changes have combined to weaken earlier patron–client relationships, as poorer sections of rural society are less likely to see an advantage in blind loyalty to powerful elites. In addition, the transition to democracy and the opening up of new opportunities in local political structures have served to bring participation in certain forms of decision-making closer to realities at the local level, while the spread of education has undermined the culture of deference that characterized relations between the powerful and the weak.

While some of these changes reflect the hidden workings of economy and society, others have been the product of purposive efforts to influence the direction and quality of change by a variety of institutional actors. The thriving NGO sector has clearly been at the forefront of these efforts, engaging with different sections of the poor in order to build their capacity to participate in newly emergent spaces. By providing alternative models of social relations that diverge to a greater or lesser degree from the earlier hierarchical models, and by disseminating new norms which help to counter older, disempowering ones, NGOs can be credited with helping to democratize the processes of social change in the country.

However, as we noted at the outset, NGOs do not constitute a homogeneous sector, and it is worth reflecting on what their differing visions, goals and strategies might imply for the kind of society that Bangladesh is evolving into. There is clearly a difference between the models of change adhered to by NGOs that focus on individual empowerment through the provision of various resources and services, and models of change that focus on collective empowerment through social mobilization, as embodied by NK.

This difference in approach reflects differences in underlying worldviews. The first is closer to the neo-liberal worldview, in which rational, self-interested individuals seek to improve their lives through the pursuit of a greater share of material goods. Competition arises because the availability of material goods is finite, but structural conflict is ruled out. Change occurs incrementally as individuals adjust to new constraints and respond to new opportunities. NK's approach, on the other hand, is very clearly rooted in a 'critical conflict' worldview. It sees the problems of society as rooted in structures that reproduce

inequalities on a systemic basis. Change can only come about through challenges to these structures, and can take a confrontational form because of the resistance likely to be encountered from those who benefit from the *status quo*.

There is no doubt that the efforts of various NGOs in providing credit and social services have played an important role in bringing about change in the lives of the poor and marginalized. However, many of these interventions have failed, because of their individualist focus, to have much effect on the deeper structures of inequality. Any improvements they may achieve in the lives of individuals are constantly undermined by various forms of unruly practice on the part of more powerful sections of society.

Moreover, the ability of NGOs to seek greater accountability to the poor on the part of government is often compromised by their own role in service delivery. A recent World Bank report on corruption in Bangladesh made this point, noting that while NGOs can play an important role in monitoring and checking government corruption, they are likely to be most effective when they do not attempt to combine this watchdog role with participation in government-funded development and service delivery programmes. The point is also made by Thornton *et al.* (2000), who note that there is a basic tension between NGO service delivery organizations (whether government-funded or not) and their capacity to demand accountability and responsiveness from public sector services.

This was precisely the rationale behind NK's decision from the outset to eschew any form of direct delivery role, leaving this to the government and other institutions. However, while NK sees the state as the only institution with the reach, the authority and the mandate to uphold the basic rights of *all* citizens, it also recognizes that the state in Bangladesh is unlikely to perform this role as long as it is dominated by powerful interests who benefit from the *status quo* and have neither the incentive nor the sanction to lead a process of change. Pressure for such change must come from those outside the state who have no stake in the *status quo*.

This is the role that NK sees for itself. By providing the poor and marginalized with knowledge about their rights, and with some degree of security in their dealings with more powerful sections of society, it seeks to shape the direction of social change through the purposive collective agency of the poor, rather than leaving it to the 'unintended consequences' of market forces or the arbitrary actions of the state. And while the size of the organization limits the scale of the change it is able to bring about, there is certainly evidence that NK's impact goes

beyond the immediate confines of its group members. Rao and Hashemi observe that the actions of NK groups in challenging instances of economic injustice have far-reaching implications, both 'in terms of increasing group solidarity as well as exhibiting the power of organisation to other poor people as well as the rural elite' (1999, p. 28). Similarly, Christensen notes that NK group mobilization around gender injustice may be leading to important changes in what are perceived as acceptable norms of behaviour: 'This change in social norms is directly linked to women's greater acknowledgement of their *rights*. They have learnt that there are rules beyond the jurisdiction of their kin and the village *shalish* that recognise rural poor women and protect them. The language of the law allows them to invoke the law to their advantage in family conflicts as well as in village struggles' (1999, p. 55).

Moreover, the transformative effects associated with membership of organizations like NK can continue long after the group may have disbanded: 'The rights of the poor may still get trampled but they do not get ignored' (Rao and Hashemi 1999, p. 35). This is because what members learned through their membership – including the possibility of challenging injustice and the hope for a better future – is not easily forgotten or abandoned. I end the chapter with what two NK members had to say on this matter:

> If I was to talk about the main strength of our struggle, I would say that before, we poor people did not realize many things. My father was a sharecropper, that is also what I did. We used to think that we would have to spend our days doing what our fathers had done. Those with assets would make money. The poor would remain poor. Since joining Nijera Kori, I have come to know the poor are not born poor, they are made poor through exploitation. They too have a right to what there is in society. As citizens of Bangladesh, the constitution gives them the right to food, shelter, education, health and housing.
>
> Nijera Kori may not be there in the future, but its ideals and objectives will remain with us. Our main strength lies in our organizational base. NK works as our umbrella. But if in the future it ceases to exist, even then the landless associations will be able to survive because of their strong identity. The basis of our existence will be what the members have learned about the difference between what is just and what is unjust.

Notes

1. I would like to thank Arif Kabir, who carried out a number of the interviews cited in this chapter.
2. Although its founding members had all been active in the field since independence in 1971 (Kabeer 2003).
3. TNO stands for Thana.

References

Ahmed, M. (1982) 'Nijera Kori in retrospect: In search of an organisation of the rural poor', Dhaka: Nijera Kori

Ali, A. K. M. Masud, A. K. M. Mustaque Ali and R. Sarkar (1998) 'Struggle in the northern plains: An impact evaluation of Nijera Kori Program in Bagatipara', prepared for the Swallows, Dhaka: INCIDIN

Christensen, R. (1999) 'Social capital in Bangladesh: Prospects and constraints', M.Sc. dissertation, Department of Political Science, University of Aarhus, Denmark

Dunn, J., P. Gain, S. Hossain, and D. Hubert (2000) 'Human rights and democracy in Bangladesh: Context for a strategy', prepared for the Royal Norwegian Embassy, Dhaka: Verulam Associates

Kabeer, N. (2003) 'Making rights work for the poor: Nijera Kori and the construction of "collective capabilities" in rural Bangladesh', IDS Working Paper No. 200

Khan, Z. R. and M. I. Khan (2000) *Field Assessment of Nijera Kori*, University of Dhaka, Dhaka

Netherlands Ministry of Foreign Affairs (1998) 'Evaluation of the Netherlands Development Programme with Bangladesh 1972–1996: Sub-report 19. Evaluation of Netherlands-funded NGOs 1972–1996', Dhaka

Rao, A. and S. H. Hashemi (1999) 'Institutional take-off or snakes and ladders', *INTRAC Occasional Papers Series* No. 30, Oxford: INTRAC

Thornton, P., J. Devine, P. Houtzager, D. Wright and S. Rozari (2000) 'Partners in development: A review of big NGOs in Bangladesh', prepared for DFID, Bangladesh

Westergaard, K. and A. Hossain (2002) 'Local institutions in Bangladesh: An analysis of civil society and local elections', in N. Webster and L. Engberg-Pedersen (eds) *In the Name of the Poor: Contesting Political Space for Poverty Reduction*, Zed Books: London

Wood, G. (2000) 'Prisoners and escapees: Improving the institutional responsibility square in Bangladesh', *Public Administration and Development* 20, pp. 221–37

World Bank (2000) *Corruption in Bangladesh: Costs and Cures*, Dhaka: World Bank

Constructing citizenship without a licence: the struggle of undocumented immigrants in the USA for livelihoods and recognition

Fran Ansley

This chapter tells the story of a legislative campaign mounted by immigrants and their allies in Tennessee, a state in the southeastern USA that has experienced a dramatic new wave of low-wage labour migration from Latin America. The campaign fought successfully for access to a state-issued driver's licence for people who could not produce proof of lawful presence in the USA. Far from focusing overtly on the 'meanings and expressions of citizenship', this effort was initiated by and designed to benefit a population of *non*-citizens. Moreover, at least in its public aspect and public rhetorical strategies, it seldom mentioned anything remotely like 'rights'. Nonetheless, the campaign and its aftermath should be of interest to those who believe that traditional ideas about citizenship and its attendant rights and duties need to be re-imagined for a global age.

The presence of low-wage Southern immigrants in the wealthy countries of the North creates a space where the contradictions of uneven development are manifested in a particularly striking way; this space offers important learning opportunities for students of citizenship. Efforts like these, where transnational migrants attempt to improve their material and legal standing, occur at a site where traditional ideas of national or territorial citizenship come into particularly sharp confrontation with the new dynamics of accelerating globalization. Since they are being initiated by some of the people most directly and adversely affected by global dynamics, these efforts provide an opportunity for scholars to listen to how such people perceive and define the unprecedented problems they face, and to see what kinds of solutions they have begun to propose. Sometimes the most interesting of such efforts will be those that are just emerging and least shaped into demands that fit existing templates.

Another reason these pro-immigrant campaigns are valuable and worthy of study is that they pose important questions about who in the global economy has the 'right to have rights' in the first place. They press more of the native-born to consider the exclusionary, 'fortress' side of Northern citizenship in today's world.

The first section of the chapter will provide some historical and factual backdrop for the Tennessee campaign. The second section will sketch some highlights of the campaign itself – or rather, of the campaign up to summer 2003, since the story is far from over. The third section will offer some reflections and tentative conclusions.

Background

Historical boundaries of US citizenship

Citizenship means many things, of course. Sometimes it signifies a formal, legal status, and, at other times, a substantive set of citizenly obligations and rights. Both of these meanings have been at the centre of past struggles for social justice in America, movements whose successes and failures alike have profoundly affected the nation's history and character.

The question of citizenship as formal legal status was a major theme during the fight to abolish and dismantle slavery, and in the process of resolving the status of peoples taken over in expansionist moments of US history. In the infamous 1856 Dred Scott case, for instance, the US Supreme Court ruled that American blacks 'are not included, and were not intended to be included, under the word "citizens" in the Constitution, and can therefore claim none of the rights and privileges which that instrument provides for and secures to citizens of the United States'.[1] It took a prolonged period of legal and extra-legal struggle before American black people won their freedom and formal citizenship under an amended constitution, and the twentieth century was half over before the basic political and civil rights of African-Americans were recognized or enforced in any serious way (Bell 2000; Foner 1988). American Indians and Puerto Ricans are only two of many groups that have been subsumed under formal US control, but whose relation to status citizenship has been circuitous and uneven (Prucha 1986; Roman 1997).

Other great arenas for contestation about status citizenship in America have been immigration and naturalization (Saito 1997). For example, the right to become a naturalized citizen was limited by federal law to 'white persons' in the Naturalization Act of 1790, a restriction not formally repealed until the mid-twentieth century (Lopez 1996). Similarly, the right to immigrate (a predicate to any later naturalization) has been subject to a long train of overtly race-based restrictions, stretching from the Chinese Exclusion Act of 1882 through to the national quota systems that were not finally abolished until 1965 (Neuman 1996). Those targeted by these exclusions did what they could to oppose them, but successes were limited (McClain 1994; Rosales 1999). To the present day, the Supreme Court remains highly deferential toward legislative action by the US Congress in this area. The Court takes the position that Congress has 'plenary power' over immigration and naturalization questions, and its exercise should not be subjected to the same standards of judicial review that the Court would apply in almost any other context (Motomura 1990; Wu 1996).

Of course, much social justice work in the USA has focused on the proper *substance* of the rights to be enjoyed by citizens, not on the formal criteria for who was eligible to be one. Organizations and citizens' movements have worked to deepen the substance of the citizenship rights accorded to groups that have been subjected to subordinating or marginalizing practices of different kinds. In good times, they have fought for more expansive understandings about things that all citizens should be able to expect from the state and from each other, and in bad times they have defended what rights they had against incursions by public and private power. While these struggles over the substance of citizenship went forward, the categories and divisions associated with outsiders' access to the status of citizenship continued, although often at the margins of mainstream national consciousness.

Present context

Today we are in a period when the status of citizenship in the USA – the line between citizen and non-citizen – is back in the spotlight, and given the turbulent global conditions that presently prevail, the task of drawing and justifying such a line is likely to prove difficult in ways not felt before. A vibrant if embattled network of new groups has emerged, and older organizations have also begun to see that low-wage immigration presents both an opportunity and an imperative for those interested in organizing for justice (Delgado 1993; Milkman 2000). Meanwhile, working for immigrants' rights has become more difficult but also more important in the atmosphere that gripped the nation after 11 September 2001 (Lawyers Committee for Human Rights 2002; 2003). The campaign to win and then to defend immigrant access to the driver's licence in Tennessee is a case in point.

Agriculture originally dominated the Tennessee economy, but in more recent times, agriculture has been complemented and partly supplanted by a strong industrial sector concentrated largely in low-wage industries like garments, textiles and consumer electronics. Many manufacturing firms first moved to Tennessee from further north in search of the low wages, docile and unorganized workers and 'business-friendly' regulatory environment for which the southeast has long been known. Today, Tennessee is experiencing trends familiar elsewhere: agriculture is increasingly mechanized and concentrated in ever fewer hands; manufacturing is in rapid decline; the service sector is on the rise; and the proportion of the workforce that is organized into labour unions is steadily slipping.

While many manufacturing jobs have moved to lower-wage locations in Mexico and elsewhere, mass in-migration and settlement of low-wage Latina and Latino workers has emerged as a major demographic phenomenon (Lowell and Suro 2002).[2] New arrivals from the global South have been entering and transforming both labour markets and the texture of daily life in many communities, large and small (Fink 2003). In Tennessee, the overall number of Latinas and Latinos is still a relatively small percentage of the population, but they are nonetheless a striking new presence. In some counties, the growth has been especially dramatic, with attendant impacts on schools and other institutions that are ill-prepared to cope equitably or competently with the newcomers they are now challenged to serve (Mendoza 2002; Smith 2001).

I teach at a Tennessee law school, where post-baccalaureate students prepare for professional practice. In the course of my research and service with local community groups,[3] and while supervising students in field placements, I became interested in Latina and Latino newcomers. My students and I began searching out opportunities to talk with immigrants about their experiences with the legal system and about their need for legal services.

As we made contact, over and over we heard the same refrain. Three main concerns predominated, and the three were closely related.[4] First, the immigrants we spoke with wanted to understand their rights (or lack thereof) in situations where they were stopped or arrested by the police. Second, they wanted to know the circumstances under which such a stop or arrest might lead to an entanglement with the immigration authorities. Third, they wanted to tell us about the impossibility of getting a driver's licence, and to explain to us what a huge impact that was having on their lives. We learned that the law in Tennessee had recently changed, so that applicants for a licence now had to provide a social security number. (Only persons who are authorized to work in the USA are assigned such a number, and for the most part this means citizens and those who have been granted Legal Permanent Residency status, with its accompanying 'green card'.) The new law effectively barred undocumented immigrants from obtaining a licence to drive.

Such a bar was significant in ways that may be difficult for non-US readers to appreciate. In Tennessee, as in many other US locations, there is basically *no* local public transportation outside the tight central core of the larger cities. For the vast majority of people, including poor people, an automobile is a virtual necessity for even the simplest acts of daily existence, including the task of getting to and from one's place of work.

Our informants were eager to explain how the pieces of this situation fitted together into an oppressive whole that greatly magnified their vulnerability:

- All undocumented people were prohibited from getting a Tennessee driver's licence
- A significant percentage of the Latina/Latino community in Tennessee was undocumented
- The chances that any given person found 'driving while brown' would also be driving without a licence were therefore astronomically increased

The simple probabilities produced by these facts could not possibly escape the notice of law enforcement officials. Under the circumstances, it seemed that the temptation for a police officer to engage in racial profiling would be almost irresistible, whether they were interested in oppressing and harassing Latinas and Latinos, hustling a personal bribe or simply enforcing the law about driving without a licence. Stories confirming the frequency of such profiling were common fare in these conversations. It seemed that any Latino then at the wheel of a car in Tennessee both felt, and was, a target for police attention, abuse, or both.

Upon hearing these stories in the field, the black law students on my courses found it easier than the white students to identify with the apprehension expressed by immigrants toward the police. They also could better imagine the stress induced by the need for constant vigilance. But all of us, black and white alike, found it bizarre to think that at the conclusion of one of our discussion sessions – at some venue such as the prosaic, fluorescent-lit and linoleum-floored fellowship hall of the local Catholic church, for instance – one group of us would get into our automobiles and return to our homes routinely, with little or no apprehension that a police stop might change our lives. Meanwhile, another group would drive home as though players in some suspense-filled war movie about life under military occupation, eyes peeled for each police cruiser, stomachs jumpy with the knowledge that any random road block might spell economic and family disaster.

The campaign

As we came to find out, we were not the only people in Tennessee who were hearing these kinds of stories. A growing population of native-born people was developing an awareness about the existence and the situation of undocumented people. Many had become staunch supporters of the immigrant community and its right to live unmolested, and many appeared to be itching for something they could do about what they saw as harsh injustice. Not a single immigrants' rights organization was yet in existence in the state, however: no informal network, list of statewide contacts, phone tree, system of referrals. There were smaller networks where new knowledge about immigrants was starting to circulate, and where people were beginning to discuss issues, compare notes and express outrage. In the spring of 2001, the driver's licence campaign provided the seed around which these emerging trends and networks could crystallize.

An *ad hoc* statewide coalition emerged, drawing support from a broad range of likely and unlikely bedfellows. A website and e-mail lists were created, and the Tennessee campaign took advantage of then-nascent national networks that had identified the issue of the driver's licence as one that was worth the time of immigrants' rights advocates. In amazingly short order, the new coalition managed to put together a legislative campaign, move a bill through the general assembly, and secure the Republican governor's signature. The programme was implemented, and soon licences were being issued once again to undocumented immigrants in Tennessee. Within days, throngs of Latinas and Latinos descended on licensing stations. Native-born people, who had not paid that much attention to immigration dynamics, got quite a jolt if they happened to show up to get their licence during that period. But the initial bottlenecks soon passed, and a new normalcy appeared to have taken hold.

Many people involved in the effort, myself included, admitted to being somewhat dumbfounded at the campaign's success. Several had been dubious about the prospects of securing this reform, especially given the conservative tenor of the Tennessee legislature and the reservoirs of anti-immigrant feeling that advocates had reason to believe existed in the state. The concerns of these doubters were not ill-founded. For instance, anti-immigrant groups in the state scrambled to respond to our campaign, and soon after the bill's passage launched a repeal effort. Then when the World Trade Center was attacked a few short months later, the impacts were wide and deep. Anger and fear among the native-born were epidemic, and immigrants of all kinds became the objects of widespread fear and suspicion.

Despite the post-9/11 climate, the pro-immigrant forces in Tennessee have succeeded so far in maintaining immigrant access to the driver's licence. However, access is now more burdened, in that people without a social security number have that fact flagged on the front of their licences. Nevertheless, our initial success, and our ability to resist full-scale repeal after 9/11, represent important victories. Several factors helped to secure them.

Perhaps the most basic contribution is that Latina and Latino immigrants themselves, together with their transnational family and friendship networks, laid the basic foundation, without which nothing would have been possible. The mass migration from Latin America to the USA is itself quite a multi-generational feat of human adventure and engineering, and it has been accomplished against stiff odds and despite sometimes intense repression, intimidation and harassment.[5] Once here, these legions of low-wage immigrants have built relationships and 'proved' themselves in ways that contain plenty of irony and ambiguity, but in any event have created a multitude of potential patrons and allies.

Second, we succeeded (to the limited and still unstable extent that we did) because the time was right. In many communities, the Latino population had reached sufficient critical mass to create free spaces for communication and planning – in places like Latino groceries, Hispanic church services, scattered radio stations and small newspapers around the state. Meanwhile, among the native-born population, the anti-immigrant forces were still relatively quiescent, but pro-immigrant individuals and emergent networks were ready and eager to sink their teeth into a concrete project. As a result, when we organized visits to the state legislature in Nashville and made our calls to legislative offices, our side represented the vast majority of contacts the legislators were receiving.

Third, we learned that support for immigrants can come from unexpected quarters. Agricultural employers, the Nashville Chamber of Commerce and the police chiefs of several major cities were on our side, in addition to more accustomed allies like church groups, service providers, civil rights organizations, labour unions and social justice groups. These unusual bedfellows had political clout, and they offered cover for legislators that the 'human rights types' could never have mustered alone. The eagerness of the Republican Party to establish ties to the Latino community undoubtedly had some influence on the outcome, increasing the willingness of our Republican governor to sign the bill into law, and later to defend it from full repeal.

A final reason I believe we won this struggle for the rights of undocumented workers in Tennessee is that we did not frame the campaign as a struggle for rights at all. Instead, at least in its visible, public face, the campaign was framed almost entirely around the desires, interests and preferences of US citizens. For instance, the *ad hoc* group that we created to push the reform was called 'Health and Safety for Tennessee Highways'. That group developed talking points that stressed things like the value of having these potentially dangerous Latino drivers properly trained, tested, licenced and insured. It also pointed out that if undocumented immigrants possessed a driver's licence, they could be tracked down more easily by police. The central messages developed by organizers focused on the training, testing and insurability of immigrant drivers, on disruptions to local business and commerce, and on the cost to the state government of forgoing licence-related fees paid by immigrants and of volunteering to shoulder the duties of federal immigration law enforcement.

The choice of a frame that left immigrants themselves so decidedly in the shadows was not uncontroversial within the campaign, but it represented a clear majority of opinion among those who developed the strategy. Certainly, the highway safety issues were not trumped up. The statistics about deaths and injuries in car crashes involving Latina and Latino immigrant motorists are alarming, and the number of people – native-born and immigrant alike – who drive uninsured in Tennessee is a scandal. Nevertheless, most people who threw themselves into our campaign did not come to it out of an involvement in issues of highway safety, but because of a strong concern for immigrants' needs and rights. The decision to frame the issue as one of highway safety grew out of the organizers' conviction that putting immigrants' rights or their welfare at the centre of the campaign (or even out toward its margins, if openly expressed) would be the kiss of death. Although I was among those who questioned this decision, in retrospect I believe we probably would have lost the campaign had we pursued a more rights-oriented or immigrant-centred approach.

For all those involved, the decision was made easier by our know-ledge of the acute difference that this particular concrete reform could make in the lives of people we knew. It would magnify freedom and decrease terror for sizeable numbers of people we knew and cared for. It seemed that success on this issue would be an educational and confidence-building win for the immigrant community, even if the framing and the official rhetoric deployed in the campaign pretty thoroughly ignored the issue of justice for immigrants.

Of course, the dilemma we faced was hardly unique. Most legislative campaigns involve trade-offs and choices about long-term goals and short-term realities. Efforts at organizing relatively powerless people from below will always have to wrestle with how much to highlight the rights or needs of the weak, and how much to appeal to the self-interest of the strong – including potential allies who have more resources and clout, as well as the decision-makers themselves. Legislative campaigns that aim to benefit undocumented immigrants are especially likely to raise these questions because such campaigns are situated at the fault-line over who should have even the 'right to have rights'. After all, undocumented immigrants cannot vote, and are therefore not part of the constituency to which an elected legislator owes formal account-ability. Further, significant numbers of the people who *are* part of the legislator's formal constituency are likely to view the concerns and well-being of non-citizens as an illegitimate object of their representative's concern.

Nevertheless, within and beneath this 'non-rights campaign', many issues of rights, justice and morality did indeed emerge. Individual campaigners with whom I have spoken echoed my own experience that actual conversations often led us naturally beyond the official theme of safety and security for native Tennesseans, and provided openings – some small and subtle, others more generous and clear – for telling other kinds of stories, and pressing other kinds of arguments. In fact, no matter what the public rhetoric on either side, everyone understood that beneath the announced issues lay a mass of other questions that profoundly challenged the current immigration regime. In any case, once the anti-immigrant organizations began to get themselves in gear, there was no way entirely to ignore the issues of immigration policy, even if the campaign had been unambivalent in wanting to do just that.

So in the end, this last ingredient of our success is something of a paradox. We did create and stick with a credible public frame that spoke to citizens and legislators about their own self-interest, and I believe that probably contributed to the success of the campaign. At the same time, the choice of this public frame was not as narrowing or chauvinistic as it may sound, because in actuality it did not banish more immigrant-centred conversations and frames from playing an important role in the life of the campaign. Sometimes by choice and sometimes by necessity, the campaign did create a space for public debate and dialogue with native-born Tennesseans about the immigrant community that has grown up in our midst, and about the justice or injustice of its circumstances.

In fact the campaign's role as the start of something bigger may be the most important point to make here. In preparation for this chapter, I contacted a number of people who had been active in the 2001 campaign and asked them for their present thoughts. All of them were pleased and proud of the victory that was won, but also acutely aware of its continuing fragility. Each remarked with amazement how gratifying it had been to participate in something that created such a dramatic, concrete change for the better in the lives of so many vulnerable people. On one final point they were particularly vocal. The best thing about the campaign, they said, was that it enabled immigrants and their supporters around the state to find each other and to begin building longer-term relationships and collaborations.

Tennessee is now home to a formal organization, the Tennessee Immigrant and Refugee Rights Coalition. It has a budget and a (very modestly) paid staff, and it holds regular state-wide meetings. The Coalition continues to be involved in the question of the driver's licence, but its agenda is now much broader and it speaks out regularly on many issues of concern to immigrants and refugees. These days, more meetings are conducted in Spanish,[6] and more leadership roles are filled by immigrants and refugees themselves than in the early days of the campaign, when most of the co-ordination was provided by citizen allies rather than by immigrants themselves. The challenges that lie ahead are serious ones, but networks and relationships among people interested in fighting for immigrants' rights are substantially ahead of where they were when the driver's licence campaign began.

Meanings and expressions of citizenship

The final section of this chapter will step back from the immediate facts of the driver's licence campaign, to ask what lessons we might take from it about the meanings and expressions of citizenship. I am looking for lessons that will advance what I take to be the fundamental project of this book: building knowledge that can be put to use by scholars and activists who want to help mount democratic, bottom-up challenges to social exclusion and injustice.

The discussion here will assume that ideas of 'citizenship' and of 'rights' are neither good nor bad in themselves. Although the concept of citizenship and the rights attendant to it may offer helpful resources for winning a more democratic, open and sustainable order (Johnston

2002; Mouffe 1992, 1993), it sometimes can and has been used for very different ends. So my question is not *whether* rights-based approaches associated with citizenship can be useful to the project I have named, but rather when, how, and under what circumstances they are most likely to be useful – or not.

The Tennessee driver's licence campaign is a paradoxical but significant site for studying rights and citizenship. It was part of a wider mobilization that continues today in the USA; one in which undocumented immigrants – people with no standing as US citizens or even as legal residents – are 'making a way out of no way',[7] offering the rest of us much-needed windows on to the global landscape, demonstrating new models, and inviting us to reinvent our own citizenship (Hair 2001; Smith and Sugimori 2003).

In many instances, those involved in this mobilization are not claiming formal legal rights, because in the context at hand they cannot point to any officially recognized rights that are available for them to claim. To be sure, there are some justiciable protections, constitutional and otherwise, that apply to immigrants in the USA (Chin, Romero and Scaperlanda 2000). Further, a number of immigrants' rights groups are attempting to win new, formally recognized rights for immigrants in specific contexts, such as access to higher education, and broader regularization of guestworkers in agriculture. Nevertheless, much of the activity pursued on behalf of immigrant welfare is pursued by necessity in a landscape of 'no rights'.

One might characterize the larger context for these campaigns as a large-scale, decentralized social experiment that combines diverse elements, including:

- The mass migration itself, which can in some ways be best appreciated as a kind of collective civil disobedience
- Political mobilizations and community and labour organizing efforts carried out with various allies (including communities of native-born and naturalized Latinas and Latinos in some regions of the country, as well as church groups, civil rights organizations and labour unions)[8]
- The building of social and economic capital through a thicket of relationships and channels that are fusing immigrants into society in ways that already appear impossible ever to undo.

The loose national network of driver's licence campaigns across the USA provides a vivid example of the still-emergent, still-inchoate work of building new claims suited to our new global economy. Sometimes such claims are based on formally realizable rights; at others they may only hint toward a possible future. Sometimes, instead of invoking rights, campaigns speak forcefully of needs, or of higher principles beyond existing domestic or international norms, or of the self-interest of those in a position to grant rights or mere concessions.

In any case, these campaigns provide spaces where immigrants are objecting to their exclusion from the licensing system, telling stories about what it means to lack a formal 'identity' sufficient to grant access to the normal workings of the national economy in which one labours. Such campaigns allow immigrants to describe in arresting detail the irrationality and strain of their situation: thoroughly integrated into the mundane workings of the aboveground economy, and at the same time legally excluded, forced to traverse daily an uneven and unpredictable minefield of simultaneous normalcy and criminality. In providing the rest of us with these narratives, immigrants help themselves and us to imagine the human rights we need for our new global condition.

There is no assurance that all immigrants' rights movements in the USA will smoothly advance toward stronger rights, or that they will develop in ways that challenge rather than sustain existing power relations. But current campaigns for access to the driver's licence are one part of a pre-legal, pre-institutional process that is helping to incubate novel rights claims appropriate for the new economy. In what follows I will sketch three citizenship norms that may be prefigured in current discussions and dialogue growing out of these concrete struggles.

The full right to international mobility of human beings

A full right to human mobility across international borders is a radical idea, one whose realization would require a direct assault on the notion that the unfettered authority to exclude non-citizens is an essential feature of national sovereignty. (Even the United Nations's International Convention on the Protection of the Rights of All Migrant Workers and Members of Their Families, which entered into force in 2003 and is a welcome new development, only guarantees international mobility as the right to *leave* any state, plus the right to return to one's country of origin.) In the US context, full international mobility would also require a confrontation with deep patterns of white racial privilege that run through the nation's legal and social history.

Nevertheless, the idea of radically more open borders has proved to be a difficult claim for wealthy states entirely to shake off, in part because it points up the sharp contradiction embedded in free trade regimes such as the North American Free Trade Agreement (NAFTA) that force signatory states to submit to the free flow of goods, capital and services but do not similarly protect the free flow of people. Whether despite or because of its unsettling implications, the call for open borders seems always just beneath the surface of every conversation on immigration. It appears simultaneously to be the only logical solution and – at least at present – a political impossibility.

The right to identity

Another emergent claim of right that may be gestating in the driver's licence campaign is a 'right to identity' – something like a transnational right to recognition of a migrating person's identity and origin. In today's high-tech world, this would include a right of entry into the computerized identity systems that exist at a national and sub-national level all over the world, but most hegemonically in core countries. Undocumented immigrants teach us that the lack of capacity to identify oneself in the information economy can be a devastating disability. Immigrants in the USA want a driver's licence first and foremost so they can engage in daily travel with less vulnerability. But many of them also want such a licence because it serves as a general identity document, needed nowadays for everything from renting a video to flying back home for a parent's funeral.

A US social security number is generally available only to citizens or legal permanent residents. In recent years, its uses have expanded, and it is now demanded for an increasing range of public and private transactions and background checks. Undocumented immigrants are by definition excluded from access to this powerful number, and yet they encounter multitudinous situations where proof of identity is required. Accordingly, both from immigrants themselves and from those who have dealings with them, the pressure for some method of identification has become intense.

Troubling questions surround the notion of a right to identity like the one sketched here. How would such a right relate to the emerging US security state and its powerful new information technologies? Surely there is some irony in the idea of vulnerable people clamouring for admittance to a computerized system that will subject them to more efficient surveillance by a hostile and powerful foreign state. Given the dramatic erosion of the rights and liberties of both citizens and non-citizens that has accompanied the Bush administration's announced war on terrorism, the cost of being integrated into state licensing systems warrants thoughtful deliberation. Still, the cost of *not* being included is also demonstrably high, as we learned from immigrant narratives in Tennessee. This dilemma about the costs of entry into information systems mirrors similar painful choices about global economic integration that presently confront poor people and poor countries around the world.

Duties of citizenship in a globalizing world

If immigrants' rights activism in countries of the North provides a hospitable environment for imagining and incubating new rights, these settings may also provide important laboratories for discerning the *duties* that should attend new conditions of global economic integration.

Some duties suggested by the situation of transnational low-wage workers make up the duties of the powerful. As many have argued, in a just legal order the shape of both rights and duties would be determined with pointed reference to power relations and would be designed to reduce and repair illegitimate disparities. With super-powers, they imply, should come super-responsibilities (Matsuda 1991; Stammers 1999). For instance, given the role that the USA has played in shaping and constraining the economies of most countries in the world, perhaps it should recognize a specifically *American* duty to admit many more economic refugees for secure and dignified employment in the USA. However, although pre-eminent, the USA is not alone in its disproportionate influence on the fate of other countries. Perhaps all the nations of the global North should take on co-ordinated duties of admission, keyed to their respective powers and histories. History-conscious, post-colonial immigration practices by some European states offer imperfect models for thinking about how such duties might be framed.

The facts of immigrants' lives also suggest that duties toward transnational migrants do not reside with states alone. Exercises of private power can affect labour migration as greatly as do exercises of state power. Accordingly, both the pushes and the pulls that affect global migrant streams point to other duty-bearers, such as multinational corporations, international financial institutions and the public/private machineries that create, embody and administer international trade agreements.

Immigrants' rights struggles also require citizens of the North to think about their own duties as persons who are in a position of relative privilege as compared to citizens of poorer countries. To be sure, workers and low-income people in the USA have many interests that are significantly aligned or at least overlapping with those of workers in other countries. But even they enjoy privileges and powers whose parameters they are seldom able to appreciate without the perspective added by looking through the eyes of others. The cauldron of immigrants' rights struggles provides one place where First World citizens can begin to discern something more about their privileges and the duties they should imply.

Speculation about pockets of immigrant activism helping to incubate not only new global rights but also new 'duties of global solidarity', takes me far beyond the Tennessee campaign for the driver's licence. As someone who learned much from being a participant observer in the one small campaign described here, I can say with confidence that many native-born citizens who become involved with immigrants – in fights that range from the mundane to the sublime – have been profoundly changed by the experience. For the most part, Americans have precious little knowledge of our own nation's immigration law, few experiences that help us understand the role our government and corporations play abroad, little familiarity with international institutions that our government dominates, and only the thinnest exposure to cultures and languages other than our own. The driver's licence fight gave many Tennesseans a chance to start knowing more about these things and to consider our own responsibilities as citizens of a thoroughly fractured and connected world.

Notes

1. Dred Scott v. Sandford, 60 U.S. 393, 404 (1856).
2. Demographics are intently watched in the USA, given their relationship to racial politics. The US Census reported that the US Hispanic population grew by 57.9 per cent between 1990 and 2000, as compared with 13.2 per cent for the population as a whole. Over half were of Mexican origin (Guzman 2001).
3. For more background on this research, on my organizational collaborator (the Tennessee Industrial Renewal Network, now renamed the Tennessee Economic Renewal Network), and on my experiences as a participant observer in some of the organization's work, see Ansley (2001); TIRN (1993).
4. The issues centred on the concerns of undocumented people, so it may be worth pointing out that many of the people we spoke to in this information-gathering process were 'legal'; that is, many of them were lawfully present in the USA and also entitled to work, because they were birthright citizens or naturalized citizens, or because they had been granted Legal Permanent Resident status, which entitled them to a (non-green) 'green card' and a social security number. But all of them, legal or not, made it clear that the concerns of the undocumented were questions of the highest priority. The vast majority, even if they were lawfully present themselves, had family members or close friends who were undocumented. In any case, the operating assumption seemed to be that the treatment accorded to undocumented immigrants directly affected all other members of the Latino community.
5. I do not mean to suggest that all Latina/Latino immigrants to the USA consider themselves to be part of a social movement for rights or any other organized social project. Latino immigrants are an extremely diverse group. They come to the USA with many different goals; they subscribe to many different ideologies and dreams; they bring with them many different levels of resources; and they are changed in many different ways after they arrive.
6. The Coalition's membership is not limited to English and Spanish speakers, nor is

it limited to issues of concern to the Latina/Latino community. There are active participants from Africa, the Middle East, Asia and Eastern Europe, and their issues are prominent on the agenda of the Coalition. Nevertheless, Spanish is by far the most numerically significant minority language spoken in the Coalition and in the state.

7. This lovely phrase is one passed on by American labour and civil rights historian Michael Honey (1999, p. 86).

8. Recently, the American Federation of Labor and Congress of Industrial Organizations (AFL-CIO), the nation's largest labour federation, announced a sharp reversal of its previous restrictive position on immigration. Now, the federation and many of its union affiliates are campaigning for broader legalization programmes and are actively recruiting among immigrant workers (Nissen 2002). Of course, many difficulties and questions about the future of organized labour and its relationship to immigrant workers remain.

References

Ansley, F. (2001) 'Inclusive boundaries and other (im)possible paths toward community development in a global world', *University of Pennsylvania Law Review* 150, pp. 353–417

Bell, D. (2000) *Race, Races and American Law* (4th edition), New York: Aspen Publishers

Chin, G., V. Romero and M. Scaperlanda (eds) (2000) *Immigration and the Constitution: Origins of Constitutional Immigration Law*, New York and London: Garland Publishing

Delgado, H. (1993) *New Immigrants, Old Unions: Organizing Undocumented Workers in Los Angeles*, Philadelphia: Temple University Press

Dred Scott v. Sandford, 60 U.S. 393: 404 (1856)

Fink, L. (2003) *The Maya of Morganton: Work and Community in the Nuevo New South*, Chapel Hill, NC: University of North Carolina Press

Foner, E. (1988) *Reconstruction: America's Unfinished Revolution, 1863–1877*, New York: Harper & Row

Guzman, B. (2001) *The Hispanic Population*, Census 2000 Brief, Washington DC: US Bureau of the Census

Hair, P. (2001) *Louder Than Words: Lawyers, Communities and the Struggle for Justice*, New York: Rockefeller Foundation

Honey, M. K. (1999) *Black Workers Remember: An Oral History of Segregation, Unionism, and the Freedom Struggle*, Berkeley, Los Angeles and London: University of California Press

Johnston, P. (2002) 'Citizenship movement unionism: For the defense of local communities in the global age', in B. Nissen (ed.) *Unions in a Globalized Environment: Changing Borders, Organizational Boundaries and Social Roles*, Armonk, NY: M. E. Sharpe

Lawyers Committee for Human Rights (2002) *A Year of Loss: Re-examining Civil Liberties Since September 11*, New York: Lawyers Committee for Human Rights (available online at www.lchr.org)

Lawyers Committee for Human Rights (2003) *Imbalance of Powers: How Changes to US Law & Policy Since 9/11 Erode Human Rights and Civil Liberties, September 2002–2003*, New York: Lawyers Committee for Human Rights (available online at www.lchr.org)

Lopez, I. H. (1996) *White by Law: The Legal Construction of Race*, New York: New York University Press

Lowell, B. L. and R. Suro (2002) *How Many Undocumented: The Numbers Behind the US–Mexico Migration Talks*, Washington, DC: Pew Hispanic Center

McClain, C. J. (1994) *In Search of Equality: The Chinese Struggle Against Discrimination in Nineteenth-Century America*, Berkeley, CA: University of California Press

Matsuda, M. (1991) 'Voices of America: Accent, antidiscrimination law, and a jurisprudence for the last reconstruction', *Yale Law Journal* 100, pp. 1329–1404

Mendoza, M. (2002) *Latino Immigrant Women in Memphis*, Memphis, TN: Center for Research on Women

Milkman, R. (2000) *Organizing Immigrants: The Challenge for Unions in Contemporary California*, Ithaca and London: Cornell University Press

Motomura, H. (1990) 'Immigration law after a century of plenary power: Phantom constitutional norms and statutory interpretation', reprinted in G. Chin, V. Romero and M. Scaperlanda (eds) (2000) *Immigration and the Constitution: Origins of Constitutional Immigration Law*, New York and London: Garland Publishing, pp. 285–613

Mouffe, C. (ed.) (1992) *Dimensions of Radical Democracy: Pluralism, Citizenship, Community*, London and New York: Verso

Mouffe, C. (1993) *The Return of the Political*, London and New York: Verso

Neuman, G. (1996) *Strangers to the Constitution: Immigrants, Borders and Fundamental Law*, Princeton: Princeton University Press

Nissen, B. (ed.) (2002) *Unions in a Globalized Environment: Changing Borders, Organizational Boundaries and Social Roles*, Armonk, NY: M. E. Sharpe

Prucha, F. P. (1986) *The Great Father: The United States Government and the American Indians*, Lincoln: University of Nebraska Press

Roman, E. (1997) 'Empire forgotten: The United States' colonization of Puerto Rico', *Villanova Law Review* 42, pp. 1119–211

Rosales, F. A. (1999) *Pobre Raza!: Violence, Justice and Mobilization Among México Lindo Immigrants, 1900–1936*, Austin: University of Texas Press

Saito, N. T. (1997) 'Alien and non-alien alike: Citizenship, "foreignness" and racial hierarchy in American law', *Oregon Law Review* 76: 261–345

Smith, B. E. (2001) *The New Latino South: An Introduction*, Memphis: Center for Research on Women

Smith, R. and Sugimori, A. (2003) *Low Pay, High Risk: State Models for Advancing Immigrants' Rights*, New York: National Employment Law Project

Stammers, N. (1999) 'Social movements and the social construction of human rights', *Human Rights Quarterly* 21, pp. 980–1008

TIRN (1993) 'From the Mountains to the Maquiladoras', Knoxville, TN: Tennessee Industrial Renewal Network (video)

Wu, F. (1996) 'A moderate proposal for immigration reform', reprinted in G. Chin, V. Romero and M. Scaperlanda (eds) (2000) *Immigration and the Constitution: Origins of Constitutional Immigration Law*, New York and London: Garland Publishing, pp. 61–100

Citizenship and Policy

The Grootboom case and the constitutional right to housing: the politics of planning in post-*apartheid* South Africa[1]

John J. Williams

Introduction

Miss Irene Grootboom was one of a group of 390 adults and 510 children living in appalling circumstances in Wallacedene, an informal housing settlement in Cape Town. In September 1998, they illegally occupied land near the settlement which had been earmarked for low-cost housing. They were forcibly evicted, their shacks bulldozed and burnt and their possessions destroyed. They could not return to their original settlement as their former homes had been occupied by others. In desperation they settled in Wallacedene sports field and in an adjacent community hall. The Legal Resources Centre, an NGO based in Cape Town, together with other legal activists decided to use their case to test the enforceability of their constitutional right to housing. The Grootboom case, as it was widely known, has been described as a landmark case in the struggle for citizenship rights in post-*apartheid* South Africa.

This chapter uses the Grootboom case to argue that the inauguration of formal democracy in 1994 in South Africa has not led to basic constitutional rights being translated into the *de facto* daily lived experience of ordinary people. It examines some of the factors which help to explain this failure, drawing attention in particular to the extent to which racist attitudes and practices continue to structure the planning process, making it extremely difficult to implement the Integrated Development Planning approach adopted by the state as its primary vehicle for delivering services at local level. Integrated Development Planning is intended as a single, inclusive and strategic plan for the development of a municipality. It links, integrates and co-ordinates plans, taking into account proposals for the development of a municipality and aligning the resources and capacity of the municipality with the implementation of plans.

The structure of the chapter is as follows. The next section briefly reviews the history of housing in the relevant community to demonstrate the deeply entrenched inequalities that characterize the South African context. The third section elaborates on the conditions which prevailed in Wallacedene housing community, which capture in microcosm the experiences of poor blacks in post-*apartheid* South Africa. The fourth section reports on the considerations which underpinned the Constitutional Court's judgement on the Grootboom case and draws out its significance for the struggle for citizenship rights. The fifth section reports the voices of the various stakeholders, both those responsible for implementing the court's judgement and those who were likely to be affected by it. The chapter concludes by noting the challenge faced by the state if it is to deliver on its commitment to provide basic services as basic rights.

The historical constitution of housing inequalities

The Grootboom case has to be understood in the context of the historically-constituted settlement patterns of Cape Town at large. In the latter half of the nineteenth century Cape Town was inhabited by people from diverse backgrounds (Le Grange and Robins, 1995, pp. 6–8), but this cultural diversity was systematically erased in subsequent years through policies of relocation and segregation. When the colonial government began the purposive settlement of the Cape Flats area between 1877 and 1910, there was initially no provision for separate 'native' settlements in Cape Town. The Reserve Locations Acts No 40 of 1902 and No 8 of 1906 signalled the first attempts by the state to create segregated African areas. These acts made it compulsory for all Africans in the municipality to live in Ndabeni, unless they were registered voters or had received permission to reside outside of the locations. The establishment of Ndabeni in 1901 was significant because it brought into Cape Town the enforced residential segregation of so-called 'Africans', a rudimentary pass system, and residence in a controlled location which offered no possibility of freehold title. However, although segregation was a legal requirement in Cape Town in 1902, it proved unenforceable: as employment opportunities grew, the city attracted more and more people.

The 1923 Native (Urban Areas) Act No 21 of 1923 was a response to this massive demographic flow. It was intended to freeze the permanent population, with additional labour requirements to be met by migrant labour. But it failed to curb the numbers of Africans seeking employment in Cape Town (Le Grange and Robins 1995, pp. 6–8). A nationwide drought lasting from 1930 to 1935 forced even more people, both black and white, into the cities. By 1927 there were 10,000 Africans officially living in Cape Town, and many more living there unofficially. As the city expanded, black people were forced further away from the city to create residential space and buffer zones for whites. Separate settlements to house Africans began to be set up: Langa in 1927, followed by Bokmakiere, Bridgetown and Kewtown.

Apartheid townships developed between 1945 and 1965. Nyanga ('the moon') was established in 1946 as one of the earliest townships for the growing African population. With the implementation of the Group Areas Act of 1950, large numbers of African families were forcibly removed from other areas and resettled in the expanded Nyanga West township, later named Guguletu. Guguletu was one of the first townships where neighbourhood town planning principles were employed (Le Grange and Robins 1995, pp. 6–12).

However, the unresolved housing shortage meant that shack settlements – informal shelters made of unconventional building materials such as plastic, scrap wood and corrugated iron sheets – sprang up both within the city limits and outside them. Many Africans preferred to live in these informal settlements because they could avoid the high rents and state regulation associated with formal townships. The shortage of accommodation meant the authorities could not stop the spread of shacks. Instead, with the 1950s began three decades of influx control – pass raids, shack clearances and the 'repatriation' of Africans to the rural 'homelands' of the Transkei and the Ciskei. From 1957 onwards, Africans were not permitted work in one area and live in another without a special permit. This led to the transfer of thousands of people between the different townships over the following 15 years. Many were moved from Nyanga to Guguletu.

The introduction of policies to favour the coloured population in 1955 exacerbated the housing problem for blacks. It led to a freeze on state provision of housing for Africans; priority was given instead to large state housing initiatives for coloured families. Manenberg, originally known as Heideveld Extension 1, was planned by the Cape Town City Council in 1963 primarily as a resettlement area for persons 'disqualified' from areas defined as 'white' by the Group Areas Act. In 1972 construction began of rental apartment blocks and houses in Hanover Park, a name chosen to reassure residents, many of whom had been displaced from District Six, by reminding them of their previous main street (Fast 1995, p. 12).

The 1970s saw growing disregard for pass laws and the further growth of informal settlements. During the 1980s there were three changes in African settlement patterns. First, many Africans were moved even further away from Cape Town to Khayelitsha. Second, there was an increasing densification within the townships, with shack areas developing within the boundaries of Nyanga and Guguletu. And third, many smaller camps developed during the decade, in contrast to the large shantytowns which had characterized the 1970s (Fast 1995, p. 33). In 1980 the official population of Langa, Guguletu and Nyanga (also called Lagunya townships) stood at 130,820. The unofficial population was much higher, with an estimated 229,000 people in Lagunya. In 1984 there were only 13,302 formal houses, which represented a shortfall of 8,897 dwellings. Africans lived in a variety of accommodations in the formal townships. Some lodged, others rented backyard shacks, and many put shacks on vacant land within and beside Nyanga and Guguletu. The number of Africans living in shacks increased again in the 1980s in the Cape Peninsula, from around 25,000 in 1978 to 250,000 in 1986 (Fast 1995, p. 34).

Acute housing shortages continue to the present time. In October 2003, the Western Cape Provincial Member of Council responsible for housing, Nomatyala Hangana, estimated that the housing backlog was between 350,000 and 400,000 units: 'Migration to the Western Cape of mostly poor people needing housing subsidies is increasing. The Western Cape is known as the shanty capital of the world... The housing budget allowed for 20,000 in the financial year, but 40,000 to 45,000 more houses were needed to fight the backlog' (*Cape Times*, 7 October 2003).

Life in Wallacedene: the persistence of racial inequalities in post-apartheid South Africa

Racially structured housing inequalities are only one aspect of the material deprivation of black South Africans more generally. Such deprivation persists in the post-*apartheid* era. Only 2% of land has been redistributed since the fall of *apartheid*. 80% of the land is still owned by white commercial farmers, depriving between 13 and 14 million people of access to land. Sixty-one per cent of Africans are poor, compared with 1% of whites. At the other end of the spectrum, 65% of white households are in the top quintile, followed by 45% of Indian households. However, only 17% of coloured families, and 10% of African, fall into this category. Racial inequalities also play out in access to work. According to a Western Cape provincial economic report,

92% of 'whites' found work in Cape Town and its environs between 1995 and 2002, compared to 22% of 'coloureds', 16% of Indians and 3% of Africans.

While there have been some improvements in access to services such as health care, these are marginal when compared to what has not been achieved. The latest report of the South African Human Rights Commission (*Cape Times*, 23 April 2003) revealed the following picture:

- despite a huge housing backlog, the housing department underspent by about R100 million [approximately $US14 million] in the 2001/02 financial year;
- less than 50% of poor people are getting the free water promised by the government before the local election of 2000;
- thousands of pensioners, who are entitled to social grants, are not getting their money;
- of the 1.2 million people identified by the Department of Social Development as deserving disability grants, only 714,000 were actually receiving them.

Given a long history of racially structured inequality, and the failure of the post-*apartheid* state to engage in redistributive measures or to plan effectively for the welfare of the marginalized, the conditions that prevailed in the Wallacedene housing community were unlikely to have been exceptional. Instead, they represent in microcosm the conditions of poor blacks elsewhere in South Africa. What the Grootboom case achieved was to draw the nation's attention in a very graphic way to what such deprivation meant in terms of everyday living conditions.

Despite its poverty, Wallacedene has continued to expand at a rapid rate, particularly since the birth of democratic South Africa in 1994. The problems associated with the over-crowded conditions have been exacerbated by the reluctance of the local authority, now the City of Cape Town, and the Provincial Administration Western Cape (PAWC) to take responsibility for providing adequate services to the community. Today the area has an estimated population of 27,000–30,000 people and a population density of 20,000 people per square kilometre. 95% of the dwellings are informal structures. The water table for the area is very high, leading to frequent flooding of the settlement, especially in winter. There are a few communal taps, no functioning toilets, no health services and minimal provision for refuse removal. There is no electricity. The use of wood and paraffin for fuel create fire hazards. There is high incidence of tuberculosis and skin disorders, particularly among children. Most of the inhabitants earn far less than the official poverty line income of R1,000 [US$140] per month. Two-thirds earn less than R500 [US$70] per month, and only 3% receive any form of state pension or grant.

Interviews with the inhabitants of Wallacedene testify to their despair that their situation would ever improve. One young inhabitant commented on the underlying causes of ill-health in the community:

> Because of the filth here people are constantly sick. And government thinks it is all just AIDS, but it is also due to our living conditions... all the stench and squalor that is here... and there is no medicine that can cure this.

The local medicine woman expressed her disappointment at the lack of progress on the part of government:

> I don't quite understand what is the difficulty for our government, because we hear that in other places there are developments taking place. We haven't seen any developments here. We are surprised this is not happening because it is long that we have been struggling .... We want our forefathers' land back. We find it difficult to comprehend this lack of progress.

An elderly man made it clear that what the community needed was support, not dependence:

> We want to work together. We want suitable houses to be built for us like it is happening elsewhere. Then after building the houses, they will have to say: 'Here is the meter box ... here is electricity and taps and it all works like this and this'. Then the people who don't want to pay can be directly approached by us ... I am a member of the community structure that attends meetings. I was at a meeting where we were asked to call a residents' meeting regarding water payment. We pointed out our dissatisfaction ... for example, what are we paying for? Where are the taps, the garbage collection? This place is filthy. Look at the toilets. People don't have any privacy.

And a young woman lamented the indifference of her municipality to the plight of Wallacedene:

> I am crying because no one cares ... especially the municipality. We don't know where else to go. We wrote a letter. We sent it; they never came back to us, except telling us they received it; but nothing tangible with regard to a meeting to address our problems (e.g., children who suffer from scabies and tuberculosis).

It is indeed the case that over the years, residents of Wallacedene had written numerous letters to the planning authorities to draw attention to their conditions, but to no avail. It was desperation, therefore, that led 900 men, women and children to move out of their overcrowded living conditions and occupy privately owned land nearby. The land owner had the squatters evicted, but they found that they were unable to return to their old dwellings, now occupied by others equally desperate. Instead, in 2000 the Grootboom community took the local authorities to court to demand their constitutional rights to housing and associated services.

The Grootboom case: the judgement

Julian Apollos, who was *pro bono* attorney at law for the Grootboom community, described his involvement during an interview on 14 October 2003:

> One morning a magistrate had to roll out an attorney for a community who were unrepresented. He required me to represent a community who were evicted in Wallacedene; I had to establish their plight as it was clear to him that it was an inequitable situation to leave the affected community to their own devices. Factually, the plight was not wholly due to circumstances of their own making but rather the failure on the part of the local authority to address acute shortage of housing in the area. Closer scrutiny revealed that not only the local authority but also provincial and national governments failed in their obligations to the people of Wallacedene. There is a Constitution to proceed against. Hence the *pro bono* support of the European Foundation for Human Rights to represent the interests of the Wallacedene community in Court.

The Cape of Good Hope High Court found that the children and, through them, their parents were entitled to shelter under Section 28(1) of the Constitution, and it ordered the national and provincial governments, as well as the Cape Metropolitan Council and the Oostenberg Municipality, to provide them immediately with tents, portable latrines and a regular supply of water by way of minimal shelter, which they did. However, the government challenged the decision, arguing that the Constitution did not require the government actually to provide shelter. The case was heard in May 2000.

Justice Zakaria Yacoob reported the unanimous judgement of the Constitutional Court as follows:

> This case shows the desperation of hundreds of thousands of people living in deplorable conditions throughout the country. The Constitution

obliges the State to act positively to ameliorate these conditions. The obligation is to provide access to housing, health-care, sufficient food and water, and social security to those unable to support themselves and their dependants. The State must also foster conditions to enable citizens to gain access to land on an equitable basis. Those in need have a corresponding right to demand that this be done (para 93).

All levels of government must ensure that the housing programme is reasonably and appropriately implemented in the light of all the provisions in the Constitution (para 82).

The proposition that rights are interrelated and are all equally important is not merely a theoretical postulate. The concept has immense human and practical significance in a society founded on human dignity, equality and freedom. It is fundamental to an evaluation of the reasonableness of State action that account be taken of the inherent dignity of human beings. The Constitution will be worth infinitely less than its paper if the reasonableness of State action concerned with housing is determined without regard to the fundamental constitutional value of human dignity... In short, I emphasise that human beings are required to be treated as human beings (para 83).

Recognizing the difficulties associated with the prevailing socio-economic conditions, the court did not oblige the state to go beyond its available resources or to realize these rights immediately. Rather, it noted that the constitution required the state to implement 'reasonable legislative and other programmes' to 'progressively realize' social and economic rights. The question therefore is always whether the measures taken by the state to realize the rights afforded by section 26 (1) are *reasonable*.

The court's judgement was that the national housing programme failed the test of reasonableness in Grootboom because it did not sufficiently address the plight of the poorest and most desperate sections of the community. It stated that a reasonable national programme to implement social and economic rights should not exclude the most resource-poor people from its service provision and should not leave out of account the degree and extent of denial of the right they endeavour to realize. Those whose needs are the most urgent, and whose ability to enjoy all rights are therefore most in peril, must not be ignored by the measures aimed at achieving realization of the right. The court stipulated that planning measures must expressly provide temporary forms of relief for people in crisis situations. Ameliorative programmes must be sufficiently flexible to respond to those in desperate need in our society and to cater appropriately for immediate and short-term requirements.

Furthermore, based on the notion of reasonable measures, the court stipulated that the national government had to monitor its constitutional obligations and ensure that appropriate financial and human resources were available for the task. In other words, it bore overall responsibility for ensuring that the state complies with its (constitutional) obligations. It was therefore essential that a reasonable part of the national housing budget be devoted to meeting constitutional obligations in respect of the poorest and most desperate: 'There must be recognition of the obligation to meet immediate needs in the nation-wide programme'. In this regard the court pointed out that '[e]ffective implementation requires at least adequate budgetary support by national government' (paragraph 68).

The Grootboom case has reverberations beyond those for the community immediately affected by it. According to Julian Appolos, the case is a watershed in the context of international jurisprudence. In his view, the court went further than most courts: it gave body to second-generation rights (ie socio-economic rights), thus making the transformation of society become seen as a necessary condition for the efficacy of political rights. The court's judgement also upheld the view that the South African state has direct responsibility to uphold the constitutional rights of ordinary citizens within the jurisdiction of a particular local authority.

The other significant aspect of the court's ruling is its assertion of a structural relationship between citizenship and the nature of planning at local level. However, exactly *how* citizenship rights are supposed to be enforced at local level is problematic. Below we reproduce some of the voices of government officials, politicians and civil society activists who were involved in the Grootboom case. These help to throw some light on the challenges involved. As will be seen, some of these challenges relate directly to policy and planning priorities and practices, while others relate to the political processes through which these priorities and practices are determined.

Planning and politics in the implementation of citizenship rights

The verdict of the court in the Grootboom case was that local authorities were obliged to provide basic services to communities such as Wallacedene. However, the implementation of this judgement was not a straightforward exercise. The Integrated Development Planning approach which had been adopted as the state's model of providing services to citizens at local level required a certain degree of consensus about the nature of the problem and the best way to solve it. What prevailed instead was considerable divergence – and some degree of conflict. This becomes evident when we consider some of the different interpretations provided by different stakeholders as to the meaning of the Grootboom case and of the court's verdict.

There were some who argued that the Grootboom case did not take the context of development planning sufficiently into consideration. Warren Smit, a researcher at Development Action Group, a non-governmental organization, argues that the Grootboom case was 'a little bit of a disappointment' in that it had not focused explicitly on the integrated approach to development. For the former Minister of Housing, Sankie Mthembi-Mahanyele, however, the Wallacedene case helped to highlight the importance of the following question: 'What do we do with people who are informally settled? How do we utilize the budget and the related resources to impact [positively] on the lives of [the squatters]?' In her view, the specific issue of housing, which the Grootboom case drew attention to, was organically linked to other development issues such as access to land and resource allocation.

Resource allocation to development issues at the local level featured prominently in comments by Seymour Bedderson, Chief Director, Department of Housing, Provincial Administration, Western Cape. He blamed the lack of development funding in the Western Cape on the rural bias of development strategies in South Africa. This view was shared by Bazil Davidson, Head of Planning, Cape Metropolitan Council, who pointed out that metropolitan Cape Town actually received only one-third of the 14,000 government subsidies originally allotted to it. The post-*apartheid* government subsequently redirected two-thirds of these subsidies to rural development programmes.

Whilst acknowledging the importance of development programmes, Anthea Houston, Director of the Development Action Group, drew attention to the ideological underpinnings of current urban development practices. She pointed out that, despite the inclusive nature of the South African constitution, urban development planning still does not take racial issues into consideration. On the contrary, it continues to operate within the restrictive parameters of *apartheid* town planning regulations.

It appears that these apartheid ideological parameters also continue to have a great purchase in largely 'white' and 'coloured' communities in the segregated townships of Cape Town. Cecil Africa, Director of Housing for the Oostenberg Municipality, pointed out that there was a

NIMBY (not-in-my-backyard) factor which often had a profound impact on housing delivery. This presumably happened in the case of the Wallacedene community. In his view, 'there is often very little a municipality can do about this because they would have endless problems from adjoining communities'. The reason for this apparently paralysing state of affairs was provided by Kobus Scott, Planning Consultant for Oostenberg Municipality:

> You see there is a stigma attached to low-cost housing or subsidized housing. And if you identify land that is suitable for that purpose then you are confronted by surrounding owners not wanting to accept a low-cost subsidy development on their doorstep. This was our first approach even before we [carried out our plans]. We first met with high-income owners and over and over their fear was: What about our property? We had to give them assurance that when we came to that stage we would look into that. And in the end they also had to approve the final plan.

According to Scott, these considerations led the Oostenberg Municipality to separate the so-called 'coloured' community and 'African' communities 'to safeguard that people would have more or less equal neighbours in value. Here I must tell you that there is some political unhappiness between the two culture groups. Your original residents ['coloured'] was [sic] of the opinion that this area had to stay in the hands of the coloured community'.

The racism of the premises underlying housing policy in Wallacedene elicited strong condemnation from Sankie Mthembi-Mahanyele. She pointed out:

> According to the constitution, no one, absolutely no one, has the right to divide people on the basis of race; no one has the right to allocate resources and services on the basis of race. There is no way in which people can bring back *apartheid* through the back-door and perpetuate racism because those policies have been refuted by our Housing Act [of 1997]. We are proceeding from the basis that housing will be provided on a non-racial basis and proceeding towards deracializing society.

The African National Congress (ANC) Councillor for Wallacedene, Lucky Gwaza, suggested that the divisiveness of planning practices in the municipality went directly against the spirit of Integrated Development Planning:

> When you construct housing for high-income earners and then on the other side you build low-low income housing for the very poor, isolated from the former, it is obvious that you are separating the haves from the

have-nots. This means that the question of integration, often spoken about, is not encouraged or practised. That's not what we want, because that is the old *apartheid* approach whereby you don't integrate people.

However, the voices of the so-called white and coloured residents living in properties adjacent to Wallacedene suggested that they were determined to continue the 'old *apartheid* approach', living in ethnic enclaves separate from the largely African community of Wallacedene. This is evident from their reactions to the proposed development plans for Wallacedene which were required by the Grootboom court case. In compliance with the court's judgement, both the City of Cape Town and the provincial administration of the Western Cape had agreed in May 2001 to take joint responsibility for the area and committed themselves to the Wallacedene Housing Regeneration Project (Williams 2003). The Wallacedene community members have been put on the City's housing waiting list. The provincial administration has provided R250,000 [US$ 35,000] while the City of Cape Town has proposed and approved a Spatial Development Framework for Wallacedene after 'numerous meetings were held with all different role players' (City of Cape Town, 18 June 2002, *Wallacedene Housing Regeneration and Densification Project*).

The reaction of surrounding 'white' and 'coloured' communities to these proposals has been vitriolic, which reveals the underlying correlation between race and politics that clearly persists in the South African population.

109 members of the Ratepayers Association of Kleinbegin, Kraaifontein signed a petition that reads:

> We, as residents of Kraaifontein, wish to register our strongest objection to the further development of Wallacedene. We shall never ever approve of it. The crime in the area is already rife. This development of Wallacedene will merely increase the crime in the area. We are already surrounded by two squatter settlements and now you still want to aggravate this situation. The noise and stench of these squatter settlements are already very bad and now you still want to bring them closer to us. Why next to us, and not elsewhere where there is enough open space for these squatters?
>
> Do you at all care about the interests of Kleinbegin or do you simply ignore us because we are not an ANC ward? Should you continue with the development of Wallacedene, we, the rate payers in the area, will withhold our taxes and service charges from the Municipality! We are no longer prepared to be shunted around! Look for another place to solve your problem.

In a follow-up petition, a Committee of Ten, elected by 48 residents of Kleinbegin on 13 October 2001, forwarded the following objections to the Municipality of Cape Town:

> The City of Cape Town and especially the Executive Committee has a misconception of the problems and trauma caused by squatter settlements in our area. Did the Executive Committee ever consider the crime statistics at the local police station? Raping, molestations, burglaries and theft are the order of the day in our area. Previous City Councils ignored our plight. Thus, we do not expect any different from the present City of Cape Town. But, this time around, we shall never accept this development. We shall fight back. Did Councillors ever have to lie awake whilst gunshots are being fired or deafening music blares throughout the night? Well, this is our plight, though we have not caused the squatter problem: the Council simply turned a blind eye to the erection of the squatter camp whilst we as ratepayers have been impoverished. The value of our properties has declined by at least 50% since the establishment of Wallacedene and Bloekombos in 1989. Who would like to live next to squatters? Thus we are demanding compensation from the Council as it is directly responsible for the squatter problem in our area.

These letters reveal some of the contradictions, tensions and fissures which inform the meaning and experience of citizenship in post-*apartheid* South Africa. In the battle for meaningful citizenship amongst historically marginalized and excluded people, such as those in Wallacedene, there are voices of clarity, such as those that were heard in South Africa's highest courts. At the same time, there are other voices within government, particularly those of planning bureaucrats who hail from the *apartheid* era, which suggest that they find the constitutional principles of equal access to basic rights deeply problematic. They have used whatever forms of red tape they have at their disposal to negate the promise of the post-*apartheid* Constitution. As the advocate Wallace Mgoqi, former Chief Commissioner of Land Claims, points out:

> The tragedy is that, even with the arrival of the new democratic dispensation throughout the country, not much has changed in the Western Cape. The powers that be, were there previously. The attitudes of your political authorities, local government authorities [show] some kind of apathy towards African people.

In a similar vein, Sankie Mthembi-Mahanyele draws attention to

> the evidence that opposition authorities in the Western Cape discriminate against ANC-oriented communities by favouring their political constituencies at the expense of the basic needs of poor communities.

Here the idea is that: if you do not vote for us, do not expect any services from us!

Miles Samuels, ANC Councillor for Wallacedene, makes even more explicit the extent to which racial party politics of the *apartheid* era continue to play out in the policy context in Western Cape:

Firstly, the whole Council of Oostenberg is DA [Democratic Alliance] controlled [favouring mostly white and coloured interests in the Western Cape]. We must understand that once a party dominates in any area, you know, its intention is to satisfy its followers' demands. Wallacedene is an ANC stronghold. Because of this, it results in fears that if this place is allowed to develop quickly, it will strengthen the ANC's support in the area. In other words, the intention is to destroy the ANC support in all the informal settlements. An impression is being created that nothing is being done, but where the DA is dominant outside of these areas there are developments in comparison to these; and I see this as a ploy to win votes for the DA and shift support towards them.

There is clearly a long way to go before the conditions exist under which an integrated approach to planning for basic services can be implemented in South Africa. But, despite the racism that continues to divide communities in South Africa and plays out in its political process, the gains represented by the Grootboom case should not be under-estimated. As the Legal Resource Centre's lawyer, Geoff Budlender, who played a pivotal role in the case, observes:

I don't think it's quite right that nothing has changed on the ground for the Grootboom community. When they started the case, they had literally nowhere to live. They had been evicted from the land where they had been living, and were truly homeless. They are now living securely on land made available by the local municipality. They are living in structures which they erected with materials provided in part by the municipality. They have access to water (communal taps) and communal toilets. It's quite true that they want better, as they should. They are on the local municipality's programme for permanent housing, which on current progress they should receive about two years from now. Negotiations are under way to attempt to accelerate the process. The implementation of the Grootboom judgement has been inadequate at a number of levels. There are a lot of lessons to be learnt from that – in particular, that cases of this kind are most effective when they are linked with social movements. But I don't think we should under-sell the actual impact of judgements on social and economic rights

Budlender, e-mail, 22 October 2003; cf. also Budlender ,2002

Conclusion

This chapter has explored the struggle to give meaning to citizenship rights in a country in transition from *apartheid* to democracy. In considering the significance of the Grootboom case, the chapter has emphasized the implications of the landmark judgement by the court for such rights, namely the state's obligation to ensure that basic rights are progressively and reasonably enforced. However, this judgement has to be realized in a context where racism continues to divide communities and where political parties have used their control of public resources to reinforce such divisions.

Quite clearly, in such a tension-ridden context, citizenship rights are not given, but interpreted and vigorously contested in a number of different arenas: we have touched briefly in this chapter on the legal arena, the political, the bureaucratic and the community. The challenge is considerable. The extent to which the courts, together with all the organs of the state, commit themselves to the progressive enforcement of rights, often in extremely hostile circumstances, will determine both the form and the substance of citizenship rights in a future South Africa. The Grootboom case, then, quite clearly, has set the stage and a remarkable precedent. The question that remains is: will the South African state be willing to follow through? Only the future will tell.

Notes

1. Disclaimer: racial terminologies. The South African Constitution, Act 108 of 1996, describes the historically disenfranchised sections of the population, the Africans, 'coloureds', and Indians, as 'black'. For the sake of historical and textual clarity, however, this chapter also refers to the Apartheid racial categories of 'Blacks' [African], 'coloureds' and 'Indians'. These racial epithets are rejected by this author as such ethnic references are not merely sociologically unsound, they are ultimately scientifically untenable.

References

African National Congress (ANC) (1994), *The Reconstruction and Development Programme*, Johannesburg: Umanyano Publishers

Budlender, Geoff (2002).'The Constitution and socio-economic rights: The nevirapine case Speaker: Constitutional Litigation Unit, Legal Resources', in *Summary Notes from the Harold Wolpe Forum Debate of 21 August 2002*, Cape Town

Budlender, Geoff (2003), e-mail, 22 October 2003

Cape Times (several editions)

City of Cape Town (18 June 2002), *Wallacedene Housing Regeneration and Densification Project*

Fast, H. (1995) *An overview of African settlement in the Cape Metropolitan area to 1990*, Urban problems research unit: University of Cape Town (UCT), project report

Grootboom vs. Oostenberg Municipality and others [Grootboom vs. State] (17 December 1999): *IN THE HIGH COURT OF SOUTH AFRICA (Cape of Good Hope Provincial Division), Case No. 6826/99 – In the matter between IRENE GROOTBOOM First Applicant et al and OOSTENBERG MUNICIPALITY First Respondent; CAPE METROPOLITAN COUNCIL Second Respondent; THE PREMIER OF THE PROVINCE OF THE WESTERN CAPE Third Respondent; NATIONAL HOUSING BOARD Fourth Respondent; GOVERNMENT OF THE REPUBLIC OF SOUTH AFRICA Fifth Respondent*, available at: http://www.suntimes.co.za/2000/05/07/politics/pol07.htm

Le Grange, L. and S. Robins (1995) *Wetton/Lansdowne road corridor area: the identification of culturally significant places and opportunities*, UCT

Republic of South Africa (1996) *The Constitution of the Republic of South Africa, 1996: Act 108 of 1996*, Pretoria: Government Printers

Republic of South Africa (2000) *South African Local Government Municipal Systems Act, No 32 of 2000*, Pretoria: Government Printers

Republic of South Africa (2001) *Government of the Republic of South Africa v Grootboom and Others 2000* (11) BCLR 1169 (CC)SA 46 (CC)

Williams, J. J. (1999) *Planning the multi-cultural city in post-apartheid South Africa: an appraisal of 'Overcoming the Group Areas Act: Social movements in Westville, South Africa'*, by Keyan Tomaselli, Occasional Paper No 3, published by the Centre for Cultural and Media Studies, University of Natal, Durban; also: www.und.ac.za/und/ccms

Williams, J. J. (2000) 'South Africa: Urban transformation', *Cities*, 17 (3), pp. 167–83

Williams, J. J. (2003) *The Grootboom Case: Oral and Video Presentation of the Wallacedene community to the Institute of Development Studies (IDS), University of Sussex*, video made by the Joint University and Educational Management Trust, South Africa; copy deposited at IDS

Citizenship and the right to water: Lessons from South Africa's Free Basic Water policy

Lyla Mehta

Needs, rights and commodities

Water is uniquely and fundamentally essential for all aspects of life, well-being and productivity. It is also the lifeblood of ecosystems, essential for many eco-hydrological functions. For poor people, access to clean and affordable water is a prerequisite for achieving a minimum standard of health and undertaking productive activities. However, it is estimated that 1.1 billion people lack access to safe water, and almost 2.5 billion people – 40 per cent of the world's population – lack access to adequate sanitation (Neto and Tropp 2000, p. 227).

Recently, a growing number of analysts have argued eloquently that water and sanitation are not just basic needs but fundamental human rights based on the criteria established in international declarations that protect the right to livelihood and well-being.[1] Curiously enough, the right to water was only implicitly endorsed in the 1948 Universal Declaration of Human Rights (UNDHR), although it is explicitly mentioned in the Convention of the Rights of the Child (1989).[2] It was only on 27 November 2002 that the United Nations Committee on Economic, Social and Cultural Rights adopted the General Comment on the right to water.[3] The Committee stressed the state's legal responsibility in fulfilling the right and defined water as a social and cultural good and not solely an economic commodity. There are several merits in endorsing the human right to water. Clearly, the provision of free and basic water, so essential for survival, could reduce the spread of diseases, as well as improve health and well-being. It could enhance poor households' sense of dignity and independence, reduce the drudgery of women and children who are responsible for water collection, and it could free time spent on water collection (one to four hours a day) for other activities.

Still, current orthodoxies in the water domain tend to focus on the need to view water as an economic good, and there is a marked lack of official endorsement of the human right to water.[4] Since the Dublin Statement of 1992,[5] water has increasingly been seen as having economic value in all its competing uses. Because water is scarce, goes the logic, it must be used judiciously and its demand must be managed. Accordingly, efficient resource management is equated with water having a price. The underlying assumption in most discourses – especially those originating in donor countries – is that there is a congruity between viewing water as a right and viewing it as an economic good. For example, the United Nations Children's Fund (UNICEF) and the World Water Council mention economic efficiency arguments and rights-based arguments in the same breath (see Nigam and Rasheed 1998, pp. 3–7). It is argued that even if something is a right, there is no denying the need to pay for it, as with food.

South Africa is one of the few countries that explicitly recognizes the right to water, and its Free Basic Water (FBW) policy goes against the grain of conventional wisdom in the water sector, which stresses cost recovery mechanisms. Since early 2000, the Department for Water Affairs and Forestry (DWAF) has been investigating providing a basic level of water free to all citizens. In February 2001, the government announced that it was going to provide a basic supply of 6,000 litres of safe water per month to all households free of charge (based on an average household size of eight people). This ties in with DWAF's overall mission to redress the inequalities of the past, overcome the backlog that it inherited in 1994 (around twelve to fourteen million people without access to water) and create universal access to water across the country. The Water Services Act 108 of 1997 states that a basic level of water should be provided to those who cannot pay, and the FBW policy emanates from the legal provisions of this Act.[6] The main source of funding for this initiative is the Equitable Share, a grant from central government to local authorities. It amounts to about 3 billion rands a year, and is from national taxes for the provision of basic services.

This chapter uses the case of water and South Africa's FBW policy to examine several challenges confronting contemporary understandings of citizenship and rights. These include universalism versus particularism, resource constraints in implementing rights, and questions of enforceability and justiciability, particularly with respect to social and economic rights. Over the past century, citizenship has increasingly been seen as encompassing social and economic rights, often known as positive rights. Advocacy for positive rights, such as access to water, food and shelter, marks a sharp change from the negative or liberal understanding of rights that underpins notions of liberal democracy. Neo-liberal traditions have viewed negative civil and political rights as essential to understanding what, for example, constitutes citizenship. But these traditions have been reluctant to award the same widespread attention to social and economic rights because such rights have strong links to social justice and imply moving away from the neo-liberal notion that people's socio-economic status is determined by the market (Plant 1998, pp. 57–8). In fact, the distinction between negative and positive rights is highly problematic because both involve state intervention and commitments for their protection. In terms of the way poor people experience rights, both are interrelated and indivisible.

Still, the distinction between civil and political rights on the one hand, and economic and social rights on the other, tends to persist. In part, this has to do with historical reasons stemming from the Cold War period, when, for ideological reasons, Western nations focused largely on civil and political rights. Consequently, social and economic rights continue to be viewed as 'second generation' rights. It is also telling that the International Covenant on Economic, Social and Cultural Rights (ICESCR) uses much weaker language than the International Covenant on Civil and Political Rights (ICCPR). It calls on states to take measures towards the progressive achievement of social and economic rights. This could suggest that there is a hierarchy in the realization of rights; that is, some are realized more gradually than others, thus weakening the imperative to see some as rights. It also has fewer signatories than the ICCPR, and the USA has not endorsed this covenant.

The South African case illustrates these contradictions nicely. Despite being the only country in the world that explicitly acknowledges the constitutional right to water, the massive policy and institutional changes needed, in parallel with strong trends towards cost recovery in the water sector, have made this policy difficult to realize. This underscores the need to look at how rights go hand in hand with political choices around responsibilities and resources. This chapter argues that even though implementing universal rights standards has been rather contradictory in the water domain, there is still value in institutionalizing access to water as a human right and viewing the right to water as an entitlement of both national and global citizenship. The right to water in principle provides justiciable components to local claims and struggles around water. Finally, universal rights language can be used as a countervailing force to the commodification of water, which impinges on poor people's right to water. The South African experience thus provides several useful lessons for understanding the key process of translating rights talk into rights practice.

Universalism vs particularism?

Stipulating allocation

Can we speak confidently of universal rights that are applicable to all human beings irrespective of age, gender, culture and geography? Despite being known as the 'global commons', it is impossible to say that water is perceived or experienced in the same way across the globe. Water is highly localized and at best regional in scope. Water availability is variable across time and space, and dependent on factors such as climate, season and temperature. Rainfall, vegetation and grass cover vary from place to place, making it difficult to provide blanket statements on the global state of water. Furthermore, most people experience and perceive water differently. In rural Kutch in western India, villagers refer to water in seven ways (sweet, saline, bland, surface, subterranean, ripe and raw), and villagers have locally-rooted notions about how water should be shared, distributed and consumed. Thus water is rooted in and defined by its locality (Mehta, forthcoming). Moreover, access to water is governed by factors such as caste, gender, status and wealth, and local water management practices can also be very conflict-ridden (Mehta, forthcoming). Thus, universalist assumptions of water as the 'global commons' often tend to romanticize the nature of local communities and gloss over how power politics can determine water management outcomes.

There are also problems around stipulating the basic allocation of a fixed quantity of litres per person. Basic water requirements have been suggested by various donor agencies, and they range from 20 to 50 litres a day, regardless of culture, climate or technology. The South Africa White Paper on Water Services, considered the state-of-the-art in water resource literature, fixes the allocation at 25 litres *per capita* per day, which works out to 6,000 litres per month per household (based on an average household of eight people). But trade union leaders and other advocates in South Africa argue that the South African state should grant everybody at least 50 litres of water per day *per capita*. This, they argue, is the only way in which poor farmers can successfully maintain their livelihoods and thus escape the trap of poverty and dependence on pension grants (Lance Veotte, interview, 15 April 2002). South Africa's

National Water Act (Act 36 of 1998) specifies a national reserve for basic needs purposes that is owned by the state (http://www-dwaf.pwv.gov.za/Documents/Legislature/nw_act/NWA.doc). It stipulates that water designated in the national reserve should not be used for 'commercial purposes', and this is in keeping with the overarching aim of the Act to redress the race and gender inequities of the past. The government also commits to guaranteeing the infrastructure to bring water to poor people within the 25-litre limit. However, whether these provisions radically redress past inequities is questionable. For example, poor black farmers who own less than one hectare, who may use the water for 'productive purposes' and for some market-based activities linked to economic survival, are not given rights to water under this national reserve. Schedule One, which permits basic water use for domestic consumption, domestic livestock use and gardening for subsistence, is ambivalent about how the basic income needs of poor producers can be met from the national water reserve (see van Koppen, Jha and Merrey 2002). In non-water-stressed areas this is not such a problem, since small users can be authorized to use the water for 'non-commercial' purposes without complicated registration procedures. However, in water-stressed basins this is more tricky, since general authorizations are avoided and the rights of small-scale producers are not granted legal and other forms of protection. Instead, they are pitted against those of large-scale users, such as mining companies, that clearly abuse limited water availability (Barbara van Koppen, personal communication, 10 January 2003).

The FBW policy was not intended to address redistribution issues, and there are other provisions in the National Water Act (for example, compulsory licensing) that deal with these. Still, we need to ask how FBW contributes to poverty reduction and wider social justice concerns. For example, it is intended that the 25 litres of water will be used primarily for drinking and cooking purposes. However, the poor also need to be assured of water during scarcity periods for their farming activities based on subsistence. The 25 litres a day policy largely focuses on domestic water supply, and not on wider concerns of livelihood security and how to restructure existing water-user practices. Thus, at times, broad and all-inclusive notions of citizenship may not adequately question existing power relations, which often benefit the dominant groups. There still remain tremendous inequalities in access to and control over land and water resources. For example, 13 per cent of the country's white population own 87 per cent of available land, and large-scale farmers control as much as 95 per cent of irrigation water (van Koppen, Jha and Merrey 2002).

Delivery

In order to achieve universal targets around economic and social rights, interventions may ignore local needs and not necessarily use locally appropriate technologies. For example, in order to overcome the backlog of the apartheid era (twelve to fourteen million people without access to water and sanitation, especially in the former homelands), DWAF initiated public–private partnerships, also known as Build Operate Train and Transfer (BOTT). These took place in the form of joint ventures, usually with consortia comprising big global water service providers, South African companies, foreign and local consultants and non-governmental organizations (NGOs). Today, several commentators acknowledge that BOTT schemes were problematic. As a senior bureaucrat at the provincial level said, 'BOTT was a joint venture between the government and the private sector, and we sought to eliminate bureaucracy, fast-track implementation procedures and streamline work. It has, however, worked out to be very expensive' (DWAF official, King William's Town, interview, 17 April 2002).

BOTT also did not really seek out local knowledge or understanding of water supply. In the Eastern Cape, kilometres of new pipeline were laid down instead of using or building on the old traditional systems (gravity feed/boreholes and pumps), and often sanitation issues were questionable (anonymous BOTT consultant, interview, 18 April 2002). As one of the consultants employed by AmanzAbantu (the BOTT consortium in the Eastern Cape) said: 'AmanzAbantu is top-down, expensive and only interested in profits. The schemes often break down because the technology is inappropriate. Unfortunately, we have brought First World technology to rural worlds. It's like giving a Rolls Royce to someone who's never seen a bicycle' (ibid). The BOTT example thus reveals the dangers of using top-down initiatives in order to meet universal standards and targets.

A more general universalism could also risk enhancing the role and status of bureaucrats and service providers. Simon Thompson and Paul Hoggart (1996, p. 21) distinguish between the *institutional model* of welfare delivery, where experts and bureaucrats are seen to be key in service delivery, and *non-institutional means* that seek to decentralize delivery processes and thus 'empower' people. Similarly, Ellison (1999) speaks of a decentralized welfare system that could be sensitive to particular needs of the disempowered. However, these authors do not try and operationalize these concepts and demonstrate how they would work in practice. To illustrate this point, let me examine decentralization and the FBW policy in South Africa.

The FBW policy was conceived by DWAF at the national level. Its critics (for example, Jackson 2002) argue that it was an ill-thought-out, populist measure announced around the 2000 elections. The now famous story is that the charismatic and dynamic Water Minister, Ronnie Kasrils, was shocked to see a woman in the Eastern Cape collecting water from an untreated stream instead of using a DWAF-sponsored water scheme. There are many interpretations of this story. One is that she could not pay the monthly fee of 10 rands. Another, argued by Ntshona (2003), is that she was using the stream because it was closer to her home than the water standpipe. Whatever the truth, the result was that the FBW policy was announced, which ostensibly took many by surprise, including some senior bureaucrats in DWAF (DWAF official, Pretoria, interview, 23 April 2002). This is because it was announced before the details had been worked out. Its implementation rests with local authorities, who are designated water services authorities and include both district municipalities (DMs) and local municipalities (LMs). They are free to interpret the policy according to the resources and capacity available. As a senior member of DWAF said, 'Free Basic Water is a non-negotiable policy statement. I realize it's a huge challenge – we have the right policy and we are proud to stand by it, but it's not easy to implement. We stand alone internationally. Local authorities just can't flick a switch and make it work. But somehow we have to deal with it and do the fancy footwork' (interview, 23 April 2002).

Operationalizing the policy has been difficult. The mere endorsement of the principle of social justice alone cannot suffice in determining how resources are to be distributed. Instead, as Hayek argues, the distribution of resources and implementing rights-based approaches are usually at the discretion of professionals and bureaucrats in the public sector, who lack clear directives on how to 'implement justice' (in Plant 1992, p. 20). This certainly echoes the experience of officials in South Africa's Eastern Cape. Many worked in bureaucracies of the former homelands and inherited a massive backlog in 1994. They also struggle to grapple with the many political and institutional changes arising from South Africa's decentralization process. The devolution of responsibility from the national level to district and local government has meant that whole administrative mechanisms have been radically restructured and new institutions created. As a DWAF official in King William's Town bemoans, 'Things are changing so much that even I can't cope. There are too many policy and political changes... For those of us working on the ground, it makes everything very uncertain' (interview, 17 April 2003).

Implementing the policy is up to each district municipality. Many of the poorer district municipalities lack financial and institutional resources to implement the policy, despite Equitable Share grants. Due to the lack of uniformity of service provision, vastly different levels of service can be observed in adjacent villages, depending on the service provider. These conflicting schemes cause considerable social tension. Powerful actors often emerge as clear beneficiaries of all these uncertainties. The private sector and metropolitan white consultants can draft complicated contracts, win tenders and make profits out of water provision 'for all'. The offices of AmanzAbantu, the consortium implementing BOTT schemes in the Eastern Cape, are located in an impressive brick building with a high barbed-wire fence in the small town of Mount Ayliff. Across the road, the office of the district municipality has been located in a camper van and temporary container since 1996. The official in charge of water provision for the district says, 'This was supposed to be a temporary solution. How do they expect us to provide services when we are still in tents?' (interview, 18 April 2002).

Clearly, deliberative welfare systems and decentralized delivery structures for the apportioning of rights can be formulated in an idealized way that ignores questions of local capacity, local 'buy in' and resource availability. Martin Rall of the Mvula Trust, a leading water provision NGO, says, 'Decentralization is taking place too quickly in South Africa. There's a gap between First World policies and the actual capacity of local authorities. Most of us in this country live in the Third World. But our policies have urban biases and draw on First World experiences. The Department of Provincial Government is advised by consultants from the USA and USAID. It is all rather impractical!' (interview 23 April 2002).

Rights, duties and responsibilities

Citizens

Do entitlements have to be earned? Critics of rights argue that rights go hand in hand with duties and responsibilities. There are concerns that rights-based approaches will not empower people but instead foster a dependency syndrome. If rights are endowed to citizens, including rights to resources, citizens in turn must fulfil obligations. This is often construed as an obligation to work, make financial contributions or partake in operation and maintenance activities. In the water debate in South Africa, some commentators argue that this policy will make people dependent on the state. For example, Martin Rall of the Mvula Trust argues that people have stopped paying for water in areas serviced by government schemes since the FBW policy was implemented. While the Mvula Trust supports the idea that those who cannot pay should be provided with free services, villages covered by the Mvula Trust do not necessarily adhere to the FBW policy, and villagers do not receive the first 6,000 litres of water free. By contrast, 'the Mvula Trust has created a sense of ownership and incentive structures so that people pay. They open bank accounts and make financial contributions. There is a strong willingness to pay and indigent families sometimes work instead of coughing up the cash' (Martin Rall, interview, 23 April 2002). In his opinion, willingness to pay has also declined in post-apartheid South Africa, especially after the FBW policy was implemented. He thus argues that obligations, in the form of either providing labour or financial contributions of 3–20 rands per month, are necessary to ensure the success of the service and to enhance people's sense of ownership in the scheme, especially in areas where local government lacks capacity. Thus the Mvula Trust believes that those who can afford the service should not get it for free, and the poor are encouraged to pay for the service, either through their unpaid labour, their time or by 'participating' in water user associations and so on.

Much has been made in the literature of households' willingness to pay for water (Altaf, Jamal and Whittington 1992; Whittington and Choe 1992). It is estimated that the willingness to pay is about 1 to 10 per cent of total household spending, and usually about 5 per cent of total consumption. But recent studies from other contexts are challenging these assumptions, and speak of linking willingness to pay to ability to pay (Ghosh and Nigam 1995; Reddy and Vandemoortele 1996). For example, in India's water-scarce Rajasthan, Reddy (1999) shows that willingness to pay is much less than 5 per cent of consumption. But willingness-to-pay proponents usually treat households as black boxes, ignoring the power dynamics within them, the naturalization of women's water-related tasks and the low opportunity costs attached to women's time. A blanket water pricing policy may not capture all these institutional dynamics and may unduly affect poor people, particularly women. Furthermore, externalities such as health issues are not really addressed. If people are unable to pay for water, their lack of access to clean water and sanitation could lead to the spread of diseases, with health implications – especially for children, women and the elderly. In addition, the low opportunity costs attached to women's time in many parts of the world, combined with their low decision-making power in households, may not lead to a pressing desire among household heads to support better water supply systems if they had to demonstrate willingness to pay for them.

Critics of cost recovery initiatives in South Africa have shown the extent to which donor influence led South African government thinking away from its Reconstruction and Development Programme commitment to basic services for all, towards a cost recovery approach, which can deprive poor communities of their basic right to adequate provision of water. Critics point to widespread service cut-offs in communities who have fallen behind with service payments, problems of profiteering, questionable motives amongst commercial service providers, and sharp price escalations since water privatization (see, for example, Bond *et al.* 2001; McDonald and Pape 2002). It must be borne in mind, however, that cut-offs also used to occur under the old arrangements, usually carried out by water boards or municipalities that were trying to balance their books. Even today, quasi-public institutions such as Rand Water have negotiated agreements on water payments, after which some cut-offs can take place. However, most criticism is directed at the private sector, due to its inability or unwillingness to serve social goals (unlike water boards, that tend to plough their profits into creating new infrastructure). Even though the private sector is involved in the management of water services in only about 5 out of 180 municipalities in South Africa, water privatization debates are intense, and are emblematic for the ways in which efforts towards achieving social justice can be contradicted by simultaneous processes of marketization and cost recovery.

States and socio-political decisions

While states are obliged to provide universal access to basic services, they often lack the resources to ensure that every woman, man and child obtains adequate food, water, health services and education. How could the human right to water be financed? Clearly, the responsibility of national governments to ensure the minimum supply required for people's well-being and survival – that is, to achieve a minimum capability – cannot be underestimated. This could take the form of a free lifeline of water to meet people's basic requirements in accordance with local conditions. The 20/20 Initiative, proposed at the 1995 World Summit for Social Development, aimed at achieving universal access to basic social services, suggests taxing the rich and allocating 20 per cent of official development assistance and 20 per cent of developing country budgets to such services (UNICEF 1994). Vision 21, drafted by the Water Supply Sanitation and Collaborative Council, recommends creating cross-subsidies, swapping debt relief for basic service delivery and reallocating resources away from high-cost, high-technology projects. Other possible financing measures include increasing donor commitments to public services and urging donors to avoid requiring private investment in public services as a condition of aid. It has been argued that if the G8 countries would double the proportion of their aid budget spent on water and sanitation, the millennium development goals on water and sanitation could be gradually realized. Current expenditure by most countries is about 5 per cent, with the UK spending a mere 2 per cent of its budget on water and sanitation (the lowest of all G8 nations).

Clearly, the resources a society assigns to health, education, defence and the legal system are all matters of 'political negotiation' (Plant 1992, p. 22). One could argue that it is not just social and economic rights that are controversial. Civil and political rights are equally contested. For example, there is growing outrage around the daily defence budget of the USA, which is about $1 billion a day. By contrast, the Water Supply Sanitation and Collaborative Council estimates that all of the world's people could be provided with an adequate water supply and sanitation with the expenditure of $9 billion a year until 2025 (Mehta 2003b). This is a lot of money for national governments and the international community. But it is the same amount spent by the USA in nine days on 'defence' matters (ibid). In a similar vein, trade union activist Lance Veotte, of the Congress of South African Trade Unions (COSATU) in South Africa, argues that the government needs to provide an assured lifeline supply of 50 litres of water per day per person. He says, '66 billion rand are spent by the South African government on arms. By contrast, only one billion is spent on water. And in the same breath the national government complains that local government lacks capacity!' (interview, 15 April 2002).[7] In sum, the resource implications of public spending on rights (be they civil, political or social) are matters of political choice and will always remain highly contested.

Needs vs rights: justiciability

Sceptics often ask how acknowledging basic rights would differ from acknowledging the importance of basic human needs, such as shelter, security and livelihoods. In the water domain, it is not clear how the human right to water would be different from the spirit of the 1970s and 1980s, when efforts were made to provide water to all. Is there any guarantee that defunct hand pumps and broken pipes are a thing of the past, and that basic needs discourses are different from the basic rights discourse?

The key difference between human needs and human rights is that the latter entail an element of entitlement. As Goldewijik and de Gaay

Forman describe it, 'A rights-based approach to social and economic security implies that people's access to basic needs is protected by law and legal mechanisms' (1999). Rights, in other words, are the basis of access to resources and commodities upon which real claims can be made. They also entail an element of justiciability, and this legal protection can in principle provide grounds for redress in cases of accountability failures, and for mobilizing resources at local and global levels (see Chapter 13).

However, do enforceable social and economic rights make a difference to people's lives and livelihoods? I have already demonstrated that rights-based approaches may not necessarily lead to the radical redistribution or reallocation of resources in a society. But do they make a difference to poor people? Take the case of two pensioners in rural South Africa who were interviewed by researcher Zolile Ntshona (2003). Mabombo is 61 years old and is entitled to a pension. Before the implementation of the FBW policy, she used to collect water from the spring far from her house, and used a ten-litre container to make two to three trips to the spring before sunrise. Collection from the spring was difficult for her because she had to wait for the sediments to settle before collecting. She now feels that since the introduction of the FBW policy, life has improved. She does not have to wake up in the morning before the livestock make the spring water murky and so she can concentrate her energy on other work. She uses the FBW for washing, drinking and cooking, though she still visits the spring to wash blankets. Mathungu, 70 years old, also supports a large family with her old age pension. Before the implementation of the FBW policy she could not afford the 10 rands needed to pay for water services in her village. She too no longer needs to go to the spring on a daily basis for her water. Clearly, FBW has made a significant difference to the everyday lives of people like Mathungu and Mabombo. However, both of them would have liked this policy to address their local livelihood concerns, including water for subsistence agriculture and livestock, since this would play a longer-term role in reducing their poverty.

Some contradictions still exist with respect to the trend towards cost recovery. After all, somebody has to pay for water delivery, even for that water which is ostensibly 'free'. This takes place either through the Equitable Share system, cost recovery, or cross-subsidization. While cross-subsidization is ideal, it may not ensure that the water supplied is safe, and it rarely works in rural areas where water usage is not as differentiated as in urban areas.

As critics of FBW policy such as Barry Jackson (2002) argue, monitoring and rationing the quota of free water is also very difficult.

Often it can cost more to install a meter than to provide water free of charge (interview with DWAF official, Mount Ayliff, 23 April 2002). Finally, the FBW policy has also made charging for water difficult. Many communities understood that they would now stop paying for water (Jackson 2002). Therefore, for cash-strapped district municipalities, raising the money to provide water is becoming increasingly difficult (see also Kihato and Schmitz 2002; Ntshona 2003), not least because historically there was a lack of clarity on how the 'equitable share' allocation should be divided up between the various arms of local government.

Do universalisms matter?

This discussion has drawn on South Africa's experience with the FBW policy to illuminate the painful contradictions of implementing universalist conceptions of social and economic rights. The chapter demonstrates that the national vision around FBW has yet to be implemented in practice. While the vision was conceived at the national level (in a rather top-down manner), the responsibility for implementing it rests with local government. There also appear to be parallel trends at local and national levels towards cost recovery. In cases where the private sector gets involved, its ability and willingness to promote access to free water are contested. Indeed, as the critical literature in South Africa indicates, private sector involvement has been very controversial, leading to disconnections (either voluntary or forced) because the service has become too expensive for consumers, or to forcing people to pay for water, something hitherto unknown (Bond 2001; McDonald and Pape 2002). In some cases, though, bringing in the private sector, at least in the short term, seems to improve service delivery. Finally, at the time of researching this chapter, South Africa's rapidly changing policy and institutional environment also engendered much uncertainty regarding rights, policies and the division of responsibility between local municipalities, district municipalities, provincial government and the national ministries. Securing the capacity to exercise these rights and responsibilities is probably a major challenge. These problems could defeat the very purpose of the policy; that is, to contribute to reducing the gap between rich and poor (Kihato and Schmitz 2002).

Does this mean that universalisms have no merits? Clearly, universalist conceptions around rights can often be blind to local priorities, needs and social dynamics. In the case of the FBW, its implementation and interpretation are often the responsibility of hapless bureaucrats (in particular at the local level), who may lack the capacity and resources to implement social justice. Still, I would argue that universalist declarations should not be rejected outright. There is still a value in seeking to have them recognized and endorsed, painful and contradictory as they may be in practice. In this respect South Africa's FBW policy needs to be applauded for its explicit focus on the basic right to water and for going against the grain of dominant global discourses.

Two further reasons emerge as important. One, the ability of citizens to mobilize around rights claims when their basic rights are violated is only possible when access to basic rights is institutionalized in the form of constitutional rights. Two, rights language can serve as a countervailing force against the commodification of water, which can in principle impinge on poor people's rights to water. This was also acknowledged by the 2002 United Nations General Comment, which states that privatization can impinge on people's rights to water and stressed that households cannot be disconnected on the basis of non-payments. Thus, countries that allow the liberalization of their water services are legally obliged to establish effective and flexible regulatory mechanisms that can secure the progressive realization of the right to water for all people.

As Donnelly says, 'markets are social institutions designed to produce efficiency' (1999, p. 628). But markets can run counter to the expansion of social and economic rights (*ibid*), since they take an aggregate view of the benefits of market-led mechanisms (such as an increase in gross domestic product and so on) and thus they 'can systematically deprive some individuals in order to achieve the collective benefits of efficiency' (*ibid*, p. 628). Seen in this light, the strong endorsement of social and economic rights can temper the market, with its emphasis on efficiency and the 'collective good'. Moreover, since the market cannot guarantee the provision of all goods, as of all rights, on a fair basis to all citizens, social and economic rights can imply limits to commodification and commercialization (Plant 1992, p. 16). In an era of increasing economic globalization, where private sector involvement in basic services is increasing (not least through pressure from bilateral and multilateral institutions such as the World Bank and the World Trade Organization), there is a need to protect citizen's rights to basic services such as water. The South African experience demonstrates both the pitfalls and positive lessons along the road to institutionalizing access to water as a human right. It also shows that making water 'public' and protecting citizens' rights to water are political choices that require strong commitment from governments and donors.

Notes

I am grateful to Renwick Irvine for his research assistance. Peter Davis encouraged me to engage with European social policy debates. The empirical material for this chapter draws on research conducted as part of the DFID-funded research programme 'Sustainable Livelihoods in Southern Africa'. I'm particularly grateful to all my interview partners for taking the time to share their ideas with me, and Zolile Ntshona, Edward Lahiff and Ian Scoones for making this research possible. John Gaventa, Neil Stammers, Barbara Schreiner, Barbara van Koppen and Barry Jackson provided useful comments on earlier drafts. Finally, I thank Naila Kabeer for her editorial suggestions.

1. For example, the Universal Declaration of Human Rights, Article 25.1 1948; International Covenant on Economic, Social and Cultural Rights (ICESCR) 11; Convention on the Elimination of All Forms of Discrimination against Women (CEDAW) 14.2h.
2. The lack of explicit references makes Gleick ask: 'Is water so fundamental a resource, like air, that it was thought unnecessary to explicitly include it at the time when these agreements were forged? Or could the Framers of these agreements have actually intended to exclude access to water as a right, while including access to food and other conditions of qualities of life? (1999, pp. 4–5). After reviewing several of the documents, he concludes that the drafter implicitly considered water to be a fundamental resource. Moreover, most other basic rights explicitly protected by international rights (around food, health and development) require access to a minimum amount of safe and adequate water.
3. General Comment 15, The right to water (articles 11 and 12 of the International Covenant on Economic, Social and Cultural Rights), UN Doc. E/C.12/2002/11 (Twenty-ninth session, 2002).
4. For example, at the 2001 Bonn Freshwater Conference, many stakeholders – including representatives of governments and business – made verbal endorsements of the human right to water, but the final conference document failed to acknowledge it explicitly.
5. Available on www.wmo.ch/index-en.html
6. The National Water Act of 1998 also explicitly tries to redress old inequalities by making the government the custodian of all water resources, and especially earmarking water for basic needs.
7. If, however, one takes into consideration the money spent on operating costs, we need to add another billion (Martin Rall, personal communication, 21 January 2004).

References

Altaf, M., H. Jamal and D. Whittington (1992) 'Willingness to pay for water in rural Punjab', UNDP–World Bank Water and Sanitation Program, Water and Sanitation Report, 4, Washington DC: World Bank

Bond, P. (2001) 'Privatisation, participation and protest in the restructuring of municipal services: Grounds for opposing World Bank promotion of "public–private" partnerships', www.thewaterpage.com/ppp_debate1.htm (accessed 4 April 2002)

Bond, P., D. McDonald, G. Ruiters and L. Greef (2001) *Water Privatisation in Southern Africa: The State of the Debate*, Cape Town: Environmental Monitoring Group

Donnelly, J. (1999) 'Human rights, democracy and development', *Human Rights*

Quarterly, 21, pp. 608–32

Ellison, N. (1999) 'Beyond universalism and particularism: Rethinking contemporary welfare theory', *Critical Social Policy*, 19 (1), pp. 57–83

Ghosh, G. and A. Nigam (1995) 'Comments on "Financing water supply and sanitation under Agenda 21" by John Briscoe and Mike Garn', *Natural Resources Forum*, 19 (2), pp. 161–5

Gleick, P. (1999) *The World's Water 2000–2001: The Biennial Report on Freshwater Resources*, Washington: Island Press

Goldewijik, B. K. and B. de Gaay Forman (1999) *Where needs meet rights: economic, social and cultural rights in new perspectives*, Geneva: WCC Publications

Jackson, B. (2002) 'FREE water – what are the chances of serving the poor', Johannesburg: mimeo

Kihato, C. and T. Schmitz (2002) 'Enhancing policy implementation: Lessons from the water sector', Research Report 96, Social Policy Series, Johannesburg: Centre for Policy Studies

McDonald, D. A. and J. Pape (eds) (2002) *Cost Recovery and the Crisis of Service Delivery in South Africa*, London: Zed Books

Mehta, L. (2003a) 'Problems of publicness and access rights: Perspectives from the water domain', in I. Kaul *et al.* (eds) *Providing Public Goods: Making Globalisation Work for All*, New York: Oxford University Press

Mehta, L. (2003b) 'Activists tapping into water row', *The Guardian*, 17 March

Mehta, L. (forthcoming) *The Naturalisation of Scarcity: The Politics and Poetics of Water in Kutch*, India, London: Zed Books/Orient Longman

Neto, F. and H. Tropp (2000) 'Water supply and sanitation services for all: Global progress during the 1990s', *Natural Resources Forum*, 24 (3), pp. 225–3

Nigam, A. and S. Rasheed (1998) 'Financing of freshwater for all: A rights-based approach', *UNICEF Staff Working Papers*, No. EPP-EVL-98_003, New York: UNICEF

Ntshona, Z. (2003) 'Realising the free basic water policy in South Africa: The case of Alfred Nzo District Municipality in the former Transkei', Brighton: Institute of Development Studies, mimeo

Plant, R. (1992) 'Citizenship, rights and welfare', in A. Coote (ed.) *The Welfare of Citizens: Developing New Social Rights*, London: IPPR

Plant, R. (1998) 'Citizenship, rights, welfare', in J. Franklin (ed.) *Social Policy and Social Justice*, Cambridge: Polity Press

Reddy, R. V. (1999) 'Quenching the thirst: The cost of water in fragile environments', *Development and Change*, 30 (1), pp. 79–113

Reddy, S. and J. Vandemoortele (1996) 'User financing of basic social services: A review of theoretical arguments and empirical evidence', *UNICEF Staff Working Papers*, Evaluation, Policy and Planning Series, New York: UNICEF

Thompson, S. and P. Hoggart (1996) 'Universalism, selectivism and particularism: Towards a postmodern social policy', *Critical Social Policy* 46

UNICEF (1994) *Implementing the 20/20 Initiative*, New York: UNICEF

van Koppen, B., N. Jha and D. Merrey (2002) 'Redressing racial inequities through water law in South Africa: Interaction and contest among legal frameworks', International Water Management Institute, mimeo

Whittington, D. and M. K. Choe (1992) 'Economic benefits available from the provision of improved potable water supplies', WASH Technical Report, 77, Washington: WASH/ USAID

Donors, rights-based approaches and implications for global citizenship: a case study from Peru

Rosalind Eyben

Introduction

How far can foreign governments go in supporting the realization of the rights of citizens of other countries? The country programmes of most bilateral aid agencies are hesitating to move from declaration to implementation of rights-based approaches. Nevertheless, innovation and enterprise flourish on the margins of the mainstream. It is here we must look for efforts to put declarations into practice. This chapter explores the challenges and risks facing a foreign aid agency when it seeks to do so. Based on interviews with the staff concerned, and illustrated with four examples from a broader range of efforts, this is the story of a small country office on the periphery of a large bilateral international aid programme: the Peru office of the UK Department for International Development (DFID).

In each and every aspect of their work, the Peru team consistently takes a rights-based approach to an extent that I have not met anywhere else in DFID. The team's effort reveals difficult issues concerning the legitimacy of action: the practice of power and lines of accountability. Illuminating these dilemmas and challenges may help development agencies contribute to an inclusive world order based on transnational notions of rights and social justice.

The Department for International Development in Peru

A bilateral aid agency such as DFID is part of a foreign, sovereign government. It provides financial and technical aid to governments of recipient countries through projects, programmes or budgetary support. It may also fund civil society activities, although perhaps preferring to channel this support through the intermediary of its own non-governmental organizations (NGOs) back home to avoid accusations of too direct an involvement in local politics (Eyben 2003b). Although the UK had been providing small amounts of aid to Peru for many years, it only opened an office in Lima in early 2000. With a total staff of seven, it is one of DFID's smallest offices, located in a continent on the periphery of DFID's interest.[1] It has adopted the unusual practice in DFID of employing senior national advisers working on equal terms with those recruited in Britain. It manages direct funding to both government and civil society programmes.

In the three to four years of its existence, this office has witnessed a dynamic and sometimes turbulent political process. Fujimori was president of Peru for a period of ten years, during which time his administration became increasingly centralized and authoritarian. Most institutions were co-opted to the regime – through bribery, blackmail or force – including Congress, the judiciary, the armed forces, much of the media and a swathe of civil society organizations, including the popular organizations used for disbursing social assistance programmes. Following Fujimori's flight in November 2000, a caretaker government paved the way for elections that brought in President Toledo in July 2001 and what the DFID office described as the 'democratic spring'. Thereafter, the office began to observe the re-emergence of long-established structures of conservatism and patronage.[2]

In its first year, and Fujimori's last, the DFID office established contact with the Peruvian academy and civil society, including human rights activists and champions of social justice. Later, during the 'democratic spring', many of these academics and activists joined the administration. DFID was encouraged by the compatibility of their agenda with its own approach to development. Thus, despite its relative paucity of staff and money, the office believed it could help shape a more inclusive and substantive democracy, informed by poor people's struggles to realize their social, economic and cultural, as well as their civil and political, rights.

The realization of rights is the conceptual lens through which DFID Peru pursues its central goal of strengthening state–society relations. This means supporting the state to become more accountable and responsive to its citizens – particularly those with the least power and the most excluded – while at the same time helping citizens' organizations develop the interest and capacity to engage with state institutions rather than confront, disregard or serve them as clients. The office developed a strategy informed by the political science literature on clientelism and citizenship in Latin America.[3] It also commissioned literature reviews and think-pieces from Peruvian social scientists and policy analysts to ground its work in a contextual understanding. It saw it was engaged in efforts to change deep structural relationships between state and society, established at the time of the Spanish conquest, and resulting in the absence of a shared vision of Peruvian society. It noted the cyclical nature of democratic moments followed by authoritarian regimes. It identified the antagonism between authoritarian and democratic tendencies running through all social life, including the low self-esteem of poor people in Peru associated with the belief that they themselves are not capable of changing their situation but are dependent on a providential leader, thus encouraging the authoritarian tendency (IEP 2003).

A paper commissioned from Francisco Sagasti (2002) distinguished between the long-term, contextual factors that change only slowly, and medium-term, institutional factors that influence the extent and direction of structural change. Examples of the latter include the extension of the franchise to women and illiterate citizens, universal and compulsory primary education, agrarian reform, the growth of the informal urban economy and substantial migration to the cities, and the economic reforms associated with the opening up of markets. Sagasti argued that foreign aid could be most effective in supporting these medium-term changes.

Lastly, the office analysed how and with whom it could promote non-party political action in favour of the realization of poor people's rights. Who makes and shapes policy, and how can DFID influence that process? Iteratively it has looked for allies within the research community, in human rights organizations and among leaders in the urban working class. It commissioned a study on elites on the premise that they may be significant agents of change (IEP 2003) and discovered that elites in Peru do not exist in any coherent sense of the word. It learned that it is rather the middle classes that may be the key agents of progressive change.

Bilateral aid and rights-based approaches

Rights-based approaches are increasingly part of the policy and practice of international development agencies (Eyben 2003a). While recognizing the importance of the internationally agreed normative framework, DFID policy and practice focus on the integration of principles of equality, inclusion, participation and empowerment into a global goal of poverty reduction (DFID 2000a). The meaning and importance of rights-based approaches are often disputed within an agency, and official *policy* statements tend to reflect a compromise between views. *Practice* may be a better indicator of emphasis and commitment. In DFID, this practice has been inadequately monitored (Piron 2003), but the extent to which a country programme practises rights–based approaches and how it does so depend significantly on the individuals appointed to the relevant office.

Rights–based approaches present different challenges for bilateral agencies as compared with those of the United Nations (UN). A donor government's own human rights record can be scrutinized and its agency subjected to the criticism that its government is not practising what it preaches. Moreover, in the case of a UN agency, the host country in some sense *owns* it, with more influence over its practice. The international framework for managing the diplomatic relationship between two governments is regulated by the Vienna Convention on Diplomatic Relations. Primarily concerned with privileges and immunities, the Convention leaves as a very grey area the extent to which a government aid agency can become involved in the domestic issues of the host country.

Of course, the *raison d'être* of foreign aid is to change the social, political and economic systems and structures of the recipient country. However, custom does not describe this as interference in domestic concerns when it is couched in technical language and the recipient government requests it. Policy conditions linked to resource transfers and even support for civil society may be welcomed if the government sees this as a means for strengthening domestic support for goals that it embraces itself. Such goals can include foreign support for the realization of human rights to which the recipient government subscribes. The concept of Westphalian sovereignty (the exclusion of external actors from domestic authority structures) is only seen to be violated when the recipient government does *not* like that interference (Krasner 1999). In such cases, it can accuse the aid agency of unwarranted or illegitimate interference in local politics and values.

This grey area of international custom is the context to the story of DFID in Peru. It is a story of how employees of a foreign government, justifying their actions by reference to an internationally agreed and domestically ratified human rights framework, became involved in supporting citizens' struggles in that country. Four illustrations are provided. These are a fund to support civil society organizations and local government action for enhancing the voice of poor people in policy-making; support for a more inclusive, representative democracy; the promotion of the right to health; and aiding the state's social investment programme to become more transparent, responsive and accountable.

Supporting a shift from clientelism to citizenship

'None of us had a very clear understanding of what we meant by rights-based approaches' [4]

During the last year of the Fujimori regime, DFID decided not to start any new projects with an administration too authoritarian and corrupt to justify support. Tactically, this meant money available in the pipeline had to be spent in other ways. Strategically, there was the challenge of how to support long-term change if the aid programme shut down every time the country reverted from democracy to authoritarianism.

The head of the office, whom I assisted (at that time working in DFID's Bolivia programme), made several visits around the country. We developed an analytical framework that understood structural poverty in Peru as a result of long-term political processes in which poor people were treated as clients of the state rather than as citizens. We saw human rights as an entry point for change. I was also eager to test and implement the newly published DFID policy on human rights that I had been instrumental in developing when at head office.[5]

What would such a policy look like in practice? We decided to design a large human rights programme that would provide funds on a competitive basis to civil society. Although in other parts of the world DFID had funded civil society programmes, this would be the first to emphasize human rights. The objective would be to strengthen poor people's organizational capacity to realize their rights, and to construct alliances so as to influence policy processes at the local, regional and national levels. DFID was particularly interested in reaching small grassroots organizations in the highlands and forest areas of Peru, and to include economic, social and cultural rights within the scope of the programme. This made it rather different from other bilateral agencies, such as the Canadian International Development Agency (CIDA) and the US Agency for International Development (USAID), who were supporting the efforts of human rights organizations in Lima to defend all citizens' civil and political rights against the abuses of the Fujimori regime, without a specific focus on the exclusion and powerlessness of poor people. Following the end of the Fujimori regime, the design of the programme shifted to a stronger emphasis on the role of the government, as well as civil society, in supporting poor people's actions.

Oxfam was appointed as management agent in late 2002.[6] Both parties felt they would benefit from the partnership. DFID, itself a government agency, more naturally tended to focus on the behaviour of central government, and Oxfam on the agenda of grassroots activists. For Oxfam, the advantage of its association with DFID was to expand its capacity to work with institutions of government as well as with civil society from the local up to the national level. For DFID, it was to gain a greater experience and understanding through Oxfam of local communities and their political processes. Both agencies saw the end of the Fujimori regime as a significant window of opportunity. Oxfam noted that one challenge for the programme was how excluded and powerless people can gain a voice at the regional and national level, bearing in mind that civil society organizations in these spaces have tended to be exclusionary, reflecting the patterns of power relations in the wider society.

By the time the programme was due to start, the political environment had become less supportive. Moreover, Oxfam was not regarded with favour by some in the Toledo government because of its campaigning on behalf of local people whose livelihoods were threatened by the state's decision to award a mining concession in the northwest of the country. How was DFID to manage its relations with the government and at the same time stay in partnership with Oxfam? Furthermore, in this case, the head of the DFID office might have found himself in trouble not only with the Peruvian government but also with his own embassy, whose principal interests in the country are commercial, and who might not want to see this kind of mining investment discouraged by grassroots protests.

Oxfam took a different position. It was interested in managing the programme *just because* it was a means to support local organizations to acquire an increased capability to challenge social injustice and unequal power relations. If it were to tone down its activities because it was now funded by an official donor, it risked compromising its very *raison d'être*.

The resulting dialogue between Oxfam and DFID revealed that their head office policy statements on rights were only the starting point for developing a mutual understanding of rights-based approaches in practice. Over time, and with increased trust, DFID and Oxfam have been working out a shared agenda, both parties coming to realize that an understanding of rights-based approaches derives from learning in practice. DFID has negotiated a common shared space with Oxfam for the project, ring-fencing it from non-shared activities undertaken by the two partners; it is a space protected from separate, other agendas.

'The challenge is how to match the democracy and the poverty agendas'

DFID is developing, as a central part of its programme in Peru, support for good governance in favour of poor people. This is seen by the office as a major challenge, because most donor-funded democracy work in

Latin America does not directly make the link with poverty reduction in the way that DFID is seeking to do.

Nearly all bilateral agencies supported the 2001 elections that followed the downfall of Fujimori, but only DFID was specifically concerned with how to help *poor* and *marginalized* people become informed *citizens*. The challenge was to change the approach of the Fujimori years, when poverty alleviation programmes had brought real material benefits to the remoter rural areas, while at the same time reinforcing poor people's status as clients of a patronage state. Thus, during the severe floods in highland Peru just before the elections took place, local people commented that if Fujimori had still been in power, disaster relief would have been much faster. The president himself would have personally visited by helicopter to show that he cared.

Was democracy thus only a concern of the educated and urban populations? In the short period of time available, DFID hastily invited civil society organizations working in the remoter rural areas to use DFID funds to work with poor populations. Activities included training in the mechanics of voting, citizenship education through workshops and mass media, and facilitating dialogues between candidates and voters.[7] Subsequent conferences in Lima shared the results with the National Election Commission and the Ombudsman's office, as well as with human rights NGOs.

Since then, DFID has funded similar activities in the local government elections in 2002, and followed these up by supporting some specific local government initiatives in participatory budgeting and monitoring along the lines of that in Porto Alegre in Brazil. It has also been working strategically at the national level to integrate concerns for inclusion into the legislature's political party and electoral reform programme. It is increasingly learning how to work indirectly on issues of political accountability by dialoguing with and funding Peruvian partners, such as academic institutions, think-tanks and national advocacy groups, who, because they are Peruvian organizations, may be judged by state institutions as more legitimate actors than DFID.

In this way, DFID is encouraging legislators and the Electoral Commission to consider specifically how to reinforce poor people's political rights. In the current reforms of the political party system, it has supported a debate on how to include the voice of people from remote and rural areas; for example, through expanding the local constituency-based system. DFID has also been involved in the discussions relating to donors' concern about the high cost of elections. It has pointed out that cost-cutting could be prejudicial to inclusiveness. It costs more for a person living in a remote rural area to vote than it does for one living in the city, and more if citizens are to vote in their own indigenous language or are to vote while illiterate. If costs were to be cut, whose rights would be diminished?

'Why force everyone into the space that DFID invented?'

Building on its prior health sector work with the Peruvian government, and some responsive and strategic funding of a civil society health policy forum, DFID decided to work with the Ministry of Health, the Ombudsman's office and with the civil society networks to build a programme of support that could strengthen Peruvian efforts to secure a rights-based approach to health care. The aim was to support greater inclusion and participation of poor and excluded people in health care processes, allowing them greater influence over public policy, expenditure and management decisions. A component of the proposed programme was the promotion of women's reproductive rights, building on the work of the civil society networks that had sprung up during the Fujimori regime and in resistance to a sterilization programme. This had been a major impulse for poor and indigenous women to shift to a new language of rights, and the establishment of networks and alliances by Peruvian feminist organizations.

A programme was designed to fund all three parties under the same umbrella. From the DFID perspective, this had the tactical advantage of simplifying administration. Strategically, the idea was that by bringing these three parties together, there would be the possibility of developing and strengthening a shared concern. However, prior to the final commitment stages, and following some changes in the Toledo administration that led to a strengthening of religious conservative views, there was a significant shift in the government's attitude on health matters, particularly with regard to women's reproductive rights. The Minister of Health indicated that he was no longer interested in DFID funding such a programme.

After details of some correspondence on this matter were leaked to the press, DFID considered how best to proceed in the light of its firm commitment to women's reproductive and other health rights. It noted that the religious conservatives were co-opting the rights language by seeking a change in the law in relation to citizens' constitutional rights concerning the claims of unborn children and health providers' right of conscience to deny women access to family planning advice. DFID also noted that there was no interest on the part of these religious conservatives in encouraging public debate on the issue. Following the publication of the leaked document, the airing of the issue in the press had the unintended effect of opening up discussion.

Meanwhile, DFID had learned that strengthening state–society relations was not a simple matter. It had tried to bring together different parts of the Peruvian system but found they were not willing to work together, however much outsiders, such as DFID, might think this a good idea. It realized that as a condition of donor funding it may be both arrogant and unrealistic to create an umbrella structure through which government and civil society organizations are required to operate jointly in a shared, DFID-created space. Partly driven by its own internal requirements, DFID had been trying to force a relationship on organizations that were not yet ready for it. It decided to switch to an alternative, more processual approach, funding civil society and government through quite separate projects, while creating spaces, such as diplomatic receptions and academic seminars, where the different parties could be invited to meet, should they wish to do so. But the Minister remained uninterested. I return to this story at the end of the chapter.

'Our aim was to help FONCODES shift to treating people as citizens rather than clients'

Peru's social investment fund, FONCODES, had been one of Fujimori's principal instruments to act as poor people's patron. Decisions were made at the centre and the funding procedures were entirely non-transparent, resulting in both corruption and an infrastructure that did not respond to local demands.

Initially the Toledo government saw the reform of FONCODES as a key matter. A former civil society activist and renowned scholar and authority on Peru's poverty alleviation programmes was appointed to manage FONCODES. He saw this as an opportunity to transform social protection policy and practice away from the Fujimori clientelist model to one based on entitlement principles. He was already well known to DFID, and the office rapidly agreed to his request for funding for Peruvian technical assistance to help restructure FONCODES procedures. With another, bigger donor (the Inter American Development Bank), it also financed Toledo's emergency employment programme, channelling the money through FONCODES to encourage a more participatory and bottom-up process.

Shortly thereafter (and before any major changes could be made to FONCODES procedures), there was a government shift towards a more populist style. The reforming head of FONCODES was dismissed, to be replaced by a party political appointment. The other, bigger donor, eager to disburse, appeared to be unconcerned about the lack of change to the status quo. The voices for reform were ignored;

no one listened any more to their case that FONCODES should be run differently. DFID learned that it could do little to support the reformers, lacking the technical credibility of prior experience in Peru concerning the reform of social investment funds.

Once again, over time, the balance shifted back in favour of the new approach. The administration of FONCODES was given to a newly created ministry and the dialogue could be re-established, but in a less transformational manner than during the 'democratic spring'. DFID was learning the importance of long-term engagement throughout the twists and turns of day-to-day, often grubby, politics.

Promoting citizenship: wider implications for donor behaviour

These examples are teaching DFID in Peru a number of significant lessons for the practice of rights-based approaches. They concern how to practise rights-based approaches through rapid and informed responses to emerging situations in which like-minded allies are seeking help in sometimes risky ventures. DFID is also learning the importance of being credible and sticking to its agenda even when the turn of events makes things more difficult than envisaged. The clear vision of supporting a shift from clientelism to citizenship as the basis for rights-based practice has allowed it to ride the roller-coaster of Peruvian politics. Some important issues are emerging concerning transparency and accountability, and the extent to which a bilateral agency can be a legitimate political actor in its host country.

Becoming more accountable

Greater accountability of state institutions to poor citizens is a key component of DFID's central policy approach to rights and good governance. This should include improving DFID's own accountability to those whom it works with and seeks to help. DFID Peru is gradually tackling this issue, and meanwhile runs the risk of being accused of playing a behind-the-scenes role by indirectly supporting policy changes through funding civil society action and academic think-tanks.

One of the challenges facing DFID in Peru was that there was no real chance of establishing clear and fairly long-term agreed rules between government and official donors concerning the extent to which external actors could be seen as legitimate agents of change. The political volatility of the regime would appear to make this impossible; what was appreciated during the 'democratic spring' was frowned upon one year later, as, for example, DFID's support to a civil society health network. The route taken by the Peru office is probably the only correct one, of being absolutely transparent and public about its own rights-based agenda. It could, however, take one more step and actively invite public debate in the country concerning its role.

Because it requires significant changes within the parent organization, becoming more accountable is much harder than becoming more transparent. DFID's White Paper (DFID 2000b) on globalization commits the UK government to work with others to build a stronger, more open and accountable international system in which poor people and countries have a more effective voice. The White Paper states: 'We need global political institutions to better manage and counterbalance global markets and to help promote global social justice'. DFID head office has not, however, sufficiently considered its own ambivalent position as a global actor.

Held (1996) points out that many decisions taken by a national government concerning actions *within* its own country (deforestation, for example) can have a wider global impact, and thus raise questions concerning the nature of democratic legitimacy. He asks whose agreement is necessary and whose participation is justified in decisions concerning, for example, the management of non-renewable natural resources or economic flows. What is the relevant constituency: national, regional or international? To whom should decision-makers have to justify their decisions? To whom should they be accountable? He notes a striking paradox. Just when the importance of democratic governance is being re-emphasized in many countries around the world, so the very efficacy of democracy as a national form of political organization appears open to question because of the impact on a country's citizenship of decisions made elsewhere and over which they have no control. The same point has been made with reference to Uganda, and the irony of the government's adoption of participatory approaches within the country, while most of the decisions that affect Ugandan people are made in global spaces (Brock *et al.* 2002).

Bilateral agency accountability is an acute example of this democratic challenge. Because these agencies *do* have clear lines of accountability back to citizens in their own countries, they have been relatively less concerned about how to be accountable to citizens in the spaces where they operate. Whatever the defects of multilateral agencies, such as the International Monetary Fund, the United Nations Development Programme and the World Bank, in terms of representation and voice, there are institutionalized arrangements for holding these agencies accountable for their actions in national and local spaces. There are no such arrangements in place for the actions of bilateral donors other than in their own countries, where by definition they do not act. Although the *raison d'être* of a bilateral donor is to make an impact on *other countries' citizens*, a bilateral donor agency considers itself as legitimate, accountable and responsive only to the citizens and taxpayers of its home country. However, its actions in any national or local space are only minimally institutionalized at the global level. A citizen of Peru cannot make a claim against DFID for failure to help secure the realization of his or her rights.

The traditional answer given to this challenge has been that donor governments are providing aid because of a request from the recipient government that itself is legitimate, accountable and responsive to its citizens. There are three problems with this answer. First, only minimal arrangements are in place for the donor to be accountable to the recipient government – and thus, by extension, to that country's citizens. Second, many recipient governments suffer from a democratic deficit, and in particular are likely to be less than legitimate, accountable and responsive in relation to the *poor* citizens that are the focus of donors' interests. Hence the popularity of aid programmes to promote democracy and better governance at the local and national level. Third, even should the first two problems be resolved, the bilateral donor is still faced with the quandary of accountability to other countries' citizens when it is operating in *global* spaces (Held 1996; Brock *et al.* 2002); for example, at the UN, when urging that the Millennium Development Goals should drive the aid agenda.

The DFID White Paper makes a commitment to ensuring that poor *people* and poor *countries* have a greater voice in these global spaces. It notes the need for a stronger *global* civil society and therefore presumes a role for global citizens. Gaventa and Edwards (2001) have explored the models of transnational citizen engagement and how the way they organize globally affects local issues, but they did not examine the implications for bilateral official donors when supporting such engagement. Who becomes accountable to whom?

Eyben and Ferguson (2004) propose that *bilateral* aid agencies are accountable to five categories of institution or persons: taxpayers in the donor country; government in the donor country; government in the recipient country; poor people in the recipient country; and, lastly, the institutions associated with the international human rights framework. Thus, a rights-based approach has the potential to offer donors a conceptual framework for addressing and managing these three problems. In adopting such an approach, donors may find themselves, almost by default, contributing to the construction of an inclusive, democratic global governance system, as well as to promoting and strengthening democratic processes in local and national spaces.

Transformation at the centre is often dependent on innovation at the periphery. What kind of example could be set by DFID in Peru? One of the problems facing such a country office is the centre's current drive in the reverse direction. Too often, practitioners see aid as about securing goals that *they* think are important. Target-driven and performance management approaches can reinforce this aim to influence others. For example, the UK National Audit Office (2002) has asked DFID to improve the way it measures the impact it is making on others.

One step towards greater donor accountability to aid recipients could be through systematic social auditing. DFID Peru could agree indicators with its partners for changed behaviour by the various intermediary organizations involved in promoting citizenship. For example, Oxfam and DFID could agree such an indicator concerning inclusive behaviour with the intermediary civil society organizations being funded through the DFID human rights programme. Such indicators would, of course, assess the extent of DFID's own behaviour as well as that of its partners. The very process of negotiation would open up space for discussion about organizational accountability and unequal power relations.

Accountability through the international human rights institutions is another, more radical, means. In addition to the committee of the International Covenant on Civil and Political Rights (ICCPR), there are five other treaty bodies that, like the ICCPR, consider reports from states that have ratified the relevant treaty (Steiner and Alston 2000, p. 773). Some donor countries already include within their reporting to some of these committees their performance on supporting the realization of human rights in recipient countries. Donor governments could take this further by inviting aid recipients to submit alternative reports on their performance. It would not only signal development agencies' commitment to supporting and strengthening the application of the human rights framework, but would also demonstrate an effort to become more accountable through those same global institutions that the world community has established to promote human rights.

Recognizing power and paradox

One of the aims of the DFID–Oxfam human rights programme was to demonstrate the importance of rights-based approaches to poverty reduction to other more powerful aid agencies. This includes those to which the UK Government was making a global contribution, such as the EC aid programme, and those in which the UK had a share, such as the World Bank and the Inter American Development Bank. These latter, the international finance institutions (IFIs), have proved difficult to secure as allies. Despite enormous personal investment by the DFID team in establishing good relationships with the IFI local offices (and securing considerable interest and engagement from the staff in these offices), decisions in Washington may prevail over local staff interest in promoting some of the principles of rights-based approaches. Interest in disbursing funds can easily override a real concern for systemic change. IFI attitudes to rights may, in turn, affect the willingness of other bilateral agencies to take a greater interest in matters that may in any case appear too blatantly political and risky.

Support from DFID's own head office may also fluctuate. Many aid bureaucrats still like the convenient pretence that aid is technical. Even the promotion of participation may be justified on the grounds of some other outcome, such as reduced maternal mortality. There is no consensus within DFID that the promotion and protection of human rights is one of its main objectives (Piron 2003).

Potentially, rights-based approaches can reveal the contradictions and complexities of donor–recipient relations. They can encourage their proponents to focus on living with these complexities, rather than ignore them by constructing imaginary worlds of technical linear planning. The contradictions in rights-based approaches could be accepted rather than smoothed away, and thus strengthen the capacity for what is now often described as *negative capability*; that is, 'When a man is capable of being in uncertainties, mysteries, doubts, without any irritable reaching after fact and reason' (Falwell 1987, quoting a letter from the poet John Keats). Rights-based approaches thus offer donors the potential for fundamental change in their behaviour, a change in which they embrace uncertainty and contradiction and allow for and encourage humility.

The need for humility has struck another observer of donor behaviour (Maxwell 2003). I have argued elsewhere (Eyben 2003b) that the current hubris and stance of absolute certainty may well be a reaction to the increasingly ambitious goals that donors have set themselves in what is self-evidently a complex and unpredictable world. The *peril* of the rights-based approach lies in the danger of proud and powerful donors co-opting the language of rights and using this to legitimize further their action while changing nothing in their behaviour. It could strengthen their hegemonic claims to understanding how to change the world in the name of poor people. Cornwall (2000) and Brock *et al.* (2002) have already noted the risk of this happening, referring to the way some donors, particularly the World Bank, use the language of *participation*. Mosse (2003) notes how donors' use of participatory development 'simultaneously confers and denies agency to the poor'. Rights-based approaches that use the international human rights standards as their normative frameworks can become an ideological weapon in the armoury of those with most *power*. It may be why some activists for social justice become confused and suspicious when they hear donors use the language of rights. Should they welcome or reject this as another example of donor hypocrisy? It may be a relief that so far the World Bank has not adopted a rights–based approach.

As a small donor in a country that is not significantly dependent on aid, DFID in Peru may have been more successful than other country offices in implementing rights–based approaches. Its success may be partially explained by its relative powerlessness and its inability to impose conditions on local partners.

Conclusion: rights-based approaches and political involvement

The relation between a donor government and a recipient's citizens is inherently problematic. Rights and their associated responsibilities are generally understood as an aspect of citizenship, and citizenship in turn is connected with the nation–state.[8] Can a foreign government justify its support to citizen action only when such support is clearly within the law and/or there are sufficient numbers of citizens who are manifestly seeking the change that the donor is promoting? Does involvement in political processes become more justified when it is apparent that citizens have little faith in their elected representatives? Does a rights–based approach necessarily lead to a foreign agency becoming a political player?

DFID in Peru decided not to adopt a judicial approach to supporting the realization of rights. Although it would appear to offer the safety of an apparent de–politicization of the issues, it can also constrain action in areas that ultimately can only be negotiated in political spaces. To pretend otherwise may well prove ultimately unhelpful. To the extent that DFID actions can be judged as political, they are to support a greater political voice for those who so far have had little influence on the decisions of their own government, including decisions on how to spend aid.

So far, DFID in Peru has worked fully within the Peruvian national legal framework, informing the government of all its major activities. It appeals not just to international human rights conventions, but also to Peruvian human rights legislation, to support the legitimacy of its actions. At the same time, DFID has respected government wishes concerning its role, nevertheless making it clear that it expects a transparent dialogue, set within the democratic process to which the government is committed. This may be classified by some as playing politics, but is not judged by DFID as transgressing national sovereignty.

I suggest that whether or not the recipient government judges any particular donor action as a transgression depends on the extent to which such action upsets power relations. Telling government – the powerful – that the agency intends to work for the disempowered creates discomfort. DFID's office in Peru has experienced the effect of that discomfort. The government might resist passively by simply not responding to letters. Or some influential persons might advise that such action would be unwelcome. DFID has taken the view that if the government does not formally object in writing, it can proceed, while aware that what is at stake is its popularity with at least some sections of the host government.

What happens if the government does say 'no' in writing? DFID in Bolivia made a decision to continue with a human rights project after receiving such a letter, gambling on the chance that the letter was from an administration at the end of its time in power, and knowing that many others in government supported the project. DFID Peru initially felt it was reaching that stage in its correspondence with the government on the health programme described earlier. The government had written requesting that the planned support to the civil society networks be channelled through the Ministry of Health. DFID planned to respond by expressing surprise at this suggestion, as it contravened the government's commitment to independent civil society monitoring of the delivery of services.

A government reshuffle and the appointment of a new health minister more favourable to the rights-based approach to health policy meant that DFID's reply was never sent. The negative letter from the previous minister was quietly forgotten. When does a ministerial letter have weight and implications? In the UK, the convention (if not always the practice) is that the authority of the letter during the same administration would have survived the change of minister. But in highly individualized, non-institutionalized, non-politically accountable Peru, a letter has less authority. It dies with the minister, especially, as in this case, when DFID could consider that the previous minister's views had limited 'legitimacy' because they deviated from the international human rights standards to which the Peruvian state has subscribed.

DFID's commitment to a rights-based approach in Peru, and the lessons it is learning from attempting to meet that commitment, have revealed some fundamental challenges for official development assistance. By acting in this way, is a small country office making a significantly greater contribution to social justice than it would have done through more conventional (apparently) non-political behaviour? I believe so, but examples of such approaches from other countries and other donors would provide more evidence to support or disprove this belief.

Notes

I am grateful to the staff of the DFID office in Lima for their views. I also thank Naila Kabeer for her helpful comments on the first draft of this chapter. However, as author, I bear the sole responsibility for its content.

1. This chapter was written in mid-2003. In November of that year, DFID head office announced cuts to its programme in middle-income countries, including the closure of the Peru office by March 2005.
2. In June 2003, the Toledo government declared a state of emergency, prompting one sociologist, Julio Cotler, to remark that democratic windows only ever last two years in Peru. However, the DFID office noted the successful popular resistance to the government clamp-down, and wondered whether such an analysis was too bleak. A further government re-shuffle has led to a more technocratic/democratic-style administration coming to the fore. DFID's constant interpretation and re-interpretation of the complex political processes taking place, and to which in a small way it was contributing, is a mark of its mainstreaming of rights-based approaches.
3. For example, Fox (1994).
4. The quotations in the subheadings of this section are taken from my interviews with staff in the DFID office in Peru.
5. In mid 2001, a full-time social development adviser was appointed to the Peru office, and I was only minimally involved after then.
6. This section draws on a meeting I held with the Oxfam management team in Lima, December 2002.
7. An account of candidates' training can be found in Eyben (2001).
8. Arguably, globalization is rendering this basis of citizenship partially obsolete. Identities are increasingly cross-border and solidarities arise as much within confessional groupings and ethnicities as within secular states (Deacon 2003). The optional protocol in some human rights conventions recognizes the rights of citizens to make claims directly to international arbiters, passing over the heads of the nation-state.

References

Brock, K., R. McGee and R. Ssewakiryanga (2002) 'Poverty knowledge and policy processes; A case study of Ugandan national poverty reduction policy', *IDS Research Report* 53, Brighton: Institute of Development Studies

Cornwall, A. (2000) 'Beneficiary, consumer, citizen: Perspectives on participation for poverty reduction', *Sida Studies* 2, Stockholm: Sida

Deacon, B. (2003) 'Global social governance reform', *GASPP Policy Brief* 1, www.gaspp.org

Department for International Development (DFID) (2000a) 'Realising human rights for poor people', *Strategies for Achieving the International Development Targets*, London: DFID

Department for International Development (2000b) 'Eliminating world poverty: Making globalisation work for the poor', *White Paper on International Development*, London: Stationery Office

Eyben, R. (2001) 'A voice for women', *Developments* 14, London: DFID

Eyben, R. (2003a) 'The rise of rights', *IDS Policy Brief* No.17, Brighton: Institute of Development Studies

Eyben, R. (2003b) 'Donors as political actors: Fighting the Thirty Years War in Bolivia', *IDS Working Paper* 183, Brighton: Institute of Development Studies

Eyben, R. and C. Ferguson (2004) 'Can donors be more accountable to poor people?', in L. Groves and R. Hinton (eds) *Inclusive Aid: Changing Power and Relationships in International Aid*, London: Earthscan

Falwell, R. (1987) *Courage to Grow*, London: Quaker Home Service

Fox, J. (1994) 'The difficult transition from clientelism to citizenship: Lessons from Mexico', *World Politics* 46 (2), pp. 151–84

Gaventa, J. and M. Edwards (2001) *Global Citizen Action*, London: Earthscan

Held, D. (1996) *Models of Democracy*, Cambridge: Polity Press

Instituto de Estudios Peruanos (IEP) (2003) 'Sistematización y Complementación del Análisis de las Relaciones Estado-Sociedad y del Cambio Pro-Pobre en el Perú', unpublished report commissioned by DFID, Lima, Peru

International Law Commission, *Vienna Convention on Diplomatic Relations, 1961* www.un.org/law/ilc/texts/diplomat.htm

Krasner, S. (1999) *Sovereignty: Organized Hypocrisy*, Princeton: Princeton University Press, quoted in H. Steiner and P. Alston (2000) *International Human Rights in Context*, Oxford: Oxford University Press, pp. 575–79

McGee, R. (2003) 'The self in participatory poverty research', in K. Brock and R. McGee (eds) *Knowing Poverty*, London: Earthscan

Maxwell, S. (2003) 'Heaven or hubris: Reflections on the new poverty agenda', *Development Policy Review* 21(1), pp. 5–25

Mosse, D. (2003) 'The making and marketing of participatory development', in P. Quarles van Ufford and A. Giri (eds) *A Moral Critique of Development: In Search of Global Responsibilities*, London and New York: Routledge

National Audit Office (2002) *Performance Management – Helping to Reduce World Poverty*, London: Stationery Office

Piron, L.-H. (2003) 'Learning from the UK Department for International Development's rights-based approach to development assistance', paper, London: Overseas Development Institute

Sagasti, F. (2002) 'Towards pro-poor change in Peru: Institutional changes and the role of the international community', unpublished paper commissioned by DFID, Lima

Steiner, H. and Alston, P. (2000) *International Human Rights in Context*, Oxford: Oxford University Press

Index